A Tortured History

A Tortured History:
The Story of
Capital Punishment in Oregon

William R. Long

The Oregon Criminal Defense Lawyers Association

The Oregon Criminal Defense Lawyers Association
44 West Broadway, Suite 403
Eugene, OR 97401
phone: (541) 686-8716
fax: (541) 686-2319
www.ocdla.org

Cover photograph: Jacksonville, 1886. Gallows set up on grounds of Jackson County Courthouse and jail for the execution of Lewis O'Neil, convicted of murder of Lewis McDaniel, Ashland, 1884. Permission to reprint granted by the Photographs Department, Oregon Historical Society, Portland, OrHi 102707/#583-i.

Library of Congress Catalog Card Number 2001095078

ISBN 0-9714035-0-3

Edited by Jennifer Root.
Designed by Tracye May.

The Oregon Criminal Defense Lawyers Association is a non-profit, educational organization dedicated to protecting constitutional rights and due process; providing scholarship in the area of legal representation in criminal, juvenile and mental commitment proceedings; and promoting public awareness as to the function and duties of criminal and juvenile defense in general.

TABLE OF CONTENTS

LANDMARKS IN OREGON
DEATH PENALTY AND U.S. HISTORY[1]

1864
Oregon enacts Deady Code, codifying the death penalty for first degree murder.
General Sherman captures Atlanta and marches through Georgia to the sea.

1873
Oregon moves executions to county courthouses.
Jesse James carries out world's first train robbery.

1902
Jack Wade and William Dalton hung at Portland's Multnomah County
Courthouse.
Charles Lindbergh and John Steinbeck born.

1912
Oregon statutory initiative to abolish death penalty fails.
Titanic sinks.

1914
Oregon statutory initiative to abolish death penalty passes.
First ship sails through Panama Canal.

1920
Special election legislative referral restores Oregon's death penalty.
19th Amendment to U.S. Constitution gives women the right to vote.

1958
Ballot Measure 4 to repeal Oregon's death penalty fails.
Alaska joins the U.S. and Senate holds McCarthy hearings.

1961
Jeannace June Freeman murders her lover's children, a crime that made her
Oregon's first woman to receive the death penalty.
Bay of Pigs invasion.

1964
Ballot Measure 1 to repeal Oregon's death penalty passes.
Civil Rights Act signed into law and Gulf of Tonkin incident.

---

[1] Source for U.S. events—http://members.theglobe.com/algis/

1977
Oregon Legislature draws up HB 2321 to restore the death penalty.
President Carter signs Panama Canal Treaty.

1978
Oregon voters pass the ballot version of HB 2321 and restore the death penalty.
President Carter hosts meeting at Camp David between Israeli Prime Minister Begin and Egyptian President Sadat.

1981
State v. Quinn decision handed down from Oregon Supreme Court.
Iran releases 52 American hostages.

1984
Oregonians pass Ballot Measures 6 and 7 to restore the death penalty and exempt it from the constitutional "cruel and unusual" provision.
President Reagan elected to second term.

1988
Oregon Supreme Court hands down decision of *Wagner I* (*State v. Wagner*).
George Bush elected to U.S. Presidency.

1989
U.S. Supreme Court decides *Penry v. Lynaugh*.
Berlin Wall falls.

1990
Oregon Supreme Court decides *Wagner II* (*State v. Wagner*).
Manuel Noriega arraigned in federal district court on drug trafficking charges.

1995
Oregon Legislature deals with mitigating and aggravating evidence, and rising victims' rights movement by amending ORS 163.150(1)(a).
Republicans control U.S. House for the first time in decades, initiating the "Republican Revolution."

1996
Ballot Measure 40 puts Oregon death penalty cases on hold until June 1998.
Unabomber Theodore Kaczynski arrested in Lincoln, Montana.

2000
Oregon effort to repeal death penalty fails to get signatures required to make the ballot.
George W. Bush elected to U.S. Presidency.

ACKNOWLEDGMENTS

One of the most pleasant tasks of an author is to express gratitude in a public manner to people who have assisted him throughout the project. This book could not have been written without the kindness and helpfulness of the following people.

Dr. Hugo Bedau, retired from Tufts University and now working on the Jeremy Bentham manuscripts at the University of London, for his insights into the movement to repeal the death penalty in Oregon in 1964.

Ms. Kathleen Cegla, Assistant Attorney General, for her description of the way in which post-conviction death penalty cases are handled in Marion County Circuit Court.

Mr. Gregory Chaimov, Legislative Counsel, for more than one conversation on the issues presented by the taping of Conan Wayne Hale's conversation/confession with a Catholic priest in the Lane County Jail in 1996.

Ms. Ann Christian, director of the State Indigent Defense Services Division program, for her helpfulness in supplying figures and data on expenditures for indigent defense generally as well as for death penalty cases over the years.

Mr. Steve Gorham, Marion County attorney, whose long experience in Marion County post-conviction cases provided perspective and insight into this aspect of the state criminal justice system.

Mr. David Groom, State Public Defender, for his generosity of time and spirit in discussing cases over the last twenty years in which he or his office has defended people sentenced to death.

The Honorable Mark O. Hatfield, former Governor and Senator from Oregon, for his ready availability to discuss political events from 1957 to 1964 in Oregon and his recollections of the McGahuey execution and Freeman case.

Justice Hans A. Linde, retired Justice of the Oregon Supreme Court, for his reminiscences of the *Wagner* cases and his life on the Oregon Supreme Court in the late 1970s and 1980s.

Chief Justice Edwin Peterson, retired Chief Justice of the Oregon Supreme Court, author of *Wagner II*, for his willingness to discuss various aspects of the *Wagner* cases.

Mr. Robert Rocklin, Assistant Attorney General and lead attorney in the appellate division for death penalty cases, for several insightful conversations on the details of arguing death penalty cases and the procedural delays often encountered in the death penalty arena.

In addition, I would like to thank Professors Ed Harri and Jeffrey Standen of the Willamette University College of Law, who lent encouragement and support during the research and writing of this project.

Several people, including lawyers working on current death penalty appeals, district attorneys from several counties and an array of staff at the Supreme Court Administrator's office, Marion County Circuit Court, Oregon State Library and Oregon State Archives have saved me from a host of errors when they answered my phone calls or clarified issues for me in a variety of areas that were unclear to me but simple for them to resolve.

Finally, I would like to express a special word of thanks to a friend and mentor, William A. Barton of Newport, Oregon. Bill Barton sought me out when I was a first-year student at Willamette University College of Law in 1997 to become my law school mentor. Since that time, our friendship has grown into a prized relationship. Bill approaches law with a scholar's intellectual concern, a practitioner's attention to detail, a writer's approach to well-chosen words and a humanist's commitment to doing justice and loving kindness. His generous words and gestures on my behalf over the last three years will forever be appreciated.

—*William R. Long*

INTRODUCTION

This book is a study in Oregon legal history. It takes one issue (capital punishment) from one jurisdiction (Oregon) and examines it in great detail. Though some articles published over the years touch a few of the topics treated here, this book, by and large, breaks new ground. It relies almost exclusively on United States and Oregon statutes, United States and Oregon Supreme Court decisions, newspaper articles over several decades, legal briefs in the Oregon Supreme Court library, a few law review articles, tapes and minutes from legislative committee meetings now housed in the Oregon State Archives, individual case files from the Marion County Circuit Court, a few excellent Web pages, and two or three helpful overviews of capital punishment in America. In addition, a plentiful source of information was a group of about a dozen people, cited in the Acknowledgments, whose specialized knowledge about some aspect of the process or workings of the death penalty in Oregon was invaluable.

The central premise of this work, unfolded throughout, is that the toll exacted on Oregonians in the last 17 years by the modern death penalty statute enacted in 1984 has far exceeded any benefits that its most zealous supporters can claim it has provided. This has occurred, in my judgment, not because the death penalty is inherently immoral or because it has been applied in a racially discriminatory way in Oregon, but because of the huge cost of unforeseen and unexpected consequences after the 1984 law was passed.

These consequences have ranged from a significant 1989 decision of the United States Supreme Court that resulted in the reversal of all death sentences for death row inmates (22 at the time) to the enormous cost of an almost invisible part of Oregon's death penalty process, called post-conviction relief, that has or will lengthen each death row inmate's appeals process by 8 to 12 years. In one of the greatest ironies of the death penalty process, the work of those involved in the victims' rights movement has already added 18 months to the length of most death penalty appeals and may end up adding several more months or years in the future. Future delays are possible because a June 4, 2001, U.S. Supreme Court decision may call into question whether a victims' rights-inspired revision of the Oregon death penalty statute in 1995 and 1997 is constitutional.

All this has resulted in a death penalty process in Oregon in which the state may pay up to ten times as much for the average death row inmate in trying to put him to death as it would if a jury had sentenced him to life imprisonment without the possibility of parole. When all is said and done, the burden of proof should now rest on those who want to maintain the death penalty in Oregon to show that such a policy represents wise stewardship of scarce government resources.

Chapter One introduces the reader to some of the basic issues mentioned in the preceding paragraph and serves as a kind of snapshot of the death penalty as it exists in Oregon as of July 1, 2001. Chapters Two through Four, Part I of the book, delve into the development of capital punishment in Oregon from the earliest days of the Provisional Government until the passage of the modern Oregon death penalty law by initiative in November 1984. Special attention will be devoted to four mini-periods in that time: 1) 1901–1903, when Oregon's executions were removed from public view at the local county courthouses to the Oregon State Penitentiary in Salem; 2) 1912–1920, when Oregon's voters abolished the death penalty by constitutional amendment and then restored it; 3) 1958–1964, when Oregonians abolished the death penalty once again; and 4) 1978–1984, when Oregonians passed the current death penalty law by a wide margin. The reason for this long historical sketch is twofold: It fills a gap in Oregon historical writing and sheds some light on how Oregonians as a distinct people have dealt with this most consuming issue.

Part II, Chapters Five and Six, will treat the subject of how a person is put to death legally in Oregon today. Very few people outside of the tight community of those who argue death penalty cases know the ten steps that are available to a death penalty defendant—beginning with affirmance of his conviction by the Oregon Supreme Court and ending with denial of clemency by the Governor. Because this process is so different from the process in the earlier days of Oregon's history, it needs to be spelled out in some detail. In addition, federal law regarding death penalty appeals has changed rather dramatically in the last five years, requiring a basic discussion of federal habeas corpus review as it relates to the death penalty appeals process.

Part III, Chapters Seven through Eleven, focuses on legal issues that have arisen since Oregon restored its death penalty in 1984. Chapter Seven treats a subject especially important for Oregon's death penalty: the development from

Introduction

xiii

1976 to 1987 in the United States Supreme Court of a jurisprudence regarding circumstances that might mitigate a possible sentence of death for defendants. The heart of Part III, however, is an attempt to understand how the Oregon Supreme Court has interpreted both the Oregon death penalty statute and the U.S. Supreme Court's requirements on the death penalty, and how the Oregon Legislature has altered the statute since 1984.

In brief, I will argue in Chapter Eight that the Oregon Supreme Court decision upholding the 1984 death penalty statute, *State v. Wagner* (1988) (*Wagner I*), was—as its dissenters powerfully and presciently pointed out— wrongly decided. In Chapter Nine I will review a most influential U.S. Supreme Court case, *Penry v. Lynaugh* (1989), and the response of the Oregon Legislature to that decision. In Chapter Ten I will argue that the subsequent *State v. Wagner* case, *Wagner* (1990) (*Wagner II*) which upholds the Oregon statute after the U.S. Supreme Court reviewed *Wagner I* and vacated it, rests on such a flimsy and poorly reasoned foundation that it ought to be abandoned by the Oregon Supreme Court today. The last point is important because several men were sentenced to death under the 1984 law during the five years after 1986. I will further contend that because of all this Oregon did not have a death penalty statute that even arguably complied with the U.S. Supreme Court's requirements *until* 1991.

Finally, in Chapter Eleven I will show how Oregon's death penalty law has changed since 1991, and will introduce the reader to the men on death row today. I will explore the current discussion on the constitutionality of Oregon's statute because of some changes made to the law in the 1995 and 1997 Legislative Assemblies. Then I will examine five cases of particular individuals convicted of aggravated murder which either have resonance beyond Oregon (Conan Wayne Hale), illustrate something of the tragedy and vagaries of the human condition (Cesar Barone and Alberto Reyes-Camarena), demonstrate some of the massive procedural complexities that can creep into death penalty cases (Dallas Ray Stevens), or show a stunning dismissal of all charges against an individual by the Oregon Supreme Court (Scott Harberts).

A concluding chapter, Chapter Twelve, discusses some of the lessons learned from this study and the effort that is underway to repeal the Oregon death penalty law by initiative petition in November 2002. In my judgment, the issue of capital punishment will be an important one in the ensuing years in Oregon. Even though the process leading to executions has been extremely slow, I project that by 2008–2012 Oregon will be confronted with a larger number of executions than at any other comparable period in its history. It would be helpful if the discussion of capital punishment in Oregon could be joined in earnest without the threat of imminent executions to prod us.

CHAPTER 1

Oregon's Death Penalty Today

On November 6, 1984, Oregon voters reinstated the death penalty by a huge margin.[1] The final vote was 75.1–24.9% (893,818–295,988), the largest margin of victory that a death penalty vote had ever secured in Oregon's history.[2] Special care was taken in wording the 1984 initiative petition because a previous initiative to restore the death penalty in 1978, approved by a 64.3–35.7% margin, was held unconstitutional by the Oregon Supreme Court in January 1981.[3] Armed with a more carefully drawn text, supplemented by fresh outrage at a spate of ghoulish murders that had taken place in the intervening years, and fueled by the burgeoning victims' rights movement, the proponents dominated the public debate on the issue and easily mustered the votes in 1984 to pass the measure.[4]

In order for the death penalty to be put into effect, however, one needed not only a statute on the books but also juries to implement it. For a while, Oregon juries made use of the law only hesitantly. Like a person dipping her feet into icy waters before deciding whether to take the plunge, Oregon juries sentenced no one to death in 1985 (the law had gone into effect on December 6, 1984) and only two people, Jeffrey Wagner and James Isom, to death in 1986. Three more were sentenced to death in 1987: Stephen Farrar in March, Ronald Moen in April and Charles Smith in June. But then, in 1988, the floodgates opened and what had begun as a trickle turned into a torrent. Or, to maintain the earlier metaphor, Oregon took the plunge. From January 1988 until June 1989, a period of 18 months, juries throughout Oregon sentenced 17 men and 0 women to death.[5]

Listing the names and dates of sentence of these 17 men might be helpful in order to let the reality of the new law's effect sink in. Reyes Miranda was sentenced to death in January 1988, Stephen Nefstad and Jesse Pratt in February 1988, Randy Guzek and Tyrone Walton in March 1988, Michael McDonnell in April 1988, Marco Montez, Mark Pinnell and Cornelius Brown in June 1988, Michael Tucker in November 1988, Dallas Ray Stevens in December 1988, Ricky Douglas early in 1989, David Simonsen in February 1989, Jeffrey Williams in March 1989, Jason Rose in May 1989, Dayton Leroy Rogers and Robert Langley in June 1989.[6]

To put these numbers in perspective, if Oregon juries had continued sentencing people to death at the rate they did from January 1988 to June 1989, and if Oregon had had a death penalty statute as long as the other 35 jurisdictions that had such a statute when Oregonians adopted theirs in 1984, Oregon would currently have nearly 300 people on death row, and would join such elite death penalty states as Texas, Florida and California vying for the greatest number of death row inmates in the nation.[7]

Thus, by June 1989 there were 22 men and 0 women on death row in Oregon.[8]

But then a series of abrupt changes happened in the summer of 1989 whose effects on the implementation of Oregon's death penalty have been dramatic and longlasting. Even the Oregon Supreme Court, which couches most of its opinions in the measured diction of judicial restraint, spoke of the "metamorphosis" in its death penalty jurisprudence after the summer of 1989.[9] One of the major purposes of this book is to examine this metamorphosis and the way it was handled by the Oregon Department of Justice, the Oregon Legislature and the Oregon Supreme Court.

In brief, the dramatic change that came about in the summer of 1989 was occasioned by the quick succession of a number of significant events: 1) a United States Supreme Court decision handed down on June 26, 1989; 2) a frantic scramble by the state Department of Justice and the Oregon Legislature in the waning days of the 1989 Legislative Assembly to try to implement the implications of that decision (June 29–July 1, 1989); 3) the rare decision of the United States Supreme Court on July 3, 1989, to grant *certiorari* and then nullify a 1988 Oregon Supreme Court decision upholding the 1984 death penalty statute; 4) the commendable celerity of the Oregon Supreme Court in hearing oral arguments in August 1989 on four death penalty cases to consider the effects of all these changes; and 5) the rapid decision of the Oregon Supreme Court in January 1990 to try to salvage Oregon's death penalty statute. All of this occurred in a time (September 1988–April 1990) of the greatest turnover of justices in the history of the Oregon Supreme Court, except for 1949–50, and during an investigation into campaign finance violations of Justice Edward N. Fadeley that would eventually lead to his being censured by his colleagues in 1990.[10]

The effects of the June 26, 1989, Supreme Court decision, often referred to as the *Penry* problem, have been immense and costly in Oregon.[11] Each of the 22 people who had been sentenced to death by June 1989, and one additional man who had been put on death row in November 1989, Stressla Johnson, were required either to have new trials to determine their guilt or innocence or new sentencing-phase trials to determine the appropriate sentence in the light of the *Penry* decision.[12] Of the 23 people either retried or resentenced, only 11 returned with death sentences (Isom, Pratt, Guzek, McDonnell, Montez, Pinnell, Stevens, Simonsen, Williams, Rogers and Langley). Eleven other men were either resentenced to life imprisonment or, through a negotiated plea, to life without the possibility of parole.[13] One, Tyrone Walton, received another arrangement.[14] Many of the 11 cases that came back with death sentences have been plagued with such severe procedural and legal difficulties in the intervening years that, as a result, in some instances it can honestly be said that ten years after *Penry* their cases are no closer to resolution. The example of the most egregious case, that of Michael McDonnell, will be given below.

Thus, for 12 of the 23 defendants who had been sentenced to death by the end of 1989, the problems occasioned by the *Penry* decision were solved within two or three years as they accepted lesser sentences than death, without a huge cost to the state or the counties. For the remaining 11, the road has been much more unpredictable and costly. Their cases were remanded to the county circuit courts that had convicted them, and their sentences of death were reaffirmed. These cases then returned to the Oregon Supreme Court because an affirmance of guilt and sentence of death by the court is necessary before the defendant can legally be put to death. In five of the 11 cases, the decision of the circuit court was affirmed by the Oregon Supreme Court by 1996 (Isom, Pratt, Montez, Pinnell, Williams). These cases then moved on to the next steps of death penalty appeals, direct appeal to the United States Supreme Court and post-conviction relief in the Circuit Court of Marion County. This process will be described in detail in Chapters Five and Six.

The other six cases that had legal problems after the *Penry* remand were reargued between 1995 and 2001 and either decided or put on hold by the Oregon Supreme Court. Four were remanded to the circuit courts once again (Guzek in 1995, McDonnell in 1999, Langley and Rogers in 2000), one was affirmed (Simonsen in 1999) and one is tied up in a procedural complexity which will be described in Chapter Eleven (Stevens). Guzek's death sentence was affirmed for a third time by a Deschutes County jury in 1997 but the record in his case is so voluminous and complex that Guzek's opening brief before the supreme court on his third direct appeal was only recently submitted and runs to the unheard-of length of 430 pages, with another 400 pages of single-spaced appendices. It is likely that his case will not even be argued until 2002 and then, for reasons stated below, be remanded once again.

The five cases that were affirmed by the Oregon Supreme Court by 1996 (Isom, Pratt, Montez, Pinnell, Williams) then marched on to the next steps of the process. Of those five men Isom has died, leaving four of those sentenced before 1989 in the next stages of their death penalty appeals. As mentioned above, all six of the cases sent back to the county courts on second remand were returned with sentences of death to the Oregon Supreme Court. But before any of them could be decided something else happened, from a most unlikely source, which delayed consideration of these cases for another 18 months. The reason for the delay was the passage of Ballot Measure 40, the so-called victims' rights initiative, in November 1996.

Ballot Measure 40, which promised greater protection of the victim in the criminal justice system, ironically slowed the process of death for those who had been convicted of murder and sentenced to death but whose convictions had not yet been affirmed by the Oregon Supreme Court. The reason for this delay was the poor wording of the measure, especially on the issue of whether its provisions would apply to pending cases or only to crimes that were committed after the effective date of the act (early December 1996). The measure did not specify the cases to which it would apply. Therefore, the Oregon Supreme Court asked for briefing on this issue from both the State Department of Justice and the Public Defenders Office in two current criminal cases, in order to determine the effect of Ballot Measure 40.

More specifically, it worked as follows: In December 1996, the state court administrator wrote to parties in death penalty cases, asking for their judgment on the applicability of Ballot Measure 40 to their cases.[15] On December 16, 1996, then-Solicitor General Virginia Linder, with consent of the state public defender, wrote to the administrator suggesting a briefing schedule that would answer two questions: 1) whether Measure 40 applied to pending cases, and 2) whether Measure 40 was constitutional. This was acceptable to the Oregon Supreme Court and, in order to give both sides time to brief the questions, the court decided that all pending death penalty appeals would be "held in abeyance" as of that date. During January and February 1997 the issue was briefed. Oral arguments were heard on the issues, in connection with a minor criminal case, in March 1997.

But it was not until June 1998 that a decision in a separate case challenging the constitutionality of Ballot Measure 40 was handed down.[16] In *Armatta*, the Oregon Supreme Court dealt only with the second of the questions briefed, and decided that although Measure 40 purported to be a single amendment to the Oregon Constitution, it contained in fact two or more amendments, and thus violated Article XVII, section 1, of the Oregon Constitution, which stipulates that two or more amendments to the constitution must be voted on separately. Since the measure was held unconstitutional, there was no need for the court to reach the issue of whether it applied to pending cases.[17] The death penalty cases were then "resubmitted" for the court's consideration in June 1998. Of the six pre-*Penry* cases resubmitted, only one of them has been affirmed by the court by July 2001 (Simonsen). McDonnell's case, which had been reargued before the court in May 1996, was remanded once again to the county circuit court (Douglas County) in October 1999 because the jury on first remand was not given the option of sentencing McDonnell to life without the possibility of parole when it resentenced him to death in 1994. Both Langley's and Rogers' cases were remanded again for the same reason as McDonnell. Guzek's case will, no doubt, be remanded sometime in 2002 for the same reason.

In the meantime (from 1992 to 2001) many more men, and no women, have been added to the growing list of death row inmates.[18] Since some of their stories will be told in Chapters Five and Eleven, I will only list the cumulative statistics regarding death row inmates as of July 1, 2001. From February 1986 to July 2001, 47 men and 0 women have been sentenced to death in Oregon under the 1984 statute. Two of the 47 have been executed: Douglas Wright in September 1996 and Charles Moore in May 1997. Both Wright and Moore refused to pursue any appeals after the mandatory appeal of their case to the Oregon Supreme Court. As will be shown in Chapters Five and Six, affirmation of one's death sentence by the Oregon Supreme Court is only the first of ten steps available to one sentenced to death before the sentence of death is actually carried out. These cases of Wright and Moore are atypical, but somewhat expected, since around 10–15% of prisoners under the sentence of death nationwide give up their appeals and "volunteer" for death.[19]

Of the 45 others sentenced to death, one, James Isom, died of cancer and difficulties relating to age while his case was on appeal. Of the 44 remaining men, 25 are currently on death row.[20] Of the 19 who are no longer on death row, two will not be returning (Grant Charboneau and Gregory Wilson) and one is still pursuing a mandamus action before the Oregon Supreme Court on the validity of Oregon's jury selection process (Stevens). Three may yet return to death row after their cases go before county juries (McDonnell, Rogers and Langley). One (Scott Harberts) has not simply been removed from death row but had the case against him dismissed altogether because the court held that by waiting five years before bringing Harberts to trial, the state had violated his constitutional right to a speedy trial.[21] All of the remaining 12 were retried or resentenced to terms less than death after the *Penry* decision. Among the death row population today there is a fairly clear line of demarcation between the pre-*Penry* defendants, sentenced to death before July 1989, and the post-*Penry* defendants, the earliest of whom (Randall Smith) was sentenced to death in 1992.

The 25 current occupants of death row consist of 6 pre-*Penry* defendants (Pratt, Guzek, Montez, Pinnell, Simonsen, Williams) and 19 post-*Penry* defendants.[22] Of the 19 post-*Penry* defendants, 8 have already had their cases affirmed by the Oregon Supreme Court (Smith, Cunningham, Hayward, Barone, Thompson, Reyes-Camarena, McNeely and Lotches). Therefore, 13 of the current 25 occupants of death row have had their cases affirmed by the Oregon Supreme Court and are on Steps 2, 3 or 4 of their appeals, and 12 have not yet been affirmed by the court.

In order to put the issue of delay, expense and process into a human form, consider the case of the first person who committed an aggravated murder under the new death penalty statute, Michael McDonnell. Perhaps oblivious to the raging public debate over the deterrent effect of the death penalty, McDonnell killed Joey Keever on December 22, 1984, a mere 16 days after the law went into effect. McDonnell had recently escaped from the Department of Corrections Farm Annex in Salem and was hitchhiking near Yoncalla high on methamphetamine when he forced himself into Keever's pickup at a stop sign. He stabbed her repeatedly and threw her out of the vehicle when a curious citizen approached them to ask some questions.

McDonnell was charged with aggravated murder in Douglas County. The judge, however, set aside the indictment because, according to him, it imposed an unconstitutional sentence—a death sentence for a prisoner who kills when he has escaped, in contrast to no death sentence for a person who is not a prisoner but who does the same thing. The Department of Justice appealed this decision to the Oregon Court of Appeals. Procedural appeals before trial in death penalty cases go to this court rather than directly to the Oregon Supreme Court. The case was argued before the court in September 1986. On March 11, 1987, the court reversed the lower court and ordered the judge to reinstate the indictment.[23]

The case then came to trial and McDonnell was convicted of aggravated murder and sentenced to death in April 1988. His appeal, according to statute, went automatically to the Oregon Supreme Court. In September 1988, the court remanded the case to the circuit court because the same judge who dismissed the indictment had failed to file the correct paperwork, even though the supreme court was pretty sure the sentence intended was a death sentence. The judge was "given leave" to enter the judgment of conviction.[24]

Documents corrected, the sentence of death was entered by another judge, and the case returned to the Oregon Supreme Court in 1989. But the court found another problem in the way the trial was conducted: the district attorney had improperly included the family of the victim in plea negotiations, thus taking away the independence of the office of the district attorney in determining his legal strategy.[25] The court remanded for a hearing on the role of the victims in the plea bargaining process. On remand the trial court, ruling without a jury, reinstated the death sentence. When the case returned to the supreme court in 1992, the court was caught up in the *Penry* problem, which relates to jury consideration of all mitigating factors before deciding whether to sentence a defendant to death. So, once again the Oregon Supreme Court remanded the case to Douglas County, telling them that the trial court's instructions on mitigating evidence in capital cases were inadequate.[26]

A second jury was then impaneled in McDonnell's case, this time to consider the full effect of mitigating evidence before resentencing him. In 1994 the Douglas County jury again sentenced him to death. Oral arguments were heard before the Oregon Supreme Court on May 3, 1996. Then, the Measure 40 problem hit, and McDonnell's case was held in abeyance until June 1998. Finally, on October 7, 1999, the supreme court handed down their decision on McDonnell. The result? Another remand. This time the court below had improperly eliminated from the jury's consideration a sentencing option of life imprisonment without the possibility of parole.[27]

It will probably be another three to five years before the Oregon Supreme Court will have a chance to affirm McDonnell's death penalty conviction if a third Douglas County jury decides to resentence him to death. That is, it may take between 18 and 20 years after McDonnell committed his crime to get him through Step 1 of a ten-step process toward death.

Though McDonnell's case is somewhat extreme, it is not unprecedented. It will take about the same length of time before the Oregon Supreme Court can affirm the conviction of Dayton Leroy Rogers, possibly the worst serial killer in Oregon's history. It will probably take nearly that long from the date of the crime until the case of Robert Langley is affirmed. Randy Guzek's case will probably take more than 20 years, and one can only guess when Dallas Ray Stevens' sentence of death will finally be affirmed. Some of the county juries, especially in the cases of Langley and McDonnell, may decide that the expense of trying the person and the extreme delay in their cases should lead to a sentence of life without the possibility of parole. Time will tell.

It should be stressed that affirmation of the death sentence by the Oregon Supreme Court is only the first of ten steps that need to be taken before the state of Oregon can legally put a person to death. Though not all ten steps are of equal duration, the sentences of death for Stevens or Langley or Guzek or

Rogers could not possibly be carried out until 30–35 years after their crimes, and that of Michael McDonnell until years after that. Even though all of these men were rather young when they committed their crimes, they, especially McDonnell, may be rather old when and if the state finally executes them. The long delay in their cases encourages consideration of the question of how long to permit cases to go on before final decisions are made concerning a person's fate.

No statistics are kept nationally regarding the average time between a person's commission of the crime and the time of his execution.[28] Yet, searching out the cases of the last 100 people executed in the United States leads to the conclusion that there is an average of 14 years between the commission of a capital crime and a person's execution. If all 580 cases (as of October 1999) of those executed since executions began again in 1977 in this country (after a ten-year hiatus) were considered, the number would probably drop to 12 or 13 years from the time of commission of the crime. The longest period in recent American history between the commission of the crime and the execution is 26 years.[29] Oregon is sure to break this record in the next decade.

And that won't be the only record that Oregon will break concerning the death penalty. At present, the oldest person executed in the United States since the death penalty was reinstated in 1977 was a 66-year-old man. The oldest man on death row in Oregon now is also the person whose case is furthest along in the march toward death: Jesse Pratt. Pratt is currently in Step 4 of the ten steps of appeal he may pursue. The Department of Corrections records place his birth date on July 4, 1934, while some police reports place it on July 3, 1944. If there are no "hitches" in his remaining appeals he will probably be executed, if he hasn't died of old age or infirmity, at an age beyond the life expectancy of the average American Caucasian male. The irony is poignant: Oregon's first involuntary execution would be a man in his mid-seventies who may need assistance to get to the death chamber, after the state has spent millions on his appeals for nearly 20 years (Pratt committed his crime in 1986); he would probably die on his own within a short time thereafter. Is this really what Oregonians had in mind when they passed the death penalty statute so overwhelmingly in 1984?

The long delays in affirming the convictions of the pre-*Penry* defendants begs a consideration of the costs of executing an inmate in Oregon. It was thought at one time that the death penalty might actually save money for the state because it meant that one would not be housing people under a sentence of death for a large number of years.[30] But because of Oregon's unique *Penry* and Measure 40 problems as well as the costs of the various levels of the trial and appeal, this is certainly not the case in Oregon. The best available numbers show that it may be ten times as costly to execute a man in Oregon as to keep him imprisoned for the duration of his life.

In Oregon, all costs for defending a death penalty inmate are borne by the state unless the person is of sufficient means to cover them himself.[31] Costs for prosecution are borne either by the state or by the counties. Only one or two of the death penalty inmates since 1986 have borne their own defense costs. Therefore, the reality is that the state and counties bear the costs of both prosecuting and defending death penalty inmates. The costs of defending inmates on appeal before the Oregon Supreme Court (Step 1 in the 10-Step process) and on direct appeal to the United States Supreme Court (Step 2) are borne by the State Public Defenders Office. They have three full-time staff working on death penalty cases and, with necessary overhead, expend about $250,000–300,000 per year defending death penalty cases.[32]

The far greater share in defense is paid out of the state indigent defense fund. This fund pays for death penalty defendants at every other stage of proceedings except for federal habeas corpus proceedings. The indigent defense budget for the state was $57 million in 1998. This fund was used to pay for the defense of more than 147,000 cases in 1998. The 25 death penalty cases claimed more than $4 million—that is, 7.5% of the indigent defense fund of the state. Each death penalty case claims annually, on average, the resources that could go to more than 4,500 other cases.[33]

But that isn't the only number that should be discussed. The total cost of defending death penalty cases in 1998, the sum of indigent defense and state public defender expenses, was about $4.3 million. Attorneys who defend death penalty cases are paid $55 per hour, with a few attorneys immediately "on call" receiving a slightly higher rate.[34] Thirty-five to forty percent of those fees go to office overhead, including secretarial staff, rent, and the myriad other expenses that go into a law practice. Therefore, the death penalty-defending lawyer makes about $35 per hour. The largest and most prestigious firms in the state require their attorneys to bill about seven hours per day (one needs to work about eleven hours to bill seven hours consistently). Therefore, if a death penalty attorney worked constantly at the pace of the highest paying firms in the state, he or she would earn about $1,000 per week. This is about 20–25% of the amount that his or her colleague partner in the big Portland firm would make. No one, on either side, has ever charged death penalty attorneys with becoming rich by defending death penalty clients or going into the field for pecuniary gain.

Therefore, $4.3 million went to defending death penalty cases in 1998, and no one is getting rich off of that amount. It is a reasonable assumption to make that the counties and the state are not spending less than that amount to prosecute death penalty cases. Precisely because Oregon district attorneys are known to be vigilant and thorough, one has good grounds for assuming that this probably underestimates the amount of money spent on prosecuting these cases. Indeed, some of their senior people at the county and state make more than $50,000 per year, and many of the district attorneys would be very reluctant to let trial costs stand in the way of an aggravated murder conviction if such a conviction were possible.[35] While the state public defender has a full-time death penalty legal staff of three, the state Department of Justice may decide to "reconstitute" a death penalty unit within the appellate division of the department. There would be far more than three attorneys working on these cases.[36] There are solid reasons for concluding that the total cost of prosecuting and defending death penalty cases in Oregon in 1998 was about $8.5 million. When one also includes the cost of the various courts along the way, noting that death penalty cases constitute about 3-5% of the case load and time of the Oregon Supreme Court, one has a conservative estimate of $9 million being spent in 1998 on death penalty cases in Oregon.

This $9 million is being spent on 25 people. The number of people on death row will no doubt grow in the ensuing years but now that money is being spent on 25 cases. That's an average expense of about $350,000 per death row inmate in 1998. Of course, some of the death row inmates surely didn't run up those kinds of costs, but some costs have exceeded that by a great deal.[37] These costs are in addition to the costs of housing the inmate in the Oregon State Penitentiary.[38]

The Oregon Department of Corrections calculated the costs of housing an inmate in 1996 to be $53.50 per day.[39] By 1999, that figure had risen to about $60 per day. The cost of housing an inmate for 30 years is therefore about $700,000 in 1999 dollars. If condemning a person to life without the possibility of parole is an average of 30 years, it would cost the state $700,000 to house him.[40] But to execute a person—for whom it takes the state 20 years to do so, a conservative time estimate according to the figures given above—the state must spend nearly $7 million. In addition, the inmate has to be housed at $60 per day for those 20 years.[41] To repeat, in Oregon it may be as much as ten times more expensive to put an inmate to death for aggravated murder than to sentence him to life imprisonment without the possibility of parole.[42]

In spite of all these figures, there are indications that the process in Oregon for post-*Penry* defendants is beginning to proceed more quickly. The Oregon Supreme Court has affirmed the sentences of five people who committed their crimes since 1990 (Smith, Cunningham, Hayward, Thompson, Barone). In a few of those cases (Hayward, Cunningham and Thompson), the affirmations came only three to five years after the crime was committed. In 1998 and 1999 the supreme court affirmed the convictions of Hayward, Thompson, Barone and Simonsen. The convictions of Reyes-Camarena, McNeely and Lotches were affirmed in 2000. Despite continuing problems with some pre-*Penry* defendants, the court seems to be moving now with greater confidence and efficiency in the newer cases. Although around three cases per year have come to the supreme court in the past seven years, there are indications that they want to increase the pace of hearing death penalty cases.[43]

In addition, the Marion County Circuit Court, which is responsible for Step 3 of the process (the post-conviction trial in the county where the prisoner is housed), is handling the cases more efficiently. The first cases that came to the county were handled in about five years or more. It took more than five years to dismiss Jesse Pratt's post-conviction case and about 4.5 years to dismiss Clinton Cunningham's. Randall Smith's case took more than six years to resolve because he refused to cooperate with his counsel and the court had to appoint a guardian for him in order to sign necessary legal papers and act for him in other ways. But the case of Jeffrey Williams was dismissed in less than three years, and the cases of Marco Montez and Michael Hayward are scheduled for hearing in the near future. Marion County is working with greater efficiency in disposing of these cases.

But this very efficiency may have the unintended effect of producing a situation where between 15 and 20 defendants could reach the end of the line, Step 10, within a four- or five-year period, probably from 2008–2012. The irony would be that the pre-*Penry* cases which should finally be settled by then (after more than 20 years from the time of the crime) will be joined by post-*Penry* defendants that the courts have been working on with greater efficiency, so that more defendants than anyone ever expected will be ready for execution beginning in about 2008. The most people that Oregon has ever executed in a period of five years is 17.[44] By the unintended confluence of the factors of finally dealing with the last of the pre-*Penry* cases and the growing efficiency with respect to the post-*Penry* cases, Oregon may face the possibility of executing more people in a coming five-year span than ever before. Finally, the true costs of the 1984 decision will confront the people of Oregon with all the gentleness of a sudden flood.[45]

Endnotes

1   Ballot Measure 7 in the general election; codified at ORS 163.150. At the same general election voters also approved Ballot Measure 6, which exempted death sentences for aggravated murder from constitutional restrictions on cruel, unusual and vindictive punishments. That ballot measure, now Article 1, section 40, of the Oregon Constitution, reads, "Notwithstanding sections 15 and 16 of this Article, the penalty for aggravated murder as defined by law shall be death upon unanimous affirmative jury findings as provided by law and otherwise shall be life imprisonment with minimum sentence as provided by law." Ballot Measure 6 passed by a 55.6–44.4% margin (653,009–521,687). *Oregon Blue Book 1999-2000* (Salem: Secretary of State, 1999), 304.

2   *Ibid.* The death penalty has been on the ballot seven times in Oregon's history (1912, 1914, 1920, 1958, 1964, 1978 and 1984). Chapters Two through Four will discuss each of these elections, some of which were by initiative petition (1912, 1914, 1978 and 1984) and some by legislative referral (1920, 1958 and 1964). In addition, some of them were constitutional amendments (1914, 1920, 1958, 1964, 1984) and some were only changes to the Oregon Revised Statutes (1912, 1978, 1984). The 1984 initiative petitions, as mentioned, included both constitutional and statutory changes.

3   *State v. Quinn,* 290 Or 383, 623 P2d 653 (1981).

4   The abduction and murder of a 14-year-old Sherwood girl, Charmel Ulrich, in August 1980, the crazed antics of the "I-5 Bandit" in sexually assaulting and killing women in the early 1980s and the Oregon Museum Tavern shooting in Salem in May 1981 where four were killed and dozens seriously injured, seemed to confirm for the vast majority of Oregonians that violent crime had spiraled out of control and that the death penalty was the appropriate and necessary measure to get control of these random or planned acts of violence.

5   Technically it is the judge who sentences a person to death, but the judge is required to implement the judgment of conviction and sentence of death given by the jury. The judge's sentence usually follows the jury decision within one or two weeks.

6   Three is no easily accessible list which provides this information. The Department of Corrections Web page, www.doc.state.or.us, lists the current men on death row in Oregon, their dates of birth, their crimes and when they were placed on death row, but the last column is inaccurate. What is listed for most of the inmates, except for Randy Guzek, is the date of their most recent placement on death row. Therefore, the Web page is not an accurate measure of how long many of the men have spent on death row. For reasons that will be evident throughout this book, many of the men on death row in Oregon have been on and off it more than once because of legal and procedural difficulties with their cases. In addition, most of those who were originally sentenced to death row (the names listed above) are no longer there. The information above was gleaned from reading their cases and newspaper articles about them. Some of this information may also be found by a search of the *Oregonian* index under these names and the articles over the years that the *Oregonian* has run on the people of death row. Among the *Oregonian* reporters, Fred Leeson, who reported on crime issues until the mid 1990s, and Ashbel Green, who covers the same issues today, have shown the greatest awareness of the legal as well as factual issues involved in the cases.

7   Even if Oregon had only kept up the pace from 1988 to the present, the number of those on death row would approximate the number in the "second tier" states of Pennsylvania, Illinois and Oklahoma. See statistics on current numbers of death row occupants on the Death Penalty Information Center's Web page, www.deathpenaltyinfo.org.

8   Of the 60 people who have been executed in Oregon's history since executions were transferred from the counties to the State Penitentiary in 1903, 60 have been men and none have been women. There has only been one woman on death row in this period, Jeannace June Freeman, and her case will be considered in some detail in Chapters Four and Five.

9   So the change was called by Chief Justice Carson in *State v. Langley,* 314 Or 247, 839 P2d 692 (1992).

10   The United States Supreme Court decision in question, *Penry v. Lynaugh,* 492 U.S. 302 (1989), will be discussed in Chapter Nine, the deliberations of the 1989 Oregon Legislature also in Chapter Nine, the 1988 decision of the Oregon Supreme Court upholding the 1984 law, *State v. Wagner,* 306 Or 115, 705 P2d 1136 (1988) (*Wagner I*) in Chapter Eight, the confusing 1990 decision of the Oregon Supreme Court seeming to uphold the 1984 law, *State v. Wagner,* 309 Or 5, 786 P2d 93 (1990) (*Wagner II*), in Chapter Ten. Information on the dates of service of Oregon Supreme Court justices is available in the *Oregon Blue Book 1999-2000* (Salem: Secretary of State, 1999), 314-18. The facts and decision of the Oregon Supreme Court regarding Justice Fadeley's censure are in *In re Fadeley,* 310 Or 548, 802 P2d 31 (1990).

11   The *Penry* problem refers to the case *Penry v. Lynaugh,* 492 U.S. 302 (1989) and has to do with the requirement that the jury consider all evidence of mitigation in defense of the guilty defendant in the sentencing phase of a capital punishment trial. The development of "mitigating measures" in the United States Supreme Court jurisprudence from 1976 to 1987 is the subject of Chapter Seven.

12   The requirement of a "two-phase" or "bifurcated" trial in the case of a person convicted of aggravated murder (as the crime is called in Oregon), the first to determine guilt and the second to determine penalty, will be discussed in Chapter Five.

13   Details on almost all of the men will be provided throughout this book. Suffice it to say that slightly over half were given life sentences which, under Oregon law, permit the possibility of parole after 30 years, and slightly under half were given other, more severe, options.

14   Walton received a life sentence but will also serve two consecutive terms for burglary.

15   Almost all of the death penalty defendants are indigent and so the state public defender argues these cases when they are on appeal before the Oregon Supreme Court.

16   *Armatta v. Kitzhaber,* 327 Or 250, 959 P2d 49 (1998).

17   Ballot Measure 40 returned to the ballot as several individual ballot measures in November 1999. Each of these new measures had a provision applying the measure to pending cases. A brief analysis of the results of the votes on these measures appears in Chapter Four.

18   One other major factor that has limited the growth of Oregon's death row since the *Penry* decision has been the use of the "true life" sentencing option in aggravated murder cases. This option, passed by the legislature in 1989, permits a jury in an aggravated murder trial to sentence a person to life imprisonment without the possibility of parole. More than 70 men and women are now imprisoned in Oregon with this sentence.

19   The most complete Web site for this information is www.deathpenaltyinfo.org.

20   Oregon is somewhat atypical in that nearly all of its death row inmates are Caucasian. Twenty-one are Caucasian males, two (Montez and Reyes-Camarena) are Hispanic, one is Native American (Lotches) and one is African-American (Gibson). Randall Smith, whose death sentence during his post-conviction hearing was recently vacated and will be removed from death row soon, is counted in this 25.

21   After he was released from the Oregon State Penitentiary late in 2000, Harberts faced a variety of sex abuse charges in Clackamas County Circuit Court. During the prosecution of those charges, significant evidence was presented that called into question Harberts' guilt for the 1989 murder for which he had been on death row. Perhaps when the Oregon Supreme Court dismissed the case against Harberts it was implicitly recognizing that substantial evidence of his guilt simply was not present in the record. Harberts is now on probation for five years, living and working in Clackamas County.

22   See page 193, Chapter Eleven, for a chart on the 19 post-*Penry* defendants.

23   *State v. McDonnell,* 84 Or App 278, 733 P2d 935 (1987).

24   *State v. McDonnell,* 306 Or 579, 761 P2d 921 (1988).

25   *State v. McDonnell,* 310 Or 98, 794 P2d 780 (1990).

26   *State v. McDonnell,* 313 Or 478, 837 P2d 941 (1992).

27   *State v. McDonnell*, 329 Or 375, 381, 987 P2d 486 (1999). The law permitting imprisonment without the possibility of parole as one sentencing option was not passed in the legislature
until 1989, but a provision in that statute made it applicable to all aggravated murders committed after December 6, 1984. Codified at ORS 163.150(5)(e)(1997). At oral arguments in
Langley's case on October 13, 1999, the justices repeatedly asked the Department of Justice
attorney, Robert Rocklin, how their decision in the *McDonnell* case would affect Langley's case.
The supreme court gave the impression in oral arguments that the *McDonnell* opinion represented a departure from some of their earlier decisions and, as indicated above, has lead to
another series of remands for the pre-*Penry* defendants.

28   Generally, organizations have been interested in collecting information about how long
people have spent on death row, or how long it has taken to execute a person from the time of
conviction in a county court until execution. The latter is usually 9–11 years. See, for example,
Mark Kramer, "Oregon's Death Penalty," *Oregon State Bar Bulletin*, December 1996, 15. Since
the time of commission of the crime is the time of familial and community disruption (the time
of suffering, if you will), it seems that this is a more realistic measure of the societal damage and
possible healing than the other information collected. Information on executions in America
since 1977 can be found at www.deathpenaltyinfo.org.

29   Robert Excell White, 61, was executed in Texas on March 30, 1999, for a crime he committed in 1973. He had been on death row since 1974, the longest of any of Texas' 460 death
row inmates.

30   On May 17, 1983, when the bill that eventually would become the 1984 initiative petition reinstating the death penalty was being considered in the House Judiciary Committee,
committee member Norm Smith, R-Tigard, testified that the costs to the state to execute an
inmate, even considering all avenues of appeal open to him, were less than the costs of keeping
him in prison for life. The testimony and exhibits of the House Judiciary Committee on HB
2294 give the impression that one of the reasons proponents sought reinstatement of the death
penalty was because it was a cost-effective way to handle a very serious problem. Committee
notes, tapes and exhibits for HB 2294 (1983 Legislative Assembly) are in the Oregon State
Archives in Salem.

31   The federal government actually bears the costs of habeas corpus appeals, discussed in
Chapter Six, but no one on death row has advanced to that stage. Jesse Pratt and Clinton
Cunningham could conceivably be in federal habeas proceedings in two or three years.

32   Interview with David Groom, State Public Defender, 16 September 1999.

33   The numbers and charts are available through Ms. Ann Christian, director of the State
Indigent Defense Services Division of the State Court Administrator's office. Interview with
Ann Christian, 5 October 1999.

34   The Indigent Defense Services Director contracts with the Marion County Association of
Defenders (MCAD) to provide much of the post-conviction indigent defense services in the
state. Mr. Steve Gorham chairs MCAD and administers the contract. Interview with Steve
Gorham, 7 September 1999.

35   Actual prosecution figures are hard to come by because, unlike the indigent defense fund,
they are scattered throughout the 36 counties and are "absorbed" in the normal costs of salaries
for the lawyers and staff in the office. The operative assumption here, however, is that the
prosecution would not spend less than the defense in these high profile cases.

36   Interview with Robert Rocklin, senior deputy for death penalty cases of the Oregon Department of Justice, 10 September 1999. The unit will be much larger than the corresponding
unit at the State Public Defender's Office because the Department of Justice, unlike the public
defender's office, is involved in all state post-conviction stages of death penalty cases.

37   The *Oregonian* has tried to keep a record of expenses in just the circuit court of Deschutes
County for Randy Guzek's case. He was convicted in March 1988 for a June 1987 murder. The
estimated costs by 1997 in circuit county defense costs alone were well over $500,000. *Orego-
nian*, 11 November 1997, D7.

38   There is some debate on whether it is more costly to house a death row inmate than a general population inmate at the Oregon State Penitentiary. death row inmates require more security, especially when they are let out of cells for exercise, transfer or meals, but general population inmates have the benefits of services, such as access to educational, chapel and recreational programs that are, by and large, not available to death row inmates. For purposes of this book, I consider the costs to be the same for each group of inmates.

39   See the figures on their Web site at www.doc.state.or.us.

40   The longest continually serving inmate among the 2,000 inmates currently in the Oregon State Penitentiary is Jerome Henry Brudos who has been in the penitentiary since 1969.

41   In addition, the actual costs of executing an inmate run into the hundreds of thousands of dollars. The execution of Henry Moore in 1997 involved the staff time, and overtime, of more than 100 corrections and legal personnel. The Department of Corrections estimated that the costs of his execution were $200,000. See the Web page at www.doc.state.or.us. It is probable that expenses for future executions would exceed this amount, especially if the people executed are not so willing to go to their deaths.

42   Comparable figures from other states, detailed at www.deathpenaltyinfo.org, list the cost of execution at about three or four times the cost of housing an inmate for life. Oregon's unique experience with the *Penry* and Ballot Measure 40 problems has increased these costs for Oregon considerably.

43   Karl Terry's 1994 murder of two Milwaukie men is scheduled for hearing early in September 2001 at Jefferson High School in Portland, as part of the Oregon Supreme Court's program to hear oral arguments at a number of schools throughout the state. 2002 then should see a large number of oral arguments as several of the next cases in the chart on page 193 should be ready for hearing.

44   Six people were executed in 1909, two in 1910, 0 in 1911, four in 1912 and five in 1913. After these executions, Oregonians promptly did away with the death penalty in 1914. See Chapter Two. More detailed analysis of these figures is in Hugo Bedau, "Capital Punishment in Oregon, 1903-64," *Oregon Law Review* 45 (1965), 8.

45   If one studies the huge number of executions from Texas over the last few years, more than 100 under the governorship of George Bush alone, one sees that these were all cases that had a long life to them. Texas didn't began to execute people in earnest until the late 1980s. Now the flood is coming there, and the rest of the nation is standing back rather nonplused at the reality of sending a person to death every month in that state.

Part I
History

Table 2–1. Oregon Death Penalty Election Tallies.

Proposal	Year	Type of Proposal	Percent in Favor	Tally in Favor	Percent in Opposition	Tally in Opposition	Effect on Death Penalty
—	November 5, 1912	Initiative petition/Statutory initiative	39.40	41,951	60.60	64,578	No effect; if passed, would have eliminated death penalty
—	November 3, 1914	Initiative petition/Constitutional amendment	50.04	100,552	49.96	100,395	Abolished death penalty
Special election	May 21, 1920	Legislative referral/Constitutional changes	55.80	81,756	44.20	64,589	Restored death penalty
Ballot Measure 4	November 1958	Legislative referral/Constitutional changes	48.70	264,434	51.30	276,487	No effect; if passed, would have repealed death penalty
Ballot Measure 1	November 3, 1964	Legislative referral/Constitutional changes	60.10	455,654	39.90	302,105	Repealed death penalty

Proposal	Year	Type of Proposal	Percent in Favor	Tally in Favor	Percent in Opposition	Tally in Opposition	Effect on Death Penalty
(HB 2321)	November 1978	Initiative petition/ Statutory initiative	64.30	573,707	35.70	318,610	Restored death penalty
Ballot Measure 6	November 6, 1984	Initiative petition/ Statutory initiative/ Constitutional and statutory changes	55.60	653,009	44.40	521,687	Exempted death sentence for aggravated murder from constitutional restrictions on cruel, unusual, and vindictive punishment
Ballot Measure 7	November 6, 1984	Initiative petition/ Statutory initiative/ Constitutional and statutory changes	75.10	893,818	24.90	295,988	Reinstated death penalty

CHAPTER 2

Capital Punishment in Oregon until 1920

Capital punishment measures have been on the ballot more times in Oregon's history—seven—than in the history of any other state.[1] The voters of Oregon have twice banned capital punishment and twice reinstated it.[2] Oregon has had capital punishment for 116 of the 142 years since statehood in 1859. Yet the greatest opposition to capital punishment as well as the most overwhelming support for it occurred in a twenty-year period, 1964 to 1984, which is within the memory of many Oregonians. It is an issue that still evokes the most eloquent arguments and the most visceral reactions.

The principal purpose of this historical survey is not simply to tell the story of capital punishment from the earliest days until passage of the current statute in 1984, but to isolate some lessons about what conditions tend to contribute to successful movements for the abolition or retention of the death penalty in Oregon. A second purpose, discussed more briefly, is to understand how Oregon's experience with capital punishment fits in with that of the other states. In order to accomplish these purposes, our focus will be upon the periods in Oregon's history of greatest turmoil and debate on the issue. After a brief introduction discussing the death penalty before statehood and the movement to transfer executions from the counties to the Oregon State Penitentiary in Salem, this section will focus on the debate over capital punishment in Oregon from 1911 to 1920, 1957 to 1964 and 1977 to 1984.

Introduction—The Earliest Period

Although most students of Oregon's history have a vague awareness that capital punishment was authorized for certain offenses in the early period, they could be forgiven if they were unsure about the source of that authorization. Howard Corning, in his *Dictionary of Oregon History*, mentions that capital punishment was authorized by the 1857 Oregon Constitution, and Hugo Bedau, a former Reed College philosophy professor and one of the leaders in the movement to abolish capital punishment in Oregon in 1964, stresses that capital punishment was *constitutional* and not *statutory* in early Oregon history.[3]

One has to do some digging to discover that this is not the case.[4] No mention was made of capital punishment in the constitution of 1857. The only mention of capital punishment at the 1857 Constitutional Convention was the rejection of a motion that would have banned capital punishment from the state.[5] The first code of criminal law enacted after statehood, the Deady Code of 1864, authorized capital punishment for first degree murder and treason.[6]

Determining the authority for executions in Oregon from the beginnings of the Provisional Government in 1843 until the Deady Code of 1864 is more complex than it ought to be and will only be indicated briefly here.[7] The Legislative Committee of the Provisional Government moved and the people accepted a motion on July 5, 1843, which provided in Article 12: "The laws of Iowa territory shall be the law of this territory in civil, military and criminal cases: where not otherwise provided for, and where no statute of Iowa territory applies, the principles of common law and equity shall govern."[8] Article 19 of the same report, however, limited the effect of Article 12 and adopted only 37 of the 74 chapters of that collection. The law of criminal offenses, from pages 109– 125 of the *Statute Laws of the Territory of Iowa 1838–39*, was adopted in Article 19. A quick check of the *Statute Laws of the Territory of Iowa 1838–39* (referred to as the *Little Blue Book* in Oregon) shows that pages 109– 125 only cover issues of criminal procedure. The enumeration of actual crimes, beginning with murder, begins on page 142.[9] The first governing authority in Oregon, therefore, officially passed no murder statute through its 1843 action.

Someone probably became aware of this rather major oversight because the next year the Legislative Committee reiterated its adoption of the *Statute Laws of the Territory of Iowa 1838–39* but then provided: "That the resolution heretofore passed, and recorded under the nineteenth article of the judiciary, be and the same is hereby repealed."[10] The effect of this act, apparently, would be to adopt the entire *Statute Laws of 1838–39*, except for those sections of a purely local character. The Iowa statute on murder, as well as other crimes as various as dueling and misprision of felony, seemingly was in place in Oregon.

Then, in 1845, the Legislative Committee passed the following: "That the Laws of Iowa Territory concerning Duelling be and the same is hereby adopted as the Law of this Territory."[11] What would be the need to adopt the Iowa law of dueling in 1845 if the effect of the 1844 statute was to appropriate the entire Iowa criminal code? Perhaps Ronald Lansing is correct when he says that it seemed generally to be understood that the Iowa laws would govern crime on the frontier, regardless of the specific language of various resolutions.[12]

By 1849 the issue was further clouded because of an act of the newly formed Territorial Legislature to adopt the *Revised Statutes of the Territory of Iowa 1842–43*.[13] Despite the controversy over whether the Iowa statutory collection of 1838–39 or 1842–43 would be adopted, the murder statute of both was fairly similar. Both defined murder as "the unlawful killing of a human being in the peace of the United States, with malice aforethought, and either express or implied." The 1838–39 statutes listed a variety of ways that such murder might be committed, but the later collection said only, "the manner of the killing is *not* material."[14] In both codes death was prescribed for one convicted of the crime of murder.

A portion of the Iowa laws adopted by the 1849 Territorial Legislature was printed, bound and distributed in the Oregon Territory in 1850.[15] Then in December 1850, the Territorial Legislature dramatically changed the murder statute and capital punishment in Oregon, adopting a "Pennsylvania-style" statute by breaking murder into two degrees and by including a felony murder component.[16] First degree murder, punishable by death, occurred when a person "purposely, and of deliberate and premeditated malice, or in the perpetration or attempt to perpetrate any rape, arson, robbery or burglary, or by administering poison...kill(s) another." Second degree murder, punishable by life imprisonment, was reserved for those who "shall purposely and maliciously, but without deliberation and premeditation, kill another."[17] This statute, adopted December 2, 1850, became the basis for the murder statute for the Code Commissioners of 1853 and the Deady Criminal Code of 1864. Therefore, the murder statute at the time of statehood in 1859 was substantially the same as in the Deady Code of 1864, even if it had changed considerably from the earliest statutes of the Oregon Provisional Government.[18]

From Public to Private Executions in Oregon

For the first 44 years of statehood, condemned murderers were executed in the counties rather than centrally.[19] In the dignified words of the Deady Code,

> When judgment of death is pronounced, a warrant, signed by the judge of the court, and attested by the clerk with the seal of the court affixed, must be drawn and delivered to the sheriff of the county; the warrant shall state the conviction and judgment, and appoint a day on which the judgment is to be executed, which must not be less than thirty nor more than sixty days from the time of judgment.[20]

Public executions, however, were anything but dignified. The *Oregonian* dispatched its special correspondent, Mr. Obenchain, to cover the hangings of four Modoc Indians who had killed General Canby and his men in the Lava Beds near the Oregon-California border in 1873. The executions were performed at Fort Klamath in Jacksonville on October 3, 1873. In the October 6 edition of the paper Obenchain breathlessly described the hundreds of people who had gathered around, the "half-smothered cry of horror" that went up from the crowd of more than 500 Klamath Indians who had gathered, the writhings of two of the victims, the burial of the dead.[21]

Perhaps as response to this mingled horror and crude interest, the Oregon Legislature in 1874 passed a statute requiring that all executions in the future should take place "within the enclosure of the jail or jail yard where the defendant is confined, and in the presence of twelve *bona fide* electors of the county, to be selected by the Sheriff of said county."[22]

If the legislature thought that bringing executions into the jail yards of the various counties would increase decorum and dignity but lessen public interest in executions, they were sorely mistaken. Crowds numbering into the thousands milled around the old Multnomah County Courthouse for executions in the 1870s and 1880s.[23] It would be two executions in Portland on January 31, 1902, however, that would become the catalyst to remove all executions from general public view and confine them to the Oregon State Penitentiary in Salem.

On November 21, 1901, Jack Wade and William Dalton, roomers in a boarding house on East Seventh Street in Portland, shot a young man named James Morrow when he was coming home after an evening with friends. Wade and Dalton claimed at trial they really had not meant to kill Morrow, but the jury quickly convicted them of murder and sentenced them to death. A January 31, 1902, execution date was set.[24] Since the Multnomah County Courthouse was the site of the county jail, the execution would be carried out, by statutory requirement, at the courthouse.

The Multnomah County Courthouse at issue was the predecessor to the current one, built in 1914. The old courthouse occupied the same square as its successor, between Fourth and Fifth and SW Salmon and SW Main in Portland, and when this two-story structure was erected in the 1860s it was the largest public building in Portland. Its early shape was like a "+" sign, with a cupola covering the center, with the entrance to the courthouse on Fourth Avenue in the center of the block. In the 1880s the old courthouse gained two additions, so that by 1890 the original "+" shape had been elongated north and south, and the wings of the courthouse stretched all the way from Salmon to Main.[25]

The executions of Wade and Dalton would take place in the northwest courtyard of the courthouse, near the intersection of Fifth and Salmon.[26] Portland had grown to be a city of 100,000 people by 1900 and so, to assure a modicum of privacy, a wooden wall twenty feet tall was erected inside the fence which ran along Fifth and Salmon where the execution would take place.[27] A nine-foot tall platform was set up along the Salmon Street wing of the courthouse, with two nooses next to each other eight feet apart, facing Fifth Avenue.

Execution was set for 8 a.m. on Friday, January 31, 1902. Already by 6 o'clock crowds were gathering outside the enclosure. Tickets had been issued to 400 special guests, and they were let inside after the sheriff and his companions from other counties had prepared the entrances, one on Fifth and one on Salmon. It was a male-only affair since, according to the beliefs of the time, the delicacy of the female frame and mind would probably be overwhelmed by the event. Observant onlookers, however, could not help noticing a crowd of eager females perched on the roof of a hotel across Fifth Avenue, straining for the most advantageous view of the proceedings.

The atmosphere at the hanging was part carnival and part martyrdom. The carnival part would be evident even to a casual viewer: people clutching rare tickets to the event, someone trying to bribe a guard to let him in, the crowd pressing forward to see the events, seven linemen from the telephone company clambering up nearby phone poles to get an unobstructed view, greetings exchanged among the crowd, all nervously expecting great and unusual things.

But there were also unmistakable signs that a martyrdom of sorts was afoot. There was a detailed account of how the prisoners had spent their last night, their hearty breakfast, the earnest attempts of the missionaries to offer consolation, and the lusty singing of classic Gospel hymns by the condemned men around 7 o'clock. The reverie of the moment was unceremoniously broken by the sheriff's reading of the death warrant. Then the prisoners were escorted to the platform for their final test of faith. One, Dalton, desired to address the crowd. A great hush fell as listeners and reporters strained for his every word, oblivious to the irony that a man to whom probably no one had listened for the balance of his life would be vouchsafed divine wisdom to shed on the crowd in his last moment.

Dalton exhorted the crowd to trust in Jesus and not to follow on the path that he had chosen. In a description that could have been lifted from an early Christian martyrology, one reporter had it:

> (t)he condemned man spoke up with an earnest appeal to young men to lead [T]he condemned man spoke up with an earnest appeal to young men to lead better lives and accept Christianity. His voice was clear and hardly a tremor was noticeable. He gestured freely and raised his eyes to Heaven in an attitude of absolute faith with his Maker. He read from the Bible Psalm 23.

The scene was replete with other indicia of verisimilitude: the leaden gray sky, a light rain that began to fall during the proceedings, the snow underfoot, the condemned men waving to acquaintances in the crowd, a prisoner nervously testing the tensility of the rope, the reporters faithfully narrating the exact moment that the traps were sprung (7:57 or 7:58, depending on the account), the exact distance that each man plunged to his death (Dalton fell 5' 6" while Wade fell 6' 2"), the precise facial expression of each man after the hoods were removed, the scramble of some members of the crowd for souvenirs of the event. The souvenirs were perhaps a piece of rope or a sliver of the platform, gathered up to show the children, wife and grandchildren to be sure, but also, in keeping with the theme of martyrdom, as if these mementos were relics of one who had passed through his final test of faith to be with God.

One Portlander who was neither amused nor entertained by the event was Multnomah County District Attorney and gubernatorial candidate George Earle Chamberlain. In his inaugural message to the 1903 Legislature, he made an unmistakable reference to the 1902 Portland hangings:

> In two cases in Multnomah County, at least four hundred invitations were issued to officials and others to witness the double execution of two notorious criminals and applica-

tions were made for as many more. The gallows were erected in the jail yard at the intersection of two of the most public streets in the city of Portland, and the morbidly curious were attracted there from the time the workmen commenced to build the scaffold until it was finally torn down. At the moment of the execution, although the ground was covered with snow, crowds of men, women and children stood in the adjacent streets to see and hear, if possible, what took place within the enclosure, and boys and men actually climbed telephone poles to look over the same. Such scenes are demoralizing and ought not to be tolerated in any civilized community.[28]

Chamberlain proposed, and the legislature adopted, a law which would require the circuit court judge in the county of the condemned man's conviction to authorize the county sheriff to deliver the condemned defendant to the superintendent of the penitentiary, who would carry out the execution out of public view at the State Penitentiary.[29] An unexpected twist in adopting the law happened when the county sheriffs balked at such a plan (their authority, of course, would be considerably curtailed through this act), and the legislature had to meet in special session to make sure that the law was only applicable to cases of *future* murders in their counties.[30] The county sheriffs would still have authority to execute people convicted of first degree murder who were currently under their care. As a result, Oregon's first person executed within the penitentiary walls in Salem was Harry Egbert, on January 29, 1904, while the last person legally executed in the counties was Norman Williams in The Dalles on July 21, 1905.[31]

The Movement to Abolish and Restore the Death Penalty (1911–1920)

An item on the agenda of many politicians during the Progressive Era was the abolition of the death penalty. The death penalty was seen by progressives as a relic of barbarism, a vestigial remnant of a primitive and less enlightened era of human experience. Between 1897 and 1917 ten states abolished the death penalty for shorter or longer periods of time.[32] When Oregonians elected the progressive Democrat Oswald West as governor in 1910, they would have reason to believe that abolition of the death penalty would be a priority in his administration. They were not to be disappointed, even though there were also larger social issues that occupied West's mind in those days. For example, the movement for women's suffrage reached its acme in 1912 in Oregon and prohibition was the "hot-button" issue in the 1914 election.

One of the lesser ironies of the story of capital punishment in Oregon is that West, whose personal opposition to the death penalty was as vigorous as any governor in Oregon's history, presided over as many executions during his four-year administration as any other governor in Oregon. Between January 1911 and January 1915 nine men were executed in Oregon. Nine also were executed in the six-year leadership of George Chamberlain (1903–1909), six had been executed in the two-year Benson-Bowerman interregnum of 1909–1911, and eight were to be executed under Earl Snell, 1943–1947.[33] That so many executions happened under West's watch is also significant because he solemnly vowed during the first year of his governorship that there would never be an execution in Oregon as long as he was governor.[34]

West came into office in 1911 as a brash, confident, energetic, progressive 37-year-old, who had cut his political teeth in the employ of the State Land Board during the timber fraud scandal of 1903–1907.[35] He saw it as his role to shake state government out of its somnolence and pursue a vigorous social agenda which, within a few years, would see dramatic wage and work-hour legislation, workmen's compensation (as it was called at the time), women's suffrage and prohibition. In his 80-minute inaugural address he devoted several paragraphs to the condemnation of capital punishment.

> Capital punishment should be abolished, in my opinion, in this state. The system of paying for a life with a life is, in my belief, merely a relic of that ancient and barbarous doctrine of an eye for an eye and a tooth for a tooth.[36]

He spoke about how juries were reluctant to assume the great responsibility of convicting a person of first degree murder because of their awareness that such a person would almost certainly be executed. A hung jury was often the result, with the convicted person going free.[37] Life imprisonment should be substituted in its stead.

But West's proposal also contained some nuance. He believed that the constitutional power of the governor to grant pardons, reprieves and commutations should be restricted in the case of a person convicted of murder.[38] Unless post-trial evidence pointed to some glaring injustice in the trial, the governor should not be able to commute or pardon such a person.[39]

West did not waste time acting on his beliefs. In July 1911 he commuted the sentence of Jesse Webb and on November 23, the day before he was to leave the state for a month, he commuted the death sentence of Jans M. Hassing to a sentence of life imprisonment.[40] During Hassing's trial the court had not allowed evidence of the history of mental illness in Hassing's family to be presented, even though it was certified by Mr. C. Moltke, Envoy Extraordinary and Minister Plenipotentiary of Denmark.[41] Such an egregious oversight justified his action, West believed.[42]

But West took the occasion of Hassing's commutation to announce a broader policy of his administration.

> There will be no hanging in Oregon as long as I am governor of the state. The belief that bloodshed must be expiated by the shedding of blood is...a relic of barbarism and not in consonance...with the spirit of the twentieth century. It is an antiquated and anachronistic remainder from the dark ages.[43]

In uttering this policy, West was relying on the notion, noted above, that the dawning of the twentieth century had banished the darkness of earlier periods and that elimination of capital punishment would be a fitting expression of this belief. The march of science, scholarship, well-intentioned reformers and people of good will would soon raise civilization to a new level. West wanted to be in the vanguard of that movement, to announce, as it were, the rosy-fingered dawn of the new day.

Perhaps not surprisingly West's chief *bete-noire* in the struggle to eliminate this dark relic was the *Oregonian*. Though its redoubtable editor Harvey Scott had died only the year before, the paper was still under the lengthened shadow of that great man. Scott had championed a death penalty that was swift and sure in its execution.[44] In holding this belief, Scott and the *Oregonian* saw themselves as the true bearer of civilization's values. Civilization for them consisted of the march of ordered liberty, where punishments were certain and convicts were spared the "everlasting meddling with the straightforward and certain operation of the law by weak-kneed Governors and by the higher courts through quibbles, technicalities, evasions and hair-splitting."[45]

The struggle over the moral high ground between West and the *Oregonian* intensified in January 1912 when West decided to propose an initiative petition to eliminate the death penalty from Oregon.[46] West had just granted a reprieve, rather than a commutation, to convicted killer Mike Morgan and promised to grant as many more reprieves that year as there were convicted first degree murderers pending a vote by the people on a ballot measure to eliminate capital punishment. To bring the matter to a head, West set a date— Friday December 13, 1912—as the day when Morgan and others reprieved would be executed if the people of Oregon did not vote to eliminate the death penalty in November. In other words, West was trying to make the people of Oregon not mere spectators but intimate participants in the raging debate over the death penalty. Their vote to maintain capital punishment would very likely send an indeterminate number of men plunging to their deaths on Friday the 13th, just before Christmas.[47]

By May 1912 the initiative petition had been drawn up. Though it proposed to amend two sections of *Lord's Oregon Laws*, it really had to do with three issues.[48] In addition to declaring life imprisonment to be the punishment for first degree murder and limiting the governor's commutation power, the law also had a "savings clause" which provided that the law would only apply to future crimes, and that the current law would be applied to acts already committed and cases already tried. The presence or absence of a savings clause would be a crucial issue during the later (1914) debate on the issue.

On November 5, 1912, the measure went down to a resounding defeat, 60.6–39.4% (64,578– 41,951). It passed in only two counties: Coos and Klamath, with Jackson being almost a dead heat. Several reasons for its defeat can be given, including the lack of campaign organization to pass the issue, the fact that only six states had abolished the death penalty by 1912, that West's challenge to Oregon's voters backfired on him, that the Republicans enjoyed a 2–1 voter registration edge and that the continuous harping of the *Oregonian* on the inconsistent approach of the governor and the need to maintain order through true and predictable sentences finally took its toll on the voters.[49]

True to his word, West let four executions go forward on December 13, 1912. The state penitentiary only had two gallows and so the four men, Mike Morgan, Noble Faulder, Jack Roberts and Frank Garrison, had to be executed in shifts in the late morning and early afternoon.[50] On the day before the executions, December 12, two delegations consisting of nearly 100 people descended on West and urged him to commute the death sentences, as he had promised to do after commuting Hassing's sentence in November 1911.[51] The exchange of views illuminates the nature of West's opposition to the death penalty and presents a more fully expressed philosophy of opposition than he had previously expressed. In brief, though he opposed it, his philosophy of capital punishment was utilitarian. He insisted, "If those men do not go to the gallows tomorrow, capital punishment will not be abolished during our lifetime." When a person pressed him on the issue, the governor challenged his guests, "(What) would you advise me to do...which in my judgment would bring about the most speedy abolition of the death penalty?"

In other words, West had used the year between the commutation of Webb and Hassing and the four executions to refine his understanding and philosophy of capital punishment. In contrast to what I will subsequently call the moralism of Robert Holmes and the legalism of Mark Hatfield, West, in good Benthamite tradition, argued for "the greatest good for the greatest number." "If we do not go through the painful process of executions now, Oregon will continue to want to execute people. The only hope rests in my showing to the people of Oregon the terrible horror of this penalty by going through with the executions. Then maybe they will become revolted by these executions, as I have become, and decide to banish them forever."[52]

Almost lost in the cacophony of words and deeds leading up to and following the December 13 executions was a December 14 editorial in the *Oregon Statesman* entitled "Against Hanging." The editorial laid out a three-point philosophy of punishment based on Article I, section 15, of the Oregon Constitution: "Laws for the punishment of crime shall be founded on the principles of reformation, and not of vindictive justice."[53] The paper argued that this basic constitutional principle, absent from most state constitutions, required that a philosophy of rehabilitation be the foundation stone for Oregon penology. As a result there should be "an absolutely indeterminate sentence or commitment for every person convicted of a crime," with reformatory treatment for prisoners with grades established based on the danger that the inmate presents. Finally, a parole system should seek to place people in jobs and reconnect him with his family and community.[54] Oregon, however, was in no mood for these suggestions in 1912.

The issue was revived in 1914 through a constitutional initiative petition drawn up by the Anti-Capital Punishment League.[55] In contrast to the statutory initiative of 1912, the 1914 proposal would add a new section to the Oregon Constitution, Article 1, section 36, which would simply say, "The death penalty shall not be inflicted upon any person under the laws of Oregon. The maximum punishment which may be inflicted shall be life imprisonment." The *Oregonian* greeted this new effort with unmitigated scorn. It pompously proclaimed that "there has been a full and free discussion of the subject." It went on,

> It would seem to be unnecessary once more to reopen this threadbare subject for discussion on these merits. The resubmission of the question, merely because a few agitators refuse to accept the verdict of the people, is a first-rate example of gross abuse of the initiative.

The editorial closed with the confident hope that the measure would be defeated by an overwhelming majority "in sheer resentment at the trifling and indefensible methods of the busy-body promoters of the measure."[56]

By 1914, however, the political landscape had changed considerably, and this change would ultimately lead to the abolition of capital punishment by a razor-thin margin in November. Women now had the vote, and instead of 106,000 people voting in 1912 there would be 201,000 voting in 1914. One of Oswald West's fondest hopes was that the presence of female voters would "humanize" the voting process and lead to abolition of the death penalty. In addition, Washington State had voted to abolish the death penalty in 1913 and the proponents of abolition in Oregon now were more organized than ever. Further, in 1913 Oregon had executed five more men, bringing to nine the number of executions within 13 months. Wavering supporters of capital punishment would surely have had their fill of executions. Editorial support was forthcoming from the *Oregon Journal* and the *Oregon Statesman,* and the unflagging efforts of organizer Paul Turner in Multnomah County provided the decisive margin of victory.[57]

But a small tempest developed two weeks before the election when the *Oregonian* noted that the initiative petition didn't have a savings clause attached. A savings clause declares how those convicted under previous laws (when the death penalty was in force) would be treated in the wake of the law's abolition. In order to maintain the appeal of simplicity, the 1914 initiative petition only proposed to amend the constitution and did not speak of the fate of those previously condemned to die after the new law was passed.

Sensing the slightest hint of blood, the *Oregonian* boldly proclaimed that two convicted murderers, John Arthur Pender and Lloyd Wilkins, would have to be let off scot-free if the initiative passed.[58] Because the initiative did away with the only punishment in the books for first degree murder, death, the logical corollary was that the elimination of the death penalty eliminated the penalty for first degree murder. Murderers go free. That would be the result of voting for the measure.

To be fair to the *Oregonian*, it had a point. At first glance, there was a good chance the 1914 initiative petition was not well crafted. It sacrificed legal completeness for brevity.[59] If nothing could be done, there was a good chance that there would be no punishment for the two after the election results were in. West rejected immediate commutation of their sentences in October 1914 because, as in 1912, he wanted to wait until the results of the election before deciding on commutation or sending the men to death.

When confronted on the issue of the lack of a savings clause, the governor was noncommittal. The ultimate resolution of the issue after the election is fascinating. The governor's legal counsel noted that the language of Article IV, section 1, on initiatives and referenda spoke only of referenda becoming effective the day of passage. Nothing was said about the effective date of initiatives.[60] Therefore, other sections of the constitution were consulted. Article XVII, section 1, stated that the secretary of state shall canvass the votes of the election before the Governor and then the Governor would proclaim that the law was in effect, but this section does not mention when that canvassing must occur. However, a section in the statutes of Oregon provided more specific guidance:

> It shall be the duty of the secretary of state in the presence of the governor, to proceed within thirty days after the election, and sooner if all the returns be all received, to canvass the votes given for each measure. The governor shall forthwith issue his proclamation...and declar(e) such measures as are approved by majority of those voting to be in full force and effect as the law of the state of Oregon from the date of said proclamation.[61]

Furnished with this statutory support, and by the fact that the election returns were so close as to make a 30-day delay after the election reasonable, the governor calmly commuted the sentences of Pender and Wilkins to life imprisonment 29 days after the election and then proclaimed the victory of the measure 30 days after the election, on December 3, 1914.[62] The *Oregonian's* point, therefore, was mooted.

The victory was by the tiniest of margins, 50.04–49.96% (100,552–100,395). It was the narrowest victory of any initiative in Oregon's history. An examination of the county-by-county voting tally shows that the largest margins of victory were 2,377 votes in Multnomah County, 1,057 in Jackson County and 713 in Coos County, while Washington, Linn, and Marion had the largest margins against the proposal.[63]

To imagine that the *Oregonian* would be gracious in defeat would be to engage in wishful thinking. Noting that there was no longer any punishment for treason since that crime, like first degree murder, merited only the death penalty before the election, the paper joyfully proclaimed, "Those treasonably disposed may now carry on their favorite amusements unhindered."[64] In 1915, an inmate released in Oregon murdered a woman in San Francisco. The *Oregonian* pounced,

> Advocates of the death penalty are met with the plea that life imprisonment is as effectual as hanging in preventing a murderer from committing another murder, but in practice there is no such penalty in Oregon as life imprisonment.[65]

When the chairman of Washington State's Industrial Insurance Commission was brutally murdered by a disgruntled injured worker in 1917, the newspaper noted that Washington, which had abolished capital punishment in 1913, would probably be changing its tune.[66] Indeed, in an ominous sign for Oregon's abolition movement, Washington voted to restore capital punishment in 1919.

The movement to restore capital punishment in Oregon began in earnest in 1917. A bill to repeal Article I, section 36, died in committee, however, and nothing came out of the 1919 legislature on the issue. Governor James Withycombe died on March 3, 1919, and was succeeded by Ben Olcott, an ardent death penalty supporter, but the legislative session had ended February 27 and proponents were resigned to waiting until 1921.[67]

The *Oregonian*, however, neither slumbered nor slept. On October 22, 1919, it published a front-page story of what purported to be an interview with a man recently convicted of murdering a Portland woman who was influential in securing his release from San Quentin shortly before.[68] In the interview he solemnly affirmed that he would not have committed his crime if Oregon had a death penalty statute. Or in his own words, "I don't believe I'd have done it if I thought there was any chance of my hanging for it." The Multnomah County District Attorney asked him about whether he knew there was a death penalty in Oregon. Displaying the learning of an accomplished legal scholar, despite being confined in San Quentin, the man replied that he not only knew that was the case but that was actually in his mind as he murdered the woman. To a question by the district attorney regarding whether these crimes would be prevented if there was a death penalty in Oregon, the man replied, with a bit too much helpfulness, "Yes, that's the reason so many of these stunts are being pulled off."

If the *Oregonian* was straining a bit too hard in October 1919, two events occurred in November that would put restoration of capital punishment in Oregon on a fast track. On November 11, 1919, several members of the I.W.W. fired on the first Armistice Day Parade in Centralia, Washington, killing four members of the American Legion. Public anger was swift and predictable, though the immediate interest was in trying to figure out methods to curb radicalism rather than restore the death penalty. On November 21, 1919, however, all that changed. That evening two outlaws held up the Cleremont Inn in Linnton just north of Portland and killed two of its patrons—the state highway commissioner, Newton Burgess, and an influential Pendleton rancher, George Perringer.

The outrage was immediate and direct. Mayor George Baker of Portland ordered the city attorney to draw up an amendment to the state constitution which would reinstate the death penalty.[69] Governor Ben Olcott called a special session of the Oregon Legislature and urged the legislators to repeal the ban on capital punishment. He intoned,

> Since the adjournment of the regular session in 1919 a wave
> of crime has swept over the country. Oregon has suffered
> from this criminal blight and during the past few months
> the commission of a number of cold-blooded and fiendish
> homicides has aroused our people to a demand for greater
> and more certain protection. . . . Because of this urgency I
> am taking the liberty of suggesting…repealing the present
> constitutional inhibition on capital punishment.[70]

The urgency of the issue was such that Olcott wanted a legislative referral to
go to the voters at a special election on May 21, 1920. Legislators quickly
acquiesced and proposed a repeal of Article I, section 36, and an adoption of
Article 1, section 37, which would read: "The penalty for murder in the first
degree shall be death, except when the trial jury in its verdict recommend life
imprisonment, in which case the penalty shall be life imprisonment."[71] Article I, section 38, of the state constitution would restore the sections implementing the death penalty from *Lord's Oregon Laws* whose effect had been
nullified by the vote to abolish capital punishment in 1914.

The debate over the proposed constitutional change was vigorous, given
the exigencies of the moment. Opposition to the proposal came from opponents of capital punishment *as well as* supporters. Objection from opponents
is easy to understand, but the opposition of capital punishment supporters is
harder to fathom at first glance. In brief, they objected to the idea that the
death penalty now would be *optional* for first degree murder. Ever since the
1840s, Oregon had a mandatory death penalty for first degree murder. Once
a person was convicted of that crime, he paid the ultimate price. But this
proposal would leave discretion on sentencing totally in the hands of the jury,
to be swayed by issues possibly extraneous to the mere guilt of the person.[72]
The conservative *Oregon Voter* likened the murderer to a rattlesnake that had
to be killed to protect mankind. Any opportunity for leniency should be es-
chewed.[73]

The May 21, 1920, special election drew only 146,000 voters, not even
75% of the vote cast in the 1914 general election. Despite the great emotion
in the wake of the previous year's shootings, the vote to restore capital punishment in Oregon was only 55.8–44.2% (81,756–64,589). Supporters of a ban
on capital punishment could take heart, perhaps, because in these strained
times they had only lost by 11%. The mood of the nation had changed, however, with Washington restoring capital punishment in 1919 and several of
the states that had experimented with it in the Progressive Era reinstating it
around the same time. Oregon would be part of that restoration, but the

closeness of the numbers should have tempered the enthusiasm of capital punishment supporters in Oregon. The issue was sure to return.

One last point, by way of a poignant epilogue to this segment on capital punishment from 1911–1920, is worthy of mention. When Burgess and Perringer were killed in Portland on November 21, 1919, one of the men who apprehended the perpetrators was Umatilla County Sheriff Tillman Taylor, who was also with his Pendleton compatriots in Portland for the Pacific International Livestock Exposition. Despite the fact that he knew he might be killed, and that no death penalty "protected" him, Taylor acted. Then in July 1920, two months after capital punishment had been restored and Taylor would therefore be "protected" by the death penalty, he was shot and killed by prisoners escaping from the Umatilla County jail. They were later found, convicted, and three of them hanged for the crime, but the death of Tillman Taylor was perhaps mute testimony for those who opposed capital punishment—that it really did not deter a criminal. Oregonians would have to wait more than a generation, however, before they broached the subject again in earnest.[74]

Endnotes

1   By initiative petitions in 1912, 1914, 1978 and 1984 and legislative referrals to the people in 1920, 1958 and 1964. The initiative petition of 1914 was for a constitutional amendment, and the initiative petitions in 1912, 1978 and 1984 were statutory initiatives. The legislative referrals in 1920, 1958 and 1964 were all for constitutional changes.

2   Abolished from 1914–1920 and 1964–1984. Even though the voters reinstated the death penalty in 1978, the Oregon Supreme Court threw out the statute in a January 1981 decision. *State v. Quinn,* 290 Or 383, 623 P2d 653 (1981). Other states, to be sure, have had and abolished the death penalty, but the most recent cases of abolition and restoration came as a result of United States Supreme Court decisions in 1972 and 1976 and not because of a movement by the people to abolish the death penalty. See Chapter Seven for a brief discussion of the role of the United States Supreme Court in the death penalty debate.

3   Corning, Howard M., *Dictionary of Oregon History* (Portland: Binfords & Mort, 1956), 44. Bedau, Hugo, *Death is Different* (Boston: Northeastern University Press, 1987), 156.

4   Helpful and easily accessible in this regard is the primer on capital punishment in Oregon on the Oregon Department of Corrections Web page: www.doc.state.or.us. A simple outline of the issue is presented there, along with pictures of the execution chambers and one of the two men executed in Oregon since capital punishment was restored by initiative petition in 1984. At present there is no comprehensive survey on this issue.

5   Carey, Charles H., ed., *The Oregon Constitution and Proceedings and Debates of the Constitutional Convention of 1857* (Salem: State Printer, 1926), 359.

6   Deady, Matthew, *General Laws of Oregon 1845–1864* (Portland: Pittock, 1866) Criminal Code, sec. 502, p. 527, defined the crime of murder in the first degree. Sec 512, page 528, declared, "Every person convicted of murder in the first degree, shall be punished with death." In addition, the General Laws of the Deady Code proscribe treason and provide: "Every person convicted of the crime of treason, shall suffer death for the same." *General Laws,* Chapter LVIII, 931. No one has ever been convicted of treason in Oregon's history.

7   Ronald B. Lansing's study of the trial of the Cayuse Indians convicted of the massacre of Marcus and Narcissa Whitman and their party in Waiilatpu in November 1847 is illuminating, but does not consider the broader question of the early development of Oregon's murder statute. *Juggernaut: The Whitman Massacre Trial* (Pasadena: Ninth Judicial Circuit Historical Society, 1993), 20–27.

8   Oregon Archives (Salem: Bush, 1853), 30–31.

9   Copies of the *Statute Laws of the Territory of Iowa 1838–39* (Dubuque: Russell & Reeves, 1839) in Oregon are rare indeed. The Oregon Supreme Court library has three copies in its vault off the main reading room.

10   *Laws of Oregon 1843–1849* (Salem: Bush, 1853), 100.

11   *Laws of Oregon 1845* (New York: Phemister, 1921), 11. The laws adopted by the Provisional Government in 1845 were inadvertently left out of the volume called *Laws of Oregon 1843–49* when it was printed by Territorial Printer Asahel Bush in 1853. Again, copies of the 1845 statutes are very rare, with the Oregon Supreme Court library in Salem having three copies.

12   *Op. cit.,* 22.

13   *Laws of Oregon 1843–1849* (Salem: Bush, 1853), 103. The 72 sections of that code specifically adopted are then spelled out in the next six pages. Interesting to note is that the section adopting the Iowa criminal law includes not only the criminal procedure of Iowa but also the substantive criminal law. See 103–104. The *Little Blue Book* vs. *Big Blue Book* controversy occasioned by this act is skillfully described in Lansing, *op.cit.,* 22–27 and Fred Leeson, *Rose City Justice* (Portland: Oregon Historical Society, 1998), 13–14.

14   *Revised Statues of the Territory of Iowa 1842–43* (Iowa City: Hughes & Williams, 1843), 166.

15   Called the *Twenty Acts,* it was published in Oregon City by Robert Moore in the summer of 1850. The criminal code of the 1843 Iowa statutes was included in this printing beginning on page 89. See 89–91.

16   Pennsylvania was widely hailed for its 1794 murder statute that differentiated between first degree murder (committed by premeditation, purposefulness, and deliberation) and second degree murder (characterized only by purpose and malice, but without deliberation and premeditation). By differentiating the degrees of murder and consigning only the perpetrators of the first to death and the second to life imprisonment, Pennsylvania started the United States on an odyssey to try to limit the class of those eligible for the death penalty who had committed deliberate acts of murder. Pennsylvania's statute, however, also included felony murder within its definition of first degree murder. In its most basic form, a felony murder statute provides that if a person kills someone while perpetrating a rape, arson, robbery or burglary, that person could be found guilty of first degree murder. The problem with felony murder is that it does away with the "mental state" element for first degree murder. All one has to do is commit an act, without consideration of one's mental state during the commission of the crime, and one might be eligible for capital punishment. The older "common law" definitions of murder, for which capital punishment was the sentence, stressed the "malice aforethought" dimension of the crime. "Malice aforethought," however, had its problems, since malice could be either express or implied. Express malice is a deliberate or premeditated murder (a "cold-blooded" murder), while implied malice shows an "abandoned or malignant heart." The biblical cadence of the last phrase cannot hide the obscurity of its meaning. Discussion of the evolution of the common law and early statutory understanding of murder can be found in Charles E. Torcia, *Wharton's Criminal Law* (New York: Clark, Boardman, Callaghan, 1994), II, secs. 140–142.

17   *General Laws of Oregon 1850–51* (Salem: Bush, 1851), 81.

18   It would have been unlikely for Oregon not to have a capital punishment statute for murder during the days of its Provisional (1843–49) and Territorial Governments (1849–59). Michigan was the first state to do away with capital punishment in 1847, followed by Rhode Island in 1852 and Wisconsin in 1853. None of these states provided the basis for the development of early Oregon law.

19   For example, the execution of the five Cayuse Indians convicted in the Whitman Massacre was held in Oregon City in June 1850. The earliest execution after statehood was that of Danford Balch of Portland, who was executed October 17, 1859 on the waterfront in Portland. Balch was executed for the November 1858 shooting on the Stark Street Ferry of his son-in-law who had eloped with his daughter contrary to Balch's wishes. See, Lansing, *op. cit.,* 95–98 and Jim Humbird, "When Hangings were a Major Pastime," *Oregonian Magazine,* 3 September 1939, 2.

20   Deady, *op. cit.,* Criminal Code, sec. 198.

21   *Oregonian,* 6 October 1873, 1.

22   *Laws of Oregon 1874* (Salem: Brown, 1874), 116.

23   Humbird, *op. cit.,* 2.

24   A description of their crime and the trial is in the rather racily entitled article in the *Daily Journal,* "Dalton Died Instantaneously, Wade Struggled in Convulsions," 31 January 1902, 1. One should note that only two months elapsed between the time of the crime and execution. This was not unprecedented at that time. Before 1960 and the huge expansion of federal habeas corpus review in death penalty cases, it was not atypical for a person to be put to death within eighteen months of committing his crime. See the helpful charts in Hugo Bedau, "Capital Punishment in Oregon, 1903–64," *Oregon Law Review* 45 (1965), 29.

25   A brief description of the Old Multnomah County Courthouse is in Kathleen M. Wiederhold, *Exploring Oregon's Historic Courthouses* (Corvallis: OSU Press, 1998), 80–81. The photo archives of the Oregon History Center have a large collection of photos of the courthouse, both in its 1860s and 1880s style, though almost all of the photos are taken from the entrance or the Fourth Avenue side.

26   Wiederhold is mistaken when she says that the executions took place to the "east" of the courthouse. *Ibid.,* 80. Her account would have the executions take place on the front lawn of the courthouse. She apparently derived her information from Humbird's 1939 *Oregonian* article on hangings in early Portland. The text of Humbird's article does not say where the executions took place, but the caption under the photograph of the old Multnomah County Courthouse says, "Gallows were rigged on the front lawn of the old courthouse building for the public executions." Captions for photos are often written not by the authors of articles but by editors. Perhaps an editor had looked at the picture of the courthouse and erroneously surmised that since he was looking at the front lawn, the lawn must have been the place where the executions took place. The only recent newspaper account of hangings in Portland's history contains the even more erroneous notion that the hangings were done in the large park bordered by Third and Fourth and SW Madison and Main, opposite from today's Portland Building. Thea Rhiannon, "History Afoot Building Timeline," *Oregonian,* 15 July 1993, Portland Zone, 1. Fred Leeson says only that executions occurred in the "courthouse yard." *Rose City Justice* (Portland: Oregon Historical Society, 1998), 25.

27   Descriptions of the scene are taken from a variety of newspaper articles from January 31 and February 1, 1902. Especially helpful for this treatment were the front-page articles of the *Oregonian* (February 1), *Daily Journal* (January 31) and the *Oregon Statesman* (February 1). My account is a conflation of the three newspaper stories and no citations to particular articles are given. Microfilm collections of these newspapers are available at the Oregon History Center. The State Library in Salem also has these newspapers on microfilm. The *Daily Journal,* which began publication in 1888, later became the *Daily Capitol Journal* and then the *Capitol Journal.* The *Oregon Journal,* which eventually merged with the *Oregonian* in the 1980s, did not begin publication until March 1902.

28   *Oregon Statesman,* 15 January 1903, 9.

29   *Laws of Oregon 1903* (Salem: Whitney, 1903), 66–67.

30   *Laws of Oregon 1903, Special Session* (Salem: Whitney, 1904), 19–20.

31   Bedau, "Capital Punishment in Oregon, 1903–64" *Oregon Law Review* 45 (1965), 5, n. 23.

32   In addition to Oregon, which abolished the death penalty from 1914–1920, Colorado abolished the death penalty 1897–1901, Kansas 1907–1935, Washington 1913–1919, South Dakota 1915–1939, Tennessee 1915–1917, Arizona 1916–1918 and Missouri 1917–1919. Minnesota abolished it permanently in 1911 and North Dakota did the same in 1915. William J. Bowers, *Executions in America* (Lexington, MA: D.C. Heath, 1974), 6.

33   There were six executions in Oregon in 1909, two of which occurred before Chamberlain left office to become U.S. Senator at the end of February. The most helpful chart on this question appears in William J. Bowers, *Legal Homicide* (Boston: Northeastern University Press, 1984), 488–89. Walter Johnson and C.Y. Timmons were executed on February 5 and February 26, 1909, respectively.

34   Statistics for executions in Oregon are also found in Bedau, "Capital Punishment in Oregon," *Oregon Law Review* 45 (1965), 8. For West's pledge, which will be described in more detail below, see *Oregonian,* 5 January 1912, 7.

35   George Chamberlain, a fellow Democrat, had appointed him to that position. Despite the fact that Oregon Republicans enjoyed a 2–1 registration edge over Democrats from 1900–1915, Democratic governors served for ten of those fifteen years.

36   Text of his inaugural address in the *Oregonian,* 11 January 1911, 8.

37   This comment assumes that a jury was often instructed only on first degree murder. That is, a jury could either convict or exonerate the defendant. If convicted of first degree murder, the statute required that the defendant be put to death. Today, jury instructions are given on any crime for which the evidence can reasonably support a conviction. A jury is rarely in the situation today of having to choose the "all or nothing" option of aggravated murder or complete freedom. In addition, under Oregon law today, even if a person is convicted of aggravated murder in the guilt phase of the trial, the jury has the power in the sentencing phase to sentence

the person either to death, life imprisonment without the possibility of parole or life imprisonment with parole possible after 25 years. ORS 163.150 (1999).
38   The power is granted to the governor under Article V, section 14, of the Oregon Constitution.
39   This part of the law was never enacted. As outgoing governor, West proposed a law in
1915 that would restrict the governor's commutation power in the following way: "no reprieve,
commutation or pardon, after conviction for murder in the first degree shall be granted, except
upon the recommendation of the judge or his successor in office of the court which originally
tried the case in which such conviction was had." *Oregonian,* 21 November 1914, 15. Oregon
has never enacted any statutory or constitutional limitation on the governor's pardon, commutation, and reprieve authority. Such wide-ranging authority is only accorded to governors in 15
states today. See list in www.deathpenaltyinfo.org. An interesting case on this issue concerned
Governor Robert Holmes' ability to commute the sentence of Billy Junior Nunn, convicted of
the 1956 sexual molestation and murder of a 14-year-old Jackson County boy. See discussion
below of *Eacret v. Holmes,* 215 Or 125, 333 P2d 743 (1958).
40   The *Oregonian* was nearly apoplectic over the commutation of Webb's sentence. See for
example, *Oregonian,* 11 September 1911, 6. West's plan to commute Hassing's sentence, as well
as the text of the commutation order, is in the *Oregon Journal,* 24 November 1911, 1.
41   The facts of the case and the court's evidentiary rulings are in 60 Or 81, 118 P 195 (1911).
42   It was also the case that a date for Hassing's execution, which would take place during
West's absence, had already been set. Ben Olcott, secretary of state, would be in charge of the
Governor's affairs when West was away, and Olcott's views on capital punishment differed
dramatically from West's. It would be Olcott who called a special session of the Oregon Legislature in January 1920 to deal with, among other things, the issue of restoring the death penalty
to Oregon. Olcott urged the legislature on that occasion to restore the death penalty. The text
of his message is in the *Oregon Statesman,* 13 January 1920, 3.
43   *Oregon Journal,* 24 November 1911, 1.
44   For example, in a May 6, 1884, editorial Scott had written: "Prompt trial and swift execution of the death penalty is the sharpest and best medicine to cure a cutthroat: the grave is a
prison more frightful to the ordinary assassin than ever the living death of life imprisonment,
whose cell is never so dark but is lighted by that ray of hope we call executive pardon."
45   *Oregonian* 11 September 1911, 6.
46   *Oregonian* 5 January 1912, 7. This ultimately would be a statutory and not a constitutional initiative petition, so it would require securing only 9,000 valid signatures.
47   Legal questions surfaced later regarding the authority of the governor to set a particular
date for execution. Under Oregon law, it was the judge of the circuit court of the county of
conviction who would draw a warrant for the date of execution, which warrant the Warden (as
he was called at the time) of the Oregon State Penitentiary would honor. This approach would
seem to require sending back each case to circuit courts after the reprieve was lifted for a new
warrant to be drawn. On the other hand, West's lawyers argued, and ultimately prevailed on the
point, that once the reprieve was lifted it would mean immediate death to the defendant, since
the reprieve had already extended the defendant's life beyond the time of the original death
warrant. This issue never made it to the Oregon Supreme Court and the execution of four men
went on, as scheduled, on December 13, 1912. The *Oregon Journal* commended the governor
for this scheme as a "fit way to settle a very old issue," but the brazenness of his proposal
probably, in the long run, gained more opponents than supporters of the measure. 26 January
1912, 8.
48   The initiative would have amended sections 1903 (regarding the penalty for first degree
murder) and 1714 (limiting the power of the governor to issue pardons, reprieves and commutations after murder convictions). *Lord's Oregon Laws* (Salem: Duniway, 1910).
49   More than five states had voted to abolish the death penalty by 1912, but two of them,
Iowa and Colorado, had also restored it. Four of the anti-capital punishment states were those

who had abolished it well before the beginning of the progressive era (Michigan in 1846, Rhode Island in 1852, Wisconsin in 1853 and Maine, after a hesitant start, in 1887). Only Kansas (1907) and Minnesota (1911) voted to abolish capital punishment in the Progressive Era before 1912. William J. Bowers, *Executions in America* (Lexington, MA: D.C. Heath, 1974), 6.

50   See the account in the *Oregon Statesman,* 14 December 1912, 1.

51   *Ibid.,* 13 December 1912, 1.

52   There is more than a bit of confidence or arrogance in this line of thinking. It presupposes that he is an unerring possessor of the truth and that the voters of Oregon need to be enlightened to see this truth. If they cannot be persuaded in the abstract, maybe the grim facts of death will change their minds. Like good visual learners, the people of Oregon will see the horrors of the gallows and quickly shrink from using them any more.

53   Page 4.

54   The editorial goes on to require something very popular in the penology and social philosophy of the day, but rejected after the horrors of the Nazi regime were exposed: compulsory sterilization of "natural-born criminals." The study of eugenics, as it was called, had an enormous following in the Progressive Era and through the 1920s, and Oregon had a Eugenics Board which would oversee individual cases of "mentally-defective" and criminal people to decide if sterilization of these people would be of long-range benefit to the people of Oregon and, perhaps, to the person him or herself. A brief description of the work of the State Board of Eugenics may be found in the *Oregon Blue Book 1919–1920* (Salem: State Printer, 1919), 95.

55   *Oregonian,* 16 April 1914, 7.

56   *Oregonian,* 21 September 1914, 6.

57   A tribute to Turner and his work appears in the *Oregon Journal,* 26 November 1914, 13.

58   20 October 1914, 13.

59   Indeed, one of the continuing criticisms of the initiative petition system, as it currently is practiced in Oregon, is that there is no check on poorly-crafted or possibly unconstitutional provisions before they go to the voters. The invalidation of the 1978 death penalty initiative petition statute, discussed below, will illustrate this.

60   This was a gap in this section of the constitution, which itself was adopted by initiative petition in 1902. The act approving the initiative and referendum in Oregon, therefore, unwittingly partook of one of the problems that has dogged the initiative since that day. It was not until 1968 that voters amended, by legislative referral, this section of the Oregon Constitution to provide that "Notwithstanding section 1, Article XVII of this Constitution, an initiative or referendum measure becomes effective 30 days after the day on which it is enacted or approved by a majority of the votes cast thereon." House Joint Resolution 16, *Oregon Laws 1967* (Salem: Legislative Counsel Committee), 1631.

61   *Lord's Oregon Laws* (Salem: Duniway, 1910), sec. 3479.

62   *Oregonian,* 3 December 1914, 7.

63   Final figures were published in the *Oregonian,* 1 December 1914, 6.

64   *Oregonian,* 2 December 1914, 14.

65   *Oregonian,* 4 May 1915, 6.

66   *Oregonian,* 3 February 1917, 6.

67   Robert Dann, "Capital Punishment in Oregon," *Annals of the American Academy of Political and Social Science* 284 (Nov. 1952), 111.

68   *Oregonian,* 22 October 1919, 1.

69   *Oregonian,* 23 October 1919, 16.

70   The text of his address to the special session is printed in the *Oregon Statesman,* 13 January 1920, 3.

71   Senate Joint Resolution 8, *Oregon Laws 1920, Special Session* (Salem: State Printer, 1920), 102.

72   Dann, *op. cit.,* discusses this opposition at 112–113.

73   *Ibid.*

74   The story of Tillman Taylor is told in the *Capitol Journal,* 2 November 1978, 5A.

CHAPTER 3

The Movement to Abolish Capital Punishment, 1957 to 1964

One has the overriding sense when the issue is joined again in the mid-1950s that 1920 and 1955 were worlds apart, not just temporally but also socially and intellectually. To be sure, some things were the same. The Bolshevik threat of 1920 had become the Soviet threat of 1955, but its perceived menace to free institutions was as strong in 1955 as it was in 1920. Capital punishment was still practiced in as many, or more, jurisdictions in 1955 as in 1920.[1] Jim Crow laws were still being enforced in the South, even though their days were numbered.

Yet the discontinuities were immense. World War II brought in its wake a new internationalism, an interventionist foreign policy, and a domestic economic expansion that lent a confidence and optimism to American life that had not been seen for a generation. It was almost as if the crises of the 1930s and 1940s were a crucible through which the nation passed and, having passed this test, the nation was ready to scale unimagined heights. To put it in terms familiar to intellectual historians, it was as if American exceptionalism had wed American innocence and produced a young, vibrant and invincible child.[2]

If optimism was the dominant mood of the times, the physical and social sciences were the academic disciplines that helped propel this optimism. They, especially the social sciences, created the intellectual underpinnings and scaffolding to fuel the sense of optimism. The fields of economics, psychology, sociology, anthropology, intellectual history and political science originated long before World War II but they all developed methods in the 1940s and 1950s which would create theoretical models and practical approaches to problems that still plagued society. Through survey techniques sociologists could describe societal problems with great precision as a prelude to providing sensible options to policy-makers. Through behavioral modification psychologists could hope to change conduct and ultimately produce a better person. Through field work anthropologists could not simply describe foreign cultures but prescribe improvements in their structures. Social scientists were, in short, secular evangelists. Their "gospel" was couched in multi-syllabic terms and learned explanations; all of it was based on "research," a term that lent an aura of credibility and authority to their pronouncements.

The message of social scientists fell on ears eager to learn. Their pulpits were the rapidly expanding universities, in the first instance, but also the societal organs which disseminated information to the educated public such as newspapers, radio and television stations, book publishers and numerous groups concerned with civic betterment. Social scientists were the experts in the democratic ocean, to use Henry Adams' phrase, the beacons to guide the ship of state through difficult shoals.

It would not be too much of an overstatement to say that the belief or hope motivating their work, their methods and their tremendous energy in the post-World War II period was the belief in the perfectability of man. America had emerged from a dark and threatening age by dint of its skill and fortitude. With the help of scientists and the commitment of a nation, the remaining obstacles that shackled us could also be conquered. We are a people who has progressed far; full victory (whatever that may entail) is within our grasp.

If one were allowed only one explanation for the ultimate success of the movement to abolish capital punishment in Oregon in 1964, it would be the triumph of this mode of thinking. This is not to take anything away from the Oregon Council to Abolish the Death Penalty or their supporters, the effect of another execution (in 1962) on the people of Oregon, or the almost unanimous support of public officials for abolition. It is only to suggest that something as gossamer as the "spirit of the times" helped create the conditions for these other commitments to flourish.

The effort to abolish the death penalty in this period can be broken up into two distinct subperiods: 1957–58 and 1961–64. Both of the movements sought constitutional amendments through legislative referrals; the repeal effort in 1958 lost by 12,000 votes while the repeal effort in 1964 succeeded by 153,000 votes.[3] So exuberant was Professor Hugo Bedau, a member of the steering committee for the 1964 campaign, that after the 1964 victory he wrote, prematurely we know now, "capital punishment in this state…may have passed into history once and for all."[4]

The 1957–58 campaign bore several similarities to the 1912 effort. The new governor, Robert Holmes, was a progressive Democrat who, like West, urged legislators in his inaugural address to abolish the death penalty.[5] In the first year of his term he pardoned two convicted killers, as did West. He stated his intention, like West, that he would not permit an execution to happen during his watch as governor. Unlike West, he kept to his word on this issue. Even though he faced a lawsuit from the grieving parents of a 14-year-old boy viciously murdered by one of the men whose sentence of death Holmes would eventually commute, Holmes stood firm to his commitment.[6]

The campaign to abolish the death penalty of 1957–58 can be best presented under three points: the legislative effort to refer an abolition amendment to the voters, Holmes' commutation strategy, and the contrast between candidates Holmes and Hatfield in 1958 on the issue.

Shortly after Holmes' inaugural address, House Democrats introduced House Joint Resolution 11, which proposed a constitutional amendment to repeal Article I, sections 37 and 38, of the Oregon Constitution and to add a provision that would fix the punishment for first degree murder at life imprisonment.[7] The House Democrats wanted to fix the penalty for first degree murder in the constitution because of the fear that if the authorization for capital punishment was simply repealed from the constitution, the legislature could still authorize it by statute. This fear came to fruition when the Senate changed the House version. Ultimately the final text of HJR 11, referred to the voters in November 1958, simply stated: "That sections 37 and 38, Article I, of the Constitution of the State of Oregon, be repealed."[8]

The passage of this amendment, however, would trigger a statute, passed as House Bill 355 in the 1957 Legislative Assembly. House Bill 355 would have amended scattered sections of the Oregon Revised Statutes to accomplish a number of things: to lengthen the period of minimum prison time from 7 to 15 years before first degree murderers would be eligible for parole, to allow the death penalty for someone who was convicted of first degree murder when he is also under sentence of death and to allow the legislature wide latitude to fix penalties for first degree murder in the future.[9]

The ballot title (Ballot Measure 4) and committee explanation also added to the confusion. The former provided: "CAPITAL PUNISHMENT BILL—Purpose: To eliminate from Oregon Constitution present provision for death penalty for first degree murder. Allows legislature to fix penalty." In its explanation the committee said, "If the amendment passes, the Legislature is thereby given power to fix the penalty for first-degree murder."[10]

To both death penalty proponents and opponents, this scheme seemed unsatisfactory. Those who favored capital punishment would have preferred to keep the authorization in the state constitution and so would naturally oppose any measure, such as Ballot Measure 4, to weaken that authority. But death penalty opponents could not have been too elated by the measure. It did not fully abolish capital punishment, and it left the distinct impression that capital punishment would be subject to legislative whim. Though the 1964 measure would ultimately accomplish the same thing, supporters of repeal in 1958 might have felt that they were being shortchanged.

To make matters worse, Governor Robert Holmes' policy of commuting death sentences shortly after appeals were exhausted gave the impression that he was blatantly nullifying the decisions of the courts out of personal preference. A case in point is the commutation of the death sentence of George Sack.[11] Sack was convicted of the murder of his wife on September 29, 1954. Not an endearing figure, Sack was also suspected in the violent deaths of his two previous wives but there was not sufficient evidence to convict him on those occasions. His conviction was affirmed by the Oregon Supreme Court in June 1956 and then the United States Supreme Court refused his appeal on May 20, 1957. He received the sentenced of death on July 1, with execution scheduled for later in the month. Holmes commuted Sack's sentence on July 2. Holmes had previously commuted the death sentence of James Jensen in March 1957, whose case the United States Supreme Court finally refused to hear in January 1957. Holmes provided no reasons for the commutation beyond his opposition to capital punishment.

An indication of the opposition which this approach provoked occurred early in 1958 after the Oregon Supreme Court affirmed the death sentence of Billy Junior Nunn, who had sexually assaulted and brutally murdered a 14-year-old Jackson County boy, Alvin Eacret, in April 1956.[12] Knowing Holmes' penchant for quick commutations, the family of the murdered boy took the unusual step of immediately filing a suit against Holmes in the Jackson County Circuit Court to prevent Holmes from exercising his constitutional power to commute sentences of death.[13] What is more surprising is that the Jackson County judge issued a temporary restraining order against Holmes in February 1958, enjoining him from commuting the death sentence of Nunn pending disposition of the complaint.[14] The case was of such importance that it was argued before the Oregon Supreme Court early in December and on Christmas Eve 1958 the court rejected the family's plea, holding in words that ring with a particular coldness forty years later: "No right, status, or legal relation of the plaintiffs (Eacret's parents) is involved, and no legal interest of theirs will be affected by the action of the Governor."[15] Fortified with this clean bill of health, Holmes promptly commuted Nunn's sentence in January 1959.

One of the criticisms of Holmes' approach to capital punishment in 1958 was that he so closely identified himself with the issue that anyone who was opposed to Holmes would probably also vote against abolition of the death penalty. Jackson County's voting record on capital punishment lends credence to that charge. It was the third most favorable county to abolishing the death penalty in the 1912 election, it supported abolition by the second largest margin of any county in 1914, and it supported it in 1964. In 1958, however, Ballot Measure 4 failed in Jackson County by a 54–46% margin.[16] Jackson County's rejection of it in 1958 did not decisively defeat the measure, but many voters in the county seemed to take out their personal pique at Holmes by voting against Ballot Measure 4.

Another interesting twist in the 1958 campaign is that the *Oregonian* finally changed sides and became a vocal supporter of repeal. In language that was seemingly taken directly from the speeches of Oswald West, the *Oregonian* now claimed that abolition of capital punishment was the "enlightened" view. Though Harvey Scott favored prompt trial and swift execution, the "modern" *Oregonian* complained that those kinds of trials and executions were not possible in 1958 and, in addition, the deterrent value of the death penalty for murder was not sufficient to justify the act of executing the few who are convicted, but who in truth are not guilty.[17] In fact, the *Oregonian* took pains to point out that the murder rate of five of the six states that had abolished capital punishment before 1958 (Rhode Island, Wisconsin, Maine, Minnesota and North Dakota) was actually lower than that of Oregon.[18] As will be evident in considering the 1964 movement, the *Oregonian's* openness to modern research on the question showed that it, too, had been swayed by the siren song of social science.

Finally, a word should be said about the different approaches of Holmes and Mark Hatfield on the question of capital punishment. *Oregonian* columnist Bob Sever wrote several articles on capital punishment in the days preceding the election, and one of them explored the nuances of agreement and disagreement between Holmes and his Republican challenger Hatfield on the issue.[19] Holmes believed, as his actions demonstrated, that he not only had the authority but also the clear-cut responsibility to commute the death penalty because of his deep-seated opposition to capital punishment. He termed as a "moral coward" anyone who shared the same beliefs but would be unprepared to commute all sentences of death in the same way.

In contrast, Hatfield, who also opposed the death penalty, observed that the mere fact of one's disagreeing with the law should not be cause for the governor to thwart that law. The decision whether to continue capital punishment was a decision of the people of the state and their decision should be carried out by responsible public officials honestly and conscientiously. In response to the charge of moral cowardice, Hatfield said that it often took more courage to uphold a law with which one disagreed than simply to avoid it. He would only use the commutation authority in a death penalty case if the facts pertinent to the case suggested that an injustice had been done.

The contrast among Holmes, Hatfield and West, all opponents of the death penalty, is a fine lesson in the different philosophies of the relationship of personal beliefs and public responsibility. As argued earlier, West's philosophy of capital punishment was utilitarian. He was vehemently opposed to the death penalty personally but took the "long view" historically and, weighing the calculus of factors like a good utilitarian, decided that the best way to assure the long-term elimination of the death penalty was to show it in all its macabre splendor to the people of Oregon. His decision was a factor, I believe, that contributed to the abolition of the death penalty in 1914, but his analysis suffers from the same weakness that afflicts all utilitarian decision-making: the inability to control future facts so as to accurately bring about long-term maximum good for the greatest number.

Holmes' approach to capital punishment may best be termed moralism. Moralism is an approach which justifies an action because of the inherent rightness of the action. Moralism is an expression of Platonic philosophy in that it argues that there is a basic, unchanging principle of goodness or justice which one is not at liberty to oppose without doing damage to one's soul. This seems to be the only charitable reading of Holmes' statement, obviously referring to Hatfield, that anyone who opposed capital punishment but would fail to commute a death sentence when he was able to do so would be a "moral coward." The problem with moralism, of course, is its arrogance and shortsightedness: arrogance because one claims for oneself a special relationship to the truth and shortsightedness because that claim often obscures the genuine personal struggles that others may have with a very problematic issue. Its benefit, for the moralist and his supporters, is blinding clarity.

Hatfield's approach to the question could best be called legalism. Hatfield comes from a religious tradition where legalism has a negative connotation, and I use the word only in a descriptive sense here.[20] Legalism may be described as adherence to the letter of the law not because the law is good or just or right but simply because it is the law. The law is the law because the people either through their duly elected representatives or through their personal votes have chosen it to be so. A governor becomes governor also through this political process. He does not stand outside of it and so must give expression to the fact that he stands within that system by affirming its choices. Hatfield held out for the possibility of commutation in the rare instance when a grave injustice had been done, but the problem with legalism in general is that the legalist really has no defensible grounds on which to deviate from what legally elected or appointed institutions (the legislature or courts) have concluded. The advantage of legalism, evident throughout Hatfield's distinguished career of public service, is that it gives fairly clear reasons for decisions, even though there may be considerable anguish in making those decisions.

When the dust had settled from the 1958 campaign, Ballot Measure 4 had suffered defeat. The vote was 276,487–264,434 or a 51.3–48.7% margin. Considering the confusion created by the legislative referral and ballot title as well as the methods used by Governor Holmes in his commutation of Sack's, Jensen's and Nunn's sentences of death, proponents of abolition knew that they had not yet given their best effort.

That effort would have to wait six years. Because Governor Holmes had commuted the sentences of all on death row, the urgency of the issue had somewhat diminished. No real energy was expended on the issue in the 1959 legislature; in 1961 a resolution introduced and strongly promoted by Representative George Van Hoomissen of Multnomah County was tabled by the House Judiciary Committee on April 25 and never revived. The issue came alive again in the fall of 1961 as three more people, LeeRoy McGahuey, Jeannace June Freeman and Larry Shipley, were placed on death row.[21] Most publicity surrounded the cases of McGahuey and Freeman, the former because his case moved the quickest toward resolution and the latter because of the extreme heinousness of her crime and the fact that she was the first woman in Oregon's history to be placed on death row.

McGahuey (pronounced McGay) murdered his girlfriend and her 2-year-old son at Central Point in February 1961.[22] He was convicted by a Jackson County jury in the summer of 1961, sentenced to death, and received on death row late in August. Freeman was convicted of beating the 6-year-old son of her lover, Gertrude Nunez Jackson, and throwing him to his death into the 300-foot chasm of the Crooked River Gorge between Madras and Bend in May 1961. What made her criminal episode so repellent to Oregonians was that after Freeman beat the boy and his 4-year-old sister, Jackson cast the girl, her own daughter, into the Gorge so that Freeman and Jackson could be rid of the children to pursue their lesbian relationship.[23]

Freeman was convicted in September and arrived on death row in October 1961. McGahuey's conviction was affirmed on automatic appeal by the Oregon Supreme Court in May 1962 and Freeman's in September. On earlier occasions in Oregon's history, what would then have happened was the judge of the court that convicted the person would draw a death warrant and the person would be put to death sometime within 30 days. Such a warrant was drawn for McGahuey, setting August 20, 1962, as the date of execution.

Normally an attorney in 1962 would then have pursued an appeal to the United States Supreme Court. Even though such an appeal would almost certainly be rejected, it would buy a person at least nine months and at most eighteen months before they were executed. As any good death penalty attorney knows, a lot can happen in that period. In fact, the chief reason that McGahuey was executed and Freeman was not was because of the thoroughness of the respective attorney in pursuing appeals. McGahuey's attorney never appealed to the United States Supreme Court and never pursued federal habeas corpus remedies available to one who could claim constitutional irregularity in the trial.

In contrast, though Freeman's death sentence was affirmed by the Oregon Supreme Court four months after McGahuey's (McGahuey's was affirmed May 23 and Freeman's on September 19, 1962), she was never executed. Governor (later Senator) Hatfield mentioned in an interview that his mail was running much stronger against Freeman than against McGahuey and that he would certainly have consented to her execution, as he did to McGahuey's.[24] Freeman's attorneys had appealed her case to the United States Supreme Court, however, which rejected her appeal in May 1963. She then filed for state postconviction relief in Marion County Circuit Court in June 1963. Her case was dismissed in August and the Oregon Supreme Court declined to review the decision in December of that year. She then, through her attorney Carl Neil, filed for habeas corpus relief early in 1964 in the federal district court of Oregon. By the time her federal habeas action would have been heard, the people of Oregon had voted to abolish the death penalty and Governor Hatfield had commuted her sentence of death.[25]

So McGahuey faced the prospect of death on August 20, 1962. Governor Hatfield was importuned to commute the sentence but true to his word he did not permit his personal predilections to override his belief that the will of the people, expressed through the law of the state, ought to be carried out. Fourteen years later he wrote that this decision was the most agonizing decision he had to make as a public official.[26] Today he confesses that he does not know if he made the right decision, even though he made the legally correct one.[27] In a terse press release on August 17, 1962, he stated:

> I have prayerfully considered all the evidence in this case and do not find any basis upon which to exercise executive clemency, except my personal opinion opposing capital punishment. But I have a higher duty and that is to the citizens of

this state, and I shall not interfere with the carrying out of the people's will as expressed in the constitution, statutes and court procedures.[28]

What Hatfield did, however, was to invite particular journalists to the execution whom he knew would give the most realistic and human account of the event to counter the macabre and ghoulish dimensions of the execution. These aspects were the midnight execution, the new and direct phone line that had been installed at the Governor's house at 883 High Street SE in Salem, the red color of the phone, and the special officer dispatched to come to his house at midnight to get the "final word" regardless of the fact that the phone was in fine working order.[29] Indeed, the stories of Scott McArthur of the *Capitol Journal* and Bob Boxberger of the *Oregon Journal* lent a touch of realism and sadness to the event that would certainly cause an intelligent reader to pause and reconsider whether the death penalty was good public policy.[30] McGahuey was executed just after midnight and pronounced dead at 12:23 a.m. on August 20, 1962.

The scene then shifted with new urgency to the Oregon Legislature in its 1963 regular session. Almost without dissent the legislature passed a resolution referring the issue to the voters in the general election of 1964. The text of Senate Joint Resolution 3, which would be on the ballot in 1964, simply stated, "Sections 37 and 38, Article I of the Constitution of the State of Oregon, are repealed."[31] As with the 1958 referendum, the 1964 referendum would trigger a statute passed by the 1963 legislature increasing from 7 to 10 years the minimum time a person convicted for first degree murder had to serve before possible parole. It also set the penalty for treason and first degree murder at life imprisonment and the penalty for second degree murder at 25 years.[32]

The campaign for repeal of the death penalty began in earnest in the winter of 1963–64.[33] Aiding the campaign was an energetic organizing committee, a hard-hitting media campaign, a speakers bureau that informed civic groups about the measure, a series of 14 short research reports on various aspects of capital punishment in Oregon, the vocal support of crucial public officials from both parties, and the lack of organized opposition.[34] Campaign organizer Bedau himself admits that the confluence of these special factors in Oregon in 1964 "may not soon reappear elsewhere."[35]

Even though Bedau is no doubt correct in crediting civic activist Janet McLennan for her tireless work as executive secretary of the Oregon Council to Abolish the Death Penalty, he understates his own role in the matter.[36] In keeping with my earlier theme of the importance of social scientific research lending authority to the generally optimistic spirit of the times, I contend that the emphasis on research and the ready availability of easily understood scholarly data that pointed to the reasonability of eliminating the death penalty contributed in a major way to the triumph in November 1964.

The first edition of Bedau's now classic work *The Death Penalty in America* was published by Doubleday in April 1964. Oregon now had its own nationally recognized expert on the question right in its front yard. Bedau's book was the first major work that systematically tried to supply the public with information on the history and use of the death penalty in America. He combed legal, criminological, penological and psychological literature on the subject. The charts throughout the book created the aura of objectivity and supplied instant and easily understood information about trends in the application of the death penalty, race and the death penalty, sex and the death penalty and a host of other crucial issues. Bedau himself was a strong opponent of the death penalty, and so a careful reader would likely conclude that all the data, collected so thoroughly and arranged so carefully, pointed inexorably to the conclusion that the death penalty ought to be abolished.[37]

One of the most faithful and careful of Bedau's readers in 1964 was the *Oregonian*. In two crucial editorials it mediated the heart of Bedau's work, both in the book and in the research reports.[38] The first editorial quoted liberally from Bedau's book:

> Nearly half the states (including Oregon) now use the death penalty so sparingly that it plays almost no part in their program of law enforcement and criminal treatment...The obvious inference is that the death penalty in our country is an anachronism, a vestigial survivor of an earlier era...

Then the paper added its own comment. "Virtually all penologists agree, including prison wardens who observe penal processes at first hand." Note the reliance on research and the deference to "experts." If historical experience shows that the death penalty is fading and if experts say that it doesn't deter crime, who are we to disagree? Then the *Oregonian* quoted some statistics, which other newspapers had quoted in 1920 in a vain attempt to keep Oregon from reinstating the death penalty.

> One need go no farther than Oregon to support this statement [that the death penalty does not deter]. During Oregon's experience without capital punishment (1915–20) 36 murderers were received in the penitentiary; in the comparable period just preceding, 59 had been received, despite the threat of death.

The paper concluded its editorial with words that no doubt sent death penalty proponent and former editor Harvey Scott spinning in his grave. After surveying the new legislation, which would among other things lengthen to 10 years the time before which a first degree murderer was eligible for parole, the *Oregonian* concluded, "That is punishment enough for a civilized society."

The confluence of statistics, experts and a commitment to "reasonable" policies in this modern age colored its approach. It was a perfect mouthpiece for the perfectionist philosophy of the early 1960s.

Even more arresting to readers today is the second editorial from October 19, 1964, just two weeks before the election. Entitled "Parole Risk Small," the *Oregonian*, relying on one of the Bedau's statistic-laden research reports, claimed:

> Since 1939, a total of 188 persons convicted in Oregon of murder (first or second degree) have been released on parole. . . . The incidence of parole revocations for any cause among this group has been, the researchers found, "significantly below" the average for all parolees, and "very significantly below" the incidence of revocations of parolees who had been convicted for robbery, larceny, forgery and auto theft.

Of the 11 people sentenced to death in Oregon since 1903 and subsequently paroled, only one was ever returned to prison, and that was for an offense of shoplifting. The bottom line from the statistics, according to the *Oregonian* was clear: "murderers can be rehabilitated and safely released under parole supervision."

The incredible naiveté of that conclusion, viewed from the perspective of more than 35 years, ought not to obscure the fundamental point that Oregonians in 1964 were more than ready to embrace the implications of the optimistic spirit of the age when those conclusions were buttressed by seemingly objective research. So, on November 3, 1964, Oregonians passed Ballot Measure 1, abolishing capital punishment by a 60.1–39.9% margin (455,654–302,105). An examination of the county-by-county returns shows that in the Tri-County area, where most of the committee's energy was concentrated, the vote swing between 1958 and 1964 was more than 100,000 votes.[39] Multnomah County, which had opposed the 1958 measure by 9,000 votes, now passed it by a 68,000 vote margin; Washington County, which had opposed the 1958 measure by 400 votes, now approved it by 13,000 and Clackamas County, which had opposed the 1958 measure by 100 votes, now supported it by 12,000 votes. Two days after the election, Governor Mark Hatfield commuted the life sentences of all those on death row.[40] Perhaps, proponents thought, the death penalty would be abolished from Oregon forever.

Endnotes

1   After Oregon had reinstated capital punishment in 1920 no other states abolished it until 1957. In addition Kansas, which had abolished it in 1907, restored it in 1935 and South Dakota, which abolished the death penalty in 1915, restored it in 1939. In 1955 only six states did not have the death penalty: Michigan (since 1847), Rhode Island (since 1852), Wisconsin (since 1853), Maine (since 1887), Minnesota (since 1911) and North Dakota (since 1915). Both Alaska and Hawaii decided, in anticipation of statehood, not to have capital punishment (1957).

2   A brief discussion of American exceptionalism is in Dorothy Ross, *The Origins of American Social Science* (Cambridge: Cambridge Univ. Press, 1991), xiii–xvii. The intellectual historian most known for his reflections on the myth of American innocence is Reinhold Niebuhr. See, especially, Richard Wightman Fox, *Reinhold Niebuhr: A Biography* (New York: Pantheon, 1985).

3   *Oregon Blue Book 1999–2000* (Salem: Secretary of State, 1999), 300.

4   "Capital Punishment in Oregon 1903–64," *Oregon Law Review* 45 (1965), 2.

5   *Capitol Journal*, 14 January 1957, 2. Although Holmes was elected in November 1956, he was only serving two years of an unexpired term of former governor Paul Patterson. The story of Oregon's governors from 1947–1959, a twelve-year period in which seven men served as governor, is complex. Earl Snell, re-elected in November 1946 was killed, along with the secretary of state and president of the Senate, in a plane crash on October 28, 1947. John Hall, Speaker of the House, became governor until the general election of 1948. Douglas McKay was elected in November 1948 to fill the two years of Snell's unexpired term, and he was re-elected in 1950 to a four-year term. McKay left office in December 1952, however, to become Secretary of Agriculture in Eisenhower's first administration. At his departure, Paul Patterson, President of the Senate, became governor. Patterson was elected in his own right in November 1954. He died of a heart attack in January 1956 at the Arlington Club in Portland and was succeeded by Elmo Smith, President of the Senate. At the general election of 1956, Holmes was elected, to fill out the two years remaining in Patterson's term. Mark Hatfield defeated Holmes in the general election of 1958 and became Governor in January 1959.

6   The case, *Eacret v. Holmes*, 215 Or 121, 333 P2d 741 (1958) will be treated below.

7   The summary is given in a lengthy editorial four years later, when a similar move was afoot. *Oregonian*, 9 April 1961, 30.

8   House Joint Resolution 11, *Oregon Laws 1957* (Salem: Legislative Counsel Committee, 1957), 1363.

9   The text of the statute and a brief discussion of it may be found in the report of the Committee on Ballot Measure 4 of the Portland City Club. See *Portland City Club Bulletin*, vol. 35, no. 20 (1958), 585–591. Even though the committee voted unanimously to support the measure, its stern words in the conclusion of its report presaged a difficulty that the measure never overcame. "Your committee was unanimous and emphatic in its condemnation of the practice employed in this case whereby the people of the State of Oregon are required to vote upon a measure by a ballot title which may bring into automatic operation another statute, the substance or title of which appears nowhere on the ballot." 587.

10   *Official Voter's Pamphlet, General Election 1958* (Salem: Secretary of State, 1958), 15.

11   *Oregonian*, 3 July 1957, 1.

12   212 Or 546, 321 P2d 356 (1958). The Oregon Supreme Court related hardly any facts surrounding the murder, considering them too "revolting" to mention.

13   That power is accorded to the Governor under Article V, section 14, of the Oregon Constitution.

14   *Oregonian*, 27 February 1958, 1.

15   *Eacret v. Holmes*, 215 Or 125, 333 P2d 743 (1958).

16   *Oregon Official Abstract of Votes, General Election 1912* (Salem: Secretary of State, 1912), cols. 366–367; *Oregonian*, 1 December 1914, 6; *Oregon Official Abstract of Votes, General Elec-*

tion 1958 (Salem: Secretary of State, 1958), 24; *Oregon Official Abstract of Votes, General Election 1964* (Salem: Secretary of State, 1964), 19.

17   *Oregonian*, 15 February 1957, 28.

18   *Oregonian*, 9 August 1958, 6.

19   *Oregonian*, 27 October 1958, 7.

20   In Baptist theology, derived from the Protestant Reformers of the Sixteenth Century, legalism is a characteristic of those who would seek to earn salvation by works of their own righteousness rather than by accepting the unmerited grace of God in Christ. A Christian from a Baptist tradition, Hatfield's tradition, wants to live by grace and not by works of law.

21   *Oregonian*, 22 October 1961, 21.

22   The facts of McGahuey's crime are narrated by the Oregon Supreme Court in *State v. McGahuey*, 230 Or 643, 371 P2d 669 (1962).

23   *Oregonian*, 31 October 1962, 1. While Freeman was sentenced to death for the crime, Jackson received a life sentence. Under the law in place in 1962, one convicted of first degree murder and given a life sentence was eligible for parole in seven years. Jackson was paroled in 1969. Part of the argument below will be that one of the factors fueling the movement to restore the death penalty in Oregon in the 1970s and 1980s was the feeling that Oregon's parole policy was without teeth, and that dangerous people were being released into the community only to commit the most egregious crimes shortly after their release. Though Gertrude Jackson was not among that number, her quick release after such a brutal crime would nonetheless stir questions about the justice of a system that would release a person from jail in such a short time after such a crime. One really cannot understand the leniency of this policy without a sense of the strong commitment of policy makers in the 1960s and 1970s, whether or not they explicitly mentioned it, to the notion of human perfectability and the possibility of human rehabilitation in almost every instance.

24   Interview with former Governor and Senator Mark O. Hatfield, 7 October 1999.

25   A factor in the prolongation of Freeman's case was the fact that 1963 saw the largest expansion of federal habeas corpus rights for prisoners in the history of the United States. In that year the United States Supreme Court decided three cases which even its most charitable supporters would admit permitted a defendant to file so many habeas petitions they could tie their cases up for years in federal courts before a final resolution was made. The cases are *Fay v. Noia*, 372 U.S. 391 (1963), *Townsend v. Sain*, 372 U.S. 293 (1963) and *Sanders v. United States*, 373 U.S. 1 (1963). The efforts of Freeman's lawyers, especially that of Carl Neil, and the lack of effort of McGahuey's lawyer, George W. Kellington, invites the question of whether Kellington's neglect constituted legal malpractice. Unless McGahuey had given explicit instructions to his attorney not to pursue appeals, a good case can be made that such neglect would constitute malpractice today. By the standards of 1962, however, this probably would not be the case. The last person executed in Oregon before McGahuey, Albert Karnes, did not even pursue an appeal to the Oregon Supreme Court before his execution in January 1953. The automatic appeal to the Oregon Supreme Court after a sentence of death did not become law until 1955. One could have had reasonable grounds to believe that arguing McGahuey's case before the Oregon Supreme Court discharged Kellington's responsibility to McGahuey. Yet Neil's efforts stand in strong and stark contrast to those of Kellington. His efforts saved Freeman's life.

26   *Between a Rock and a Hard Place* (Waco, TX: Word Books, 1976), 111.

27   7 October 1999 interview with Senator Hatfield.

28   *Oregon Statesman*, 18 August 1962, 1.

29   Interview, 7 October 1999.

30   Both stories appear on page 1 of the respective papers on October 20, 1962. Boxberger also had a more reflective piece on page 4 of the *Oregon Journal* of that day, which began with the question, "What is the color of death?" and contrasted the gray-white cloud of cyanide gas that billowed around McGahuey's head with the "soft summer night in the Willamette Valley" where "the sky over Salem was a deep blue emptiness studded with stars—an incongruous

night for death." Thirty-five years later, Scott McArthur was still writing about the event. See his article, "The Ultimate Penalty: A History of Capital Punishment in Oregon," *Oregon State Bar Bulletin* 57 (Oct. 1996), 38.

31   Senate Joint Resolution 3, *Oregon Laws 1963* (Salem: Legislative Counsel Committee, 1963), 1373–74.

32   *Ibid.*, ch. 625, 1323–24.

33   Hugo Bedau describes the campaign in some detail in *Death is Different* (Boston: Northeastern University Press, 1987), 156–163.

34   Bedau makes special mention of the role of Multnomah County Sheriff Donald Clark and District Attorney George van Hoomissen.

35   *Ibid.*, 163.

36   28 September 1999 phone interview with Hugo Bedau at University College, London, where he is editing the works of 19th century utilitarian philosopher Jeremy Bentham.

37   Oxford University Press came out with a third edition in 1982 and a fourth in 1997.

38   *Oregonian*, 4 October 1964, F2; *Oregonian*, 19 October 1964, 26.

39   *Oregon Official Abstract of Votes, General Election 1964* (Salem: Secretary of State, 1964), 19.

40   The three who had their sentences commuted to life imprisonment were Jeannace June Freeman, Larry W. Shipley and Herbert F. Mitchell. The last had been sent to death row during while Freeman and Shipley were pursuing their federal appeals. *Oregonian*, 6 November 1964, 1. Freeman was ultimately paroled from prison in 1983, broke her parole by certain actions in Washington State, was recommitted to the Oregon Women's Correctional Center and then received her final parole in 1985. She was only 43 years old. The subsequent story of her release from prison, parole violations, reincarceration and pleas for her ultimate release can be found in a number of articles in the *Statesman Journal*. 13 January 1984, 1A; 28 January 1984, 3B; 16 February 1984, 1A; 12 April 1984, 1A; 19 July 1984, 5D; 16 August 1984, 1C and 27 September 1984, 8C. Shipley was paroled in 1973.

CHAPTER 4

Reinstating the Death Penalty in 1978 and 1984

Oregon's abolition of the death penalty in 1964 proved to be a harbinger of future trends. Five other states (Iowa, West Virginia, Vermont, New York and New Mexico) abolished the death penalty in the next four years and a few more would do so in the early 1970s. By the late 1960s there was a significant national movement to abolish the death penalty completely, and the *Furman* decision by the United States Supreme Court in 1972 held that the death penalty as it was then applied in the U.S. violated the Eighth Amendment protection against cruel and unusual punishment.[1] Because of the uncertainty surrounding the constitutionality of state death penalty statutes, there were no executions in America from 1968 to 1976. When one considers that there were more than 3800 people executed in America from 1930 to 1967, the total elimination of executions for a decade stands as the most signal triumph for death penalty opponents in American history.[2]

The Supreme Court struck down a Georgia statute in *Furman* because it gave juries unlimited discretion in the imposition of the death sentence. Most state laws at the time provided that after a jury found a person guilty of first degree murder it could decide without further guidance on whether the person should receive life imprisonment or death. Oregon's pre-1964 murder statute also provided this. Finding that this led to "freakish" and inconsistent results, the Supreme Court declared that unlimited jury discretion in death penalty cases did not meet constitutional requirements.

In response to this decision, the 35 or so states that still had the death penalty revised their statutes in one of three ways. By far the most popular rewriting of statutes was based on the suggested framework of the Model Penal Code (MPC), a criminal code revision approved by the American Law Institute in 1962 and adopted in most states over the next decade.[3] The system presented in the Code includes the method of "guided discretion" of the jury in death penalty cases.

The MPC death penalty statute guided jury discretion in two ways. First, it required a "bifurcated" trial in a death penalty case, the first phase to determine a defendant's guilt and the second to determine the penalty. By so doing, it hoped to keep separate the questions of guilt and punishment in jury deliberations. Second, in the penalty phase of a death penalty case, the MPC suggested that the jury be presented a series of factors that either aggravated or mitigated the defendant's culpability, and that the jury be required to find at least one aggravating circumstance and no mitigating circumstances in order to impose a sentence of death.[4]

A second response to the Supreme Court's decision was to rewrite a death penalty statute to reimpose a mandatory death penalty if the defendant was found guilty of committing a particularly heinous crime. Since the Supreme Court found fault with Georgia's statute because it permitted too much discretion in jury sentencing, a few states thought that the complete elimination of jury discretion was required. The few states that did this had these statutes struck down by the Supreme Court in 1976.

A final response was Texas' answer. Texas decided that it would guide the jury's discretion in a death penalty case in two ways: by narrowing the class of crimes eligible for the death penalty (either particularly heinous murders or murders of personnel in the justice or corrections system) and by asking the jury to answer three questions about the nature of the crime.[5]

Four years later, in 1976, the U.S. Supreme Court upheld the Model Penal Code-type death penalty statutes, overturned the mandatory death penalty statutes and upheld the constitutionality of Texas' statute.[6] In January 1977, Gary Gilmore was executed in Utah, and executions began again in the United States. Since January 1977 around 600 people have been executed in the United States, nearly one-third of them in Texas.[7]

Oregon was spared a good deal of this national turmoil occasioned by the Supreme Court decisions because it did not have a death penalty during this period and therefore did not have to try to rewrite its statute to comply with the Court's requirements. Yet Oregon was not insulated from these national developments. As many states were rewriting their statutes, the movement to bring the death penalty back to Oregon began in earnest. The Achilles heel of the Oregon abolition movement in the 1960s was the *Oregonian's* claim, based on "research" to be sure, that convicted murderers were good parole risks. Oregon's experience in the 1970s would sadly refute this claim.

It often only takes one or two high-profile murders to get a reinstatement movement going. The murder of a Eugene couple in Washington State in 1974 by convicted murderer Carl Cletus Bowles, after he took advantage of a social pass to escape from the Oregon State Penitentiary, led to calls for the resignation of Superintendent Hoyt Cupp as well as for the return of the death penalty.[8] The indictment and conviction of Richard L. Marquette for the mutilation murder of a Scio woman in 1975 after he had been paroled in 1973 for a similar murder in 1961 added fuel to the flame. In an editorial that seems to realize that the tide was quickly turning, the *Oregonian* urged caution rather than haste. Restoration of the death penalty in the heat of public passion should not be the answer, it argued.[9]

By 1977 the hopes of those desiring to restore the death penalty were rekindled when a survey conducted by Bardsley & Haslacher and published in the *Oregonian* showed the rather astonishing result that Oregonians by a 65–28% margin (7% undecided) wanted a return of the death penalty.[10] A bill to reinstate the death penalty had been introduced in the Oregon Legislature a month before the survey was published, but after an emotional hearing before the State Government Operations Committee in February the issue never made it out of committee.[11] The bill, HB 2321, would instead become the basis for the statutory initiative petition eventually approved by the voters in November 1978.

Before discussing that initiative petition, a few words need to be said about the passage of another law in the 1977 legislature. This bill was intended to blunt the effect of HB 2321, but had the unintended effect of contributing toward the tossing-out of the 1978 death penalty law by the Oregon Supreme Court in January 1981.[12] House Bill 2011, would create the crime of aggravated murder. A person would be guilty of the crime of aggravated murder if he either committed a most heinous murder (murder for hire, by means of a bombing, murder after already being convicted of a murder) or killed a police officer or a person in the justice system. The penalty for aggravated murder would be life imprisonment with a minimum of 30 years without the possibility of parole if it was committed in a heinous manner, and twenty years without the possibility of parole if it was committed against a protected person.[13] Parole could be granted earlier, after 20 or 15 years, upon the unanimous vote of the State Board of Parole.

Before passage of this bill, parole for the first degree murderer was obtainable after 10 years of incarceration. By passing this bill late in the session, the legislators hoped to show the people of Oregon that they were responsive to their pleas and that they could be tough on crime. They refused, however, to consider the possibility of reinstating the death penalty.

This legislative strategy backfired on everybody in the next few years. An initiative petition to institute the death penalty for murder was hastily drawn up in July from the shards of HB 2321. Because HB 2321 had been buried in committee since February, the section of the initiative on the death penalty did not reflect the new aggravated murder law that was passed at the end of the 1977 session. That is, the most serious crime in Oregon in January was murder; by July it was aggravated murder. The death penalty statute passed by initiative petition in November 1978, modeled on the January 1977 proposal, still assumed that the most severe crime in Oregon was murder. The 1978 law therefore imposed the death penalty for murder, without a word about aggravated murder. Death could be imposed for the second-worst crime in Oregon but not for the worst crime.

These legal niceties had little effect on the voters in November 1978. By a margin of 64.3–35.7% (573,707–318,610), Oregonians overwhelmingly restored the death penalty. Or so they thought. It was a most stunning turnaround in just 14 years. Such a dramatic reversal in so short a time, coupled with what would become an even larger victory in 1984, marks a significant repudiation of a liberal penological theory and perfectionist philosophy that permeated the 1964 election.

The statute passed by the voters in 1978 consisted of seven sections, only one of which, section 3, will concern us in any detail. The first section expanded the definition of murder in ORS 163.115 and provided that a person convicted of murder could, in accordance with section 3, be sentenced either to death or life imprisonment with a 25-year minimum before parole.[14] Section 2 simply incorporated section 3 into a particular place in the Oregon Revised Statutes (ORS 163.005 to 163.145). Sections 4–7 reiterated the necessity of the death warrant and the administration of lethal gas as the chosen mode of execution.[15]

Section 3 authorized the death penalty. Although this part of the Act was held unconstitutional by the Oregon Supreme Court in 1981, it needed only minimal clean-up to meet the standards articulated by the court before being presented to the voters again in 1984. The most stunning realization upon reading section 3 is that when the voters of Oregon decided to reinstate a death penalty they decided to choose the Texas statute as a model rather than the Model Penal Code. In short, of the approximately 35 states that had the death penalty after 1977, 33 had an MPC-type statute and two had a Texas-style statute—Texas and Oregon.

Oregon chose the Texas statute no doubt because it had been upheld by the United States Supreme Court in 1976. One would have hoped that legislative debate in 1977 when HB 2321 was introduced would have brought out the point that it would have been more appropriate, had Oregon wanted to restore the death penalty, to choose an MPC model rather than a Texas model. Indeed, as one prominent Oregon jurist told me, Oregonians and Texans have nothing in common when it has to do with their philosophy or approach to issues of the death penalty. Yet, because the hearings on HB 2321 were scuttled after February 1977 and the bill languished in committee, when it was taken up as an initiative petition there really could be no informed public debate on the type of statute the initiative proposed. One had a Texas-style statute and very few people knew, or cared, about that. They simply wanted to restore the death penalty.

Section 3 of the 1978 Act gave guidance on how to conduct the sentencing or penalty phase hearing after guilt was found. It read, in relevant part,

SECTION 3. (1) Upon a finding that the defendant is guilty of murder, the court shall conduct a separate sentencing proceeding to determine whether the defendant shall be sentenced to life imprisonment or death. The proceeding shall be conducted in the trial court before the trial judge as soon as practicable. In the proceeding, evidence may be presented as to any matter that the court deems relevant to sentence. This subsection shall not be construed to authorize the introduction of any evidence secured in violation of the Constitution of the United States or of the State of Oregon. The state and the defendant or his counsel shall be permitted to present arguments for or against a sentence of death.

(2) Upon conclusion of the presentation of the evidence, the trial court shall consider:

a. Whether the conduct of the defendant that caused the death of the deceased was committed deliberately and with the reasonable expectation that death of the deceased or another would result;

b. Whether there is a probability that the defendant would commit criminal acts of violence that would constitute a continuing threat to society. In determining this issue, the trial judge shall consider any mitigating circumstances offered by the defendant, including, but not limited to, the defendant's age, the extent and severity of his prior criminal con-

duct and the extent of the mental and emotional pressure under which the defendant was
acting at the time the offense was committed;
and

c. If raised by the evidence, whether the conduct of the defendant in killing the deceased
was unreasonable in response to the provocation, if any, by the deceased.[16]

The section went on to mention that the state must prove each issue submitted by the judge beyond reasonable doubt (Sec. 3(3)), that a unanimous
jury finding on all three questions would require the judge to impose a death
sentence (Sec. 3(4)) and that the conviction and sentence shall be reviewed in
the Oregon Supreme Court automatically within 60 days (Sec. 3(5)).

Four criticisms of the statutory language emerged almost as soon as the
initiative petition was passed. The first three are drawn from the text of section 3. First, as noted above, the statute improperly authorizes a worse punishment for murder than for aggravated murder. Second, unlike the Texas
statute that Oregon imitated, the Oregon statute does not narrow the class of
people eligible for the death penalty.[17] Third, and more technically, by permitting the trial judge to answer the three statutory questions and impose a
death sentence, the statute usurped from the jury the traditional role of considering all the evidence before deciding on a sentence.[18] A fourth criticism
was more philosophical and ultimately much more difficult for proponents of
the death penalty to overcome, even though it was finally overcome in an
interesting way in the campaign of 1984.

The fourth criticism was articulated in an eloquent article in the *Willamette
Law Review* by Professor Stephen Kanter from Lewis & Clark's Northwestern
College of Law.[19] In brief, Kanter argued that when the United States Supreme Court in *Gregg* (1976) permitted the death penalty to be imposed once
again, it did so based on a theory of retribution and utility. That is, the Supreme Court decision stated that both utilitarian and retributionist justifica-
tions were essential in upholding the constitutionality of the death penalty.
However, the Oregon Constitution had a fairly unique provision in Article I,
section 15, which prohibits retribution as a motive for punishment in Oregon.[20] Because retribution as a penological theory was disallowed by the Oregon Constitution, and the constitutionality of the death penalty rested on a
retributivist theory, the death penalty was unconstitutional under the Oregon
Constitution.[21]

In making this argument, Kanter was quite aware that he was pitching his
argument not to the general reading public, or even to the legal community at

large, but to the seven justices on the Oregon Supreme Court, and especially to Justice Hans Linde who had pioneered the so-called "state constitutional revolution" in a number of law review articles, when he was a professor at the University of Oregon Law School, and in a number of cases, after he was appointed to the Oregon Supreme Court in 1977.[22] Linde, who was at the height of his influence on the court from 1980 to 1986, argued that state supreme courts had the duty to interpret their own constitutions independently from the federal constitution when the wording of the former was different, or even identical, to the latter. What Kanter was trying to do was to show that the Oregon Constitution, which the Oregon Supreme Court was now interpreting *before* it interpreted the United States Constitution on a constitutional case, ought to decide the issue. The Oregon Constitution did not permit the death penalty.

These four criticisms swirled around during 1979-80 as the legislature, judges, attorneys and others weighed in on the constitutionality of the death penalty statute.[23] Finally, on January 20, 1981, the Oregon Supreme Court invalidated the law on state constitutional grounds.[24] But they were not the state constitutional grounds urged on the court by Professor Kanter. The court held, in an opinion not altogether convincing in its rationale, that the 1978 statute indirectly reestablished a crime of deliberate first degree murder which the legislature, by eliminating the distinction between first and second degree murder in 1971, had discarded. This new indirect deliberate first degree murder statute gave only the judge the power to impose a sentence of death. But first degree murder requires the showing of an evil "mental state" and this mental state can only be determined by the jury. Therefore, the statute authorized a sentence (death) to be imposed by a judge while the Oregon Constitution requires a jury to determine the mental state of the defendant who committed the crime.[25]

If opponents of the death penalty in Oregon thought that this decision would end the debate, they were sorely mistaken. Proponents of the death penalty tried to push for a bill in the 1981 legislature to clean up the statute invalidated by the Oregon Supreme Court, but their effort failed there. Then they were unable to secure enough signatures to put the issue on the 1982 ballot. So, they returned to the legislature in 1983, determined to get a revised and constitutional death penalty statute out of the session. They had strong support from Governor Victor Atiyeh, who personally appeared before the House Judiciary Committee and urged them to pass on to the voters two bills that had been submitted for their consideration.[26] In order to get such a measure through the Democrat-controlled House Judiciary Committee, however, supporters would have to outwit the shrewd committee chairman, Hardy

Myers, which they were ultimately unable to do. A bill that arguably had the
support of more than 65% of the Oregon electorate died in the House Judiciary Committee in 1983.

Angered by legislative temporizing, stung by Oregon Supreme Court rejection, and enraged by a fresh spate of ghoulish murders in Oregon in the
early 1980s, proponents of the death penalty decided in the summer of 1983
to circulate two initiative petitions.[27] One of the two was a statutory initiative
that cleaned up the language of the 1978 statute in response to the *Quinn*
decision of 1981, and the other was a constitutional initiative petition which
responded particularly to the issue brought up by Professor Kanter in his law
review article. The statutory corrections were minor: the change of "murder"
to "aggravated murder" in subsection (1), the change of "trial judge" to "trial
jury" in subsection (1), and a few additional changes in the jury instructions
of subsection (1) to eliminate repetitive evidence. The most fascinating issue,
however, was how proponents decided to deal with Professor Kanter's theory.

In both the 1983 Legislative Assembly and the constitutional initiative
petition of 1984, the proponents decided they needed to add a section to the
Oregon Constitution which would blunt the effect of sections 15 and 16 of
Article I in death penalty cases. That is, they recognized the convincing nature
of Kanter's argument and decided that the best thing to do was to say that the
death penalty was exempt from the requirements of Article I, sections 15 and
16. They proposed a new section (Article I, section 40) to the Oregon Constitution which provided:

> Notwithstanding sections 15 and 16 of this Article, the pen-
> alty for aggravated murder as defined by law shall be death
> upon unanimous affirmative jury findings as provided by law
> and otherwise shall be life imprisonment with minimum sen-
> tence as provided by law.[28]

The proposal was quite radical and was intended to suggest that this new
section of the constitution would override earlier sections only with respect to
cases of aggravated murder. In the wake of Kanter's article, this was the only
thing that proponents could do, short of eliminating sections 15 and 16 from
the Oregon Constitution or changing their wording to include retributionist
language in addition to reformation language in dealing with convicted criminals.

There is no reason to believe that Oregonians understood that this is what
they were doing when they voted on both ballot measures, 6 and 7, in the
general election of 1984. Ballot Measure 6 was the constitutional change, to
add section 40, while Ballot Measure 7 was a reprise of the 1978 statute, now

cleaned up to pass constitutional muster. Oregonians certainly understood that they wanted to restore capital punishment, and they did so by an astonishing 75.1–24.9% margin (893,818–295,988). It was supported by a larger majority than the state lottery received in the same election.

But the vote on Measure 6 was much more ambiguous. It passed by only 653,009–521,687 (55.6–44.4%). Though opponents of the death penalty might have tried to take solace in this small margin, it appears that the closeness of the vote was due more to the complexity of the issue than to any principled voter stand to affirm the style of constitutional interpretation performed by the Oregon Supreme Court under the leadership of Justice Linde. If an elated Hugo Bedau could have expressed the hope in 1964 that the death penalty in Oregon might have just passed out of our history for all time, an elated supporter of the death penalty in 1984 could have had good reason for celebrating the opposite. A brief analysis of the meaning of Oregon's experience with the death penalty, which concludes this part, will bring both those perspectives into question.

Historical Analysis and Conclusion

Hugo Bedau has noted that one of the paradoxes of the death penalty debate in the twentieth century is that the very reforms in the administration of capital punishment sought by abolitionists have become the obstacles to further statutory repeal of capital punishment.[29] The twentieth century brought discretionary, rather than mandatory, death penalty verdicts; the protection of the general public from viewing executions; the introduction of more "humane" ways of carrying out the sentence; and the limitation of the death penalty to the highest degree of murder.[30] In addition to all these paradoxes, Oregon has had paradoxes or ironies of its own. Three that have been mentioned in the text are Oregonians' use of the Texas death penalty statute as a model both in 1978 and 1984, Oswald West's presiding over as many executions in Salem as any other Oregon governor, and Robert Holmes' moralistic opposition to capital punishment that perhaps contributed to the failure of the 1958 abolition effort.

But life and history consist of more than paradox or well-intentioned efforts gone awry. Two kinds of lessons may be derived from Oregon's experience: those gleaned from a comparison of Oregon's experience with that of other states and those learned by examining Oregon's unique historical experience. One might call these the horizontal and vertical lessons of the death penalty.

When comparing Oregon's experience with that of other states, the horizontal dimension, it becomes evident that Oregon has been at the forefront of two of the three great waves of death penalty abolition in American history. In addition, except for the years after 1984, whenever there have been ten or more states without the death penalty, Oregon has been in that number.

Abolition of capital punishment in America has been the product of three periods of intense effort: the decades preceding the Civil War, the Progressive Era at the beginning of the twentieth century and the 1960s. The communitarian impulse of the 1840s, a time which Emerson once described as when every farmer had a utopian plan in his back pocket as he plowed his field, led to abolition in Michigan, Rhode Island, Wisconsin and Maine.[31] Each of these states has no death penalty today.

During the Progressive Era from 1907 to 1917, no fewer than nine states abolished capital punishment in whole or in part.[32] Had Oregon's 1912 effort passed, it would have been the third on that list. As it turned out, Oregon was the fourth. Only two of those nine states, Minnesota and North Dakota, never reinstated the death penalty, though it took Kansas and South Dakota to the late 1930s to restore theirs.

In the 1960s and early 1970s before the *Furman* decision was handed down, eight more states abolished the death penalty.[33] Oregon was at the head of this parade and was the only state that had abolished the death penalty in the Progressive Era that also abolished it in the 1960s. In addition, before statehood Alaska and Hawaii both voted in 1957 that they would not have the death penalty. Of the ten which abolished the death penalty in this period, if Alaska and Hawaii are included, five do not have the death penalty today (Alaska, Hawaii, Iowa, West Virginia and Vermont).

From a national perspective, then, the movement to abolish the death penalty comes in waves and Oregon is usually brought in with the tide. Each successive wave recedes and leaves behind a few more abolitionist states than the previous wave. There were four abolition states after the first wave receded, six after the second and eleven after the third.[34]

The result of these three waves has left what one might call three groups of states, membership in a group calibrated by one's vigor in maintaining the death penalty. Group I, the hard-core abolitionist states, consists of about eight: Michigan, Rhode Island, Wisconsin, Maine, Minnesota, North Dakota, Hawaii and Alaska. These states have not had the death penalty either since statehood or for the last 85 or more years. Group II, the "swing" states, consists also of about eight: Iowa, West Virginia, Vermont, Massachusetts, Oregon, Washington, South Dakota, Kansas and perhaps a few others like New York or California. The other 32 or 34 states, Group III, may be termed hard-core death penalty states.[35]

Table 4–1. State Attitudes on the Death Penalty.

States Without Death Penalty (date of abolition)

1   Michigan (1846)
2   Rhode Island (1852)[1]
3   Wisconsin (1853)
4   Maine (1887)[2]
5   Minnesota (1911)
6   North Dakota (1915)[3]
7   Hawaii (1956)[4]
8   Alaska (1957)[5]
9   Vermont (1965)
10 Iowa (1965)[6]
11 West Virginia (1965)
12 Massachusetts (1984)

[1] Rhode Island also briefly legalized the death penalty from 1973-1979. See Christopher E. Friel et al., 4 Roger Williams U L Rev 596 (1991) (reviewing Patrick T. Conley, *Liberty and Justice: A History of Law and Lawyers in Rhode Island*, 1636-1998) (1998)).
[2] Maine also abolished the death penalty in 1876, only to restore it in 1883 and to abolish it again in 1887. See Christopher Q. Cutler, "Death Resurrected: The Reimplementation of the Federal Death Penalty," 23 Seattle U L Rev 1189, 1194 n. 34 (2000) (citation omitted).
[3] See Andrea Shapiro, "Unequal Before the Law: Men, Women, and the Death Penalty," 8 Am U J Gender Soc Pol'y & L 427, 432 n. 33 (2000).
[4] See Deborah W. Deeno, "Getting to Death: Are Executions Constitutional?," 82 Iowa L Rev 319, 365 n. 274 (1997).
[5] *Ibid.*
[6] Iowa also abolished the death penalty from 1872 to 1878. See *supra* Cutler.

Swing States (dates when death penalty in effect)

1   California (statehood to 1972, 1977-present)
2   Delaware (at least 1831-1958, 1961-1972, 1974-present)
3   Kansas (to 1907, 1935-1972, 1994-present)
4   New York (to 1965, 1995-present)
5   Oregon (to 1914, 1920-1964, 1978-1981, 1984-present)
6   South Dakota (to 1915, 1939-present)
7   Washington (to 1913, 1919-1972, 1975-present)

See www.deathpenaltyinfo.org for pages on each state, but the quality of the historical information varies.

"Hard Core" States

(Thirty-one states with death penalty since statehood and after *Furman*)

Alabama, Arkansas, Arizona, Colorado, Connecticut, Florida, Georgia, Idaho, Illinois, Indiana, Kentucky, Louisiana, Maryland, Mississippi, Missouri, Montana, Nebraska, Nevada, New Hampshire, New Jersey, New Mexico, North Carolina, Ohio, Oklahoma, Pennsylvania, South Carolina, Tennessee, Texas, Utah, Virginia, Wyoming.

Sources: Death Penalty Information Center (www.deathpenaltyinfo.org) and William J. Bowers, *Legal Homicide* (Boston: Northwestern University Press, 1984).

Oregon has not had a death penalty for 26 years of its history. It is usually in the forefront of national movements to abolish the death penalty. That is, it usually helps to get the wave of abolition going. When Oregon abolished the death penalty in 1914 it was the eighth state without a death penalty, and when it abolished capital punishment in 1964 it was the ninth state without such a penalty. One can derive from this experience that even though Oregon is a "swing" state on the death penalty, Oregon is usually in the list of states without a death penalty when there are 10 or more states without capital punishment. Now there are 12. If one considered horizontal statistics alone, Oregon should be primed for another abolition movement.

When one looks at the vertical dimension of the problem, Oregon's unique historical experience, the news is not at first glance as encouraging for abolitionists. Five features seem to have been of particular importance in the debate over capital punishment in Oregon's history: 1) gubernatorial attitude and action toward abolition, 2) organization of the campaign for abolition or retention, 3) the role of research in the campaign, 4) the proximity of grisly murders or legal executions to the time of the campaign, and 5) the larger social values of the people of Oregon during the time of the campaign. When any two of the five have been present in such a way as to encourage retention of capital punishment, capital punishment has been retained. However, it has taken four of the five factors to be present for abolition of capital punishment to succeed.

If one examines the campaign of 1912, one has strong gubernatorial support and the proximity of executions to the campaign, but the other factors are fairly weak. Oswald West was among the strongest gubernatorial opponents of capital punishment, and he had scheduled four executions for a few weeks after the election, but nowhere does one read about the importance of campaign organization, or specific studies or information that was presented to aid the abolitionist cause. The social environment of 1912 was increasingly open to the progressive message in Oregon; indeed, the equal suffrage vote passed by a 51.8–48.2% margin (61,265–57,104) that year.[36] The fact that the largest number of ballot measures in Oregon's history appeared on the ballot in 1912 (37) also indicates a progressive frame of mind. So, for the election of 1912, there were probably two or at most three factors favoring abolition, but there were also two or three favoring retention.

The 1914 election saw some changes. West's commitment was still there, but in contrast to 1912 the abolition campaign was more organized. Also, between 1912 and 1914 the largest number of executions occurred in Oregon's history—nine—than in any comparable period. A strong indication that the progressive spirit was still evident was the overwhelming passage of the prohibition amendment that year, 57.7–42.3% (136,842–100,362).[37] Though one cannot say with certainty that the huge number of executions repulsed the populace, since there had been eight in 1909-1910 and abolition was not an issue in those years, West thought that continual exposure to capital punishment would change the hearts and minds of the people of Oregon. Therefore, the first successful abolition effort had four or five of the factors present, while opponents perhaps had one.

Capital punishment was restored by a vote of the people in May 1920. The six years between 1914 and 1920 saw a huge change in the national psyche, especially as it related to attitudes toward foreign-born people and those who through physical or mental disability or criminal activity did not fit into the American system. Almost all the states which experimented with abolition of capital punishment in the Progressive Era restored the death penalty by 1920.[38] In addition, the murders of Burgess and Perringer in November 1919, just six months before the vote, certainly set the stage to restore capital punishment. There was a fairly vigorous campaign by both supporters and opponents, but the new Governor, Ben Olcott, was a strong supporter of the death penalty. Supporters of the penalty had three or four factors in their favor, while opponents only had about two.

The campaign of 1958 came very close to eliminating the death penalty in Oregon. The governor was strongly opposed to it and the social environment, reflected in the *Oregonian's* volte-face on the issue, bespoke a willingness to change. Research was available regarding the murder rates in Oregon during times of abolition and retention, showing that the presence of the death penalty did not seem to affect the murder rate (countering the claims of proponents that the death penalty deterred murder). Unlike 1920, there were no ghastly murders just before the campaign, even though Holmes' handling of the commutations of Jensen and Sack probably alienated some voters from him. Though there was a campaign steering committee consisting of many prominent Oregonians, it did not seem to have the confidence of 1964's. Thus there were three or four factors favoring abolition and one or two favoring retention and, true to the model, the vote was very close.

By 1964, however, everything was going right for the abolitionists. Mark Hatfield was an opponent of the death penalty even though he was not an active participant in the campaign to abolish it. The campaign was energetic and focused. Research was available in easily digestible form to influential leaders throughout the state. Hugo Bedau stresses that there was no organized opposition to the abolition movement.[39] The execution of McGahuey in August 1962 and the thoughtful treatment of the story by Scott McArthur and Bob Boxberger brought home to Oregonians the reality of what an execution was and that more executions might be in the offing.[40] Finally, the optimistic spirit of the times so pervaded the campaign that even the *Oregonian* was convinced that murderers could be rehabilitated in the space of ten years. All five factors were in favor of the abolitionists in this campaign.

By 1978, however, the tables had turned. Though Governor Bob Straub opposed the death penalty, several changes had occurred that led to the dramatic turnaround at the polls. The principal changes were the steady parade of grisly murders committed by paroled people (especially Bowles and Marquette) and the overwhelming sense that the problem of crime had gotten out of control and had to be dealt with by citizen action. The credibility of the optimistic 1964 research findings was undermined. Though there was strong legislative opposition to restoring the death penalty, this opposition was swept away by the incoming tide of death penalty proponents. The proponents had probably four factors in their favor, with only an opposed governor in the abolitionists' column.

The campaign of 1984 was 1978-redux but intensified. Nothing had changed except to the advantage of death penalty suppporters. There had been even more ghastly murders. Now the legislature *and* the Oregon Supreme Court seemed to oppose the will of the people. The new Governor, Victor Atiyeh, personally appeared before the House Judiciary Committee to plead for a referral of the issue to the voters. When he was rebuffed, he became a major force in the campaign supporting restoration of the death penalty. The nascent victims' rights movement was galvanized by this campaign. Supporters had all five factors in their column and the overwhelming victory was testimony to that fact.

It is hard to say how all of the factors are to be weighed in the middle of 2001. Some are relatively clear at this point. Governor Kitzhaber opposes the death penalty, even though he has not been an active campaigner against it. There have been no ghoulish murders that have enraged the people of Oregon of late, even though aggravated murders keep being committed and men (but no women) keep getting sent to death row.[41] The executions of Douglas Wright in September 1996 and Harry Moore in May 1997 certainly were protested by opponents of capital punishment, but they did not have the desired effect of galvanizing a huge opposition to the death penalty.[42]

Harder to measure are the role of research, the strength of campaigns to repeal or maintain capital punishment, or the "spirit of the times" in Oregon at present. Much of that will emerge in the next few years as proponents and opponents of capital punishment square off on the issue. Most elusive but probably most outcome determinative will be the "spirit of the times," though this might well be affected by research and the strength of support or opposition movements. The central question in determining the spirit of the times on the issue is whether the crime victims' movement, with its call for harsher and longer sentences for convicted criminals and important roles for crime victims in the criminal justice system, has reached its peak in Oregon. The passage of Ballot Measure 40, the crime victims' "Bill of Rights," by a 59–41% margin in 1996 was an indication of the continued strength of the movement.[43]

That measure was struck down by the Oregon Supreme Court in June 1998 and returned to the voters in November 1999 in seven individual ballot measures. Though the results of the votes have passed from most Oregonians' consciousness, five comments on the election are appropriate.[44] First, a general comment. Four of the measures passed and three failed. The four that passed were Measure 69, giving victims access to information and opportunities to participate in the legal proceedings relating to their victimization; Measure 71, limiting pretrial release of persons accused of felonies; Measure 74, requiring terms of imprisonment announced in court to be fully served, with exceptions; and Measure 75, prohibiting jury service for felons and certain misdemeanants. Each of these passed with a majority of 56–59%. The three measures that failed—Measure 70, allowing prosecutors to demand a jury trial; Measure 72, allowing a conviction for murder by an 11–1 jury vote; and Measure 73, changing the nature of immunity from prosecution in Oregon—failed by margins of 53–57%.

The four measures that passed amended the Oregon Constitution. Voter participation for this mail-only election was around 35% of registered voters, the smallest percentage since mail elections were instituted. Therefore, the Oregon Constitution has been amended four times by fewer than 20% of registered Oregon voters. Those who have regard for the diminishing integrity of the Oregon Constitution may want to give heed to those numbers. How foundational can a document be when it can be amended by so few?

Second, victims' rights supporters can take heart because the four measures that seemed to offer most immediate protection to victims passed by almost the same margin as Ballot Measure 40 passed in 1996. It shows that there still were significant issues in the minds of many Oregonians relating to victim participation in the criminal justice system and offender sentencing that needed to be addressed. The appeal of victims' rights measures, therefore, had not lost its luster in three years.

Third, the voters of Oregon who participated in the election showed their ability to distinguish between efforts that would seem to aid and protect victims and the community and measures that would change the fundamental balance of power between prosecutors and defense attorneys in criminal trials.

Opponents of the ballot scored some points when they claimed that many of the measures were not real victims' rights measures but were designed to enlarge prosecutorial power, perhaps even at the expense of victims.

Fourth, opponents of the ballot measures can take heart that three of the measures were rejected and the rather vigorous rhetoric of the commercials in favor of all seven did not push the citizens of Oregon beyond what they voted for in 1996. Opponents of these measures may be cautiously optimistic in seeing these ballot measures as the last big push for the victims' rights movement after their signal successes in lengthening minimum sentences, compelling prisoners to work, and amending the constitution to make sure that principles beyond rehabilitation are foundations of Oregon's criminal justice system.

It is certainly not correct to say that the momentum of the victims' rights movement has waned; it is more accurate to say that the tremendous energy that directed their cause in the past decade is not quite as focused anymore.

Finally, the mixed results of the election on November 3, 1999, suggest that Oregonians are interested in moving to other issues, both in the criminal justice and non-criminal justice arenas. Two issues in the criminal justice arena that will emerge in the next few years are what to do with offenders *after* they have served their mandatory terms and are now coming back to live in the community, and what to do about the death penalty. Although a ballot measure to eliminate the death penalty did not secure enough signatures to make the ballot in 2000, a 2002 measure, almost identical to the 2000 measure, has already been drawn up and certified by the Oregon Supreme Court. In 2000 proponents only had a little more than six months to collect signatures; this time around they will have more than a year. When they collect sufficient signatures, which appears likely in 2002, opponents of the death penalty may find that the coming years provide the most congenial setting in more than 25 years to bring the issue to the people of Oregon. When this happens, however, the outcome of the election will be affected not simply by the feelings of Oregonians on any particular fall day in 2002 or 2004 but also by the historical experience of the inhabitants of America's Eden.[45]

Endnotes

1   *Furman v. Georgia*, 408 U.S 238 (1972).

2   Bedau's charts in *The Death Penalty in America* (3rd ed; Oxford University Press, 1982), 56–64, are especially helpful in breaking down these executions into a host of categories.

3   *Model Penal Code* (Philadelphia: American Law Institute, 1962). A multi-volume commentary on the Code, complete with copious case citations, was published 1980–85.

4   *Model Penal Code*, 210.6(2)–(4).

5   The questions had to do with the deliberateness of the act of murder, the future dangerousness of the offender, and whether the defendant's conduct in killing the deceased was unreasonable in response to the provocation.

6   The Model Penal Code-type statute was upheld in *Gregg v. Georgia*, 428 U.S. 153 (1976). Mandatory death penalty statutes were overturned in *Roberts v. Louisiana*, 428 U.S. 325 (1976) and *Woodson v. North Carolina*, 428 U.S. 280 (1976). Texas's death penalty statute was upheld in *Jurek v. Texas*, 428 U.S. 262 (1976).

7   Current statistics on the death penalty in America are in the Death Penalty Information Center's Web page: www.deathpenaltyinfo.org.

8   *Oregonian*, 21 June 1974, 30.

9   24 April 1975, D2.

10   *Oregonian*, 27 February 1977, B3.

11   Instead of referring the measure to the House Judiciary Committee, the normal place where such a measure should go, Speaker Phil Lang, who supported the death penalty, referred it to this committee, perhaps hoping to get a more favorable hearing than he could in the Judiciary Committee. On February 10, 1977, however, prominent political leaders from both parties descended on the committee and unanimously opposed the reintroduction of the death penalty. Testimony was given by Secretary of State Norma Paulus, State Treasurer Clay Myers and Superintendent of Schools Verne Duncan, all Republicans, and Attorney General James Redden, a Democrat. In addition, Governor Robert Straub, a Democrat, vowed to veto any capital punishment bill that would come to his desk. As if this were not enough, someone had crafted the testimony at the hearing so that a prominent representative from the state's largest Protestant (the Methodists) and Jewish (Rabbi Rose of Portland's Temple Beth Israel) groups at the time as well as a person speaking with the approval of the Archbishop of Portland (Rev. Michael Sprauer, a chaplain at OSCI) all unanimously spoke in opposition to the death penalty. See Phil Cogswell's informative reflections on the issue in *Oregonian*, 5 February 1977, A18 and the news story on 11 February 1977, C1.

12   When the Oregon Supreme Court declared that the 1978 law passed by initiative petition to reimpose the death penalty was invalid, it actually rested its argument on state constitutional grounds—that the initiative violated the right to jury trial assured by Article I, sec. 11 of the Oregon Constitution. Making the court's decision easier, however, was the fact that the 1978 law was inconsistent with the 1977 aggravated murder law and simply could not be reconciled with it.

13   *Oregon Laws 1977* (Salem: Legislative Counsel Committee, 1977), ch. 370, secs. 1, 2, 370–71.

14   *Ibid.*, sec. 1.

15   Execution by lethal injection, the current mode of execution in Oregon and most states with the death penalty, was authorized by the 1984 initiative petition, discussed below.

16   Oregon Laws 1979 (Salem: Legislative Counsel Committee, 1979), Ch. 2, sec. 3, 4–5.

17   The class of "death eligible" people according to the Texas statute was limited either by the heinousness of the crime or by the relation of the person murdered to the justice system. Interestingly, the aggravated murder statute narrowed the class of those who could be convicted of aggravated murder but the murder statute did not. The aggravated murder statute, as we have seen, provided for less severe penalties than this new statute.

18   These criticisms were leveled at a conference organized by criminal defense lawyers and law professors in Portland in February 1979. *Oregonian*, 24 Februar   73 of the murder of a woman but was suspected in the deaths of several women and sexual abuse of dozens, and the horrific Oregon Museum Tavern shootings in Salem in May 1981, just four months after the Supreme Court decision, where a man with a history of mental problems, Lawrence William Moore, opened fire in a popular crowded night spot killing four people and seriously wounding twenty.

28   *Official 1984 General Election Voters' Pamphlet* (Salem: Secretary of State, 1984), 28.

29   *The Death Penalty in America* (2nd ed.; New York: Anchor Books, 1967), 14–15.

30   These have all been present in Oregon's experience. Oregon went from mandatory to discretionary sentencing for first degree murder in 1920, it introduced aggravated murder in 1977 and made it the sole crime for which the death penalty could be invoked in 1984, it moved from public to private executions in two stages, first to enclose the hangings in the county jail yard in 1874 and then to move executions to the Oregon State Penitentiary in 1903, and it went from hanging as the method of execution to gas in 1937 and then to lethal injection in 1984.

31   Maine did not finally abolish the death penalty until 1887, though it had made partial efforts to do so in 1837 and in the 1870s.

32   Those states are Kansas in 1907, Minnesota in 1911, Washington in 1913, Oregon in 1914, North and South Dakota and Tennessee in 1915, Arizona in 1916 and Missouri in 1917. Colorado briefly flirted with abolition from 1897 to 1901. William J. Bowers, *Legal Homicide* (Boston: Northeastern University Press, 1984), 9.

33   Oregon in 1964, Iowa, West Virginia, Vermont and New York in 1965, New Mexico in 1969, New Jersey and California in 1972. Delaware had experimented with abolition in 1958 but restored the death penalty in 1961.

34   Massachusetts has also abolished the death penalty, bringing to twelve the number of abolitionist states today.

35   A few of the "hard core" or Group III states have abolished the death penalty for a few years in their history, but never for more than a decade. If a state has abolished the death penalty for fewer than ten years in its history, it is according to this classification, a Group III state. Washington State could go either way, having abolished the death penalty in the Progressive Era and for a few years in the late 1970s.

36   Other progressive ballot measures passing in 1912 were the eight-hour work day on public works (64,508–48,078) and statewide public utilities regulation (65,985–40,956). *Oregon Blue Book 1999–2000* (Salem: Secretary of State, 1999), 291.

37   *Ibid.*, 292.

38   Only Minnesota and North Dakota never restored the death penalty, while Kansas and South Dakota restored it in the 1930s.

39   He mentioned in a phone interview that even one of his opponents in a public debate approached him after the meeting and told Bedau that he was an opponent of capital punishment but had taken the retention position just so there might be a debate. Phone interview with Dr. Hugo Bedau, 28 September 1999.

40   The last execution before McGahuey's was of William Karnes, a Salem ax-murderer, in January 1953. Governor Paul Patterson permitted this execution to go forward, even though he commuted the death sentence of 19-year-old Donald Imlah in 1955.

41   As of July 1, 2001, there were 25 men and 0 women on death row in Oregon. Four men, Jeffrey Tiner, Eric Running, David Cox and Travis Gibson, have been added to death row in the past two years and four men, Scott Harberts, Dayton Leroy Rogers, Robert Langley and Michael McDonnell have been removed in the same period. Randall Smith will be removed shortly from death row because his death sentence was vacated during his post-conviction appeal in Marion County. See statistics of death row inmates on the Oregon Department of Corrections

Web page: www.doc.state.or.us. The four murders by Kipland Kinkel of Springfield in May 1998 have not rekindled the debate on the death penalty to any large measure. Most reactions to that killing has been one of shock and anger, but because of Kinkel's age at the time of the crime (15), the focus in his sentencing has been how long to keep him away from society and not whether his crime ought to renew the debate about the death penalty for young offenders.

42   One of the reasons for this is that both Wright and Moore went to death willingly and both refused to pursue appeals to which they were statutorily entitled. As a matter of fact, they appealed to death penalty opponents *not* to stand in their way. Opponents find that it is hard to lead a movement when those going to death do so willingly, and even eagerly.

43   The final vote tally was 778,574–544,301. *Oregon Blue Book 1999–2000* (Salem: Secretary of State, 1999), 308.

44   Brief reviews of how each measure did at the polls can be found in the *Oregonian*, 3 November 1999, A1.

45   For the metaphor "Eden" to describe Oregon, see Malcolm Clark, *Eden Seekers: The Settlement of Oregon, 1818–1862* (Boston: Houghton Mifflin, 1981).

Part II
Procedure

CHAPTER 5

Putting a Person to Death in Oregon—Legally

One of the most dramatic changes concerning the death penalty that came about in the twentieth century is the length of time between commission of a first degree or aggravated murder and execution of the convicted person. We saw earlier that it took a mere ten weeks from the time that Dalton and Wade killed Morrow until they were hanged at the Multnomah County Courthouse on January 31, 1902.[1] That was not an unusual occurrence a century ago. In his survey of executions in Oregon from 1903 to 1964, Hugo Bedau shows that the average time served under death sentences in Oregon during this period was 14 months.[2] What was the case in 1900, however, is definitely not the case in 2000. What took three months in 1900 may easily take 20 years a century later. What happens in those 20 years will be covered in this chapter.[3]

This section on procedure begins with a brief description of the current "10-Step" system of death penalty appeals in Oregon, then proceed to a description of the "old" system so that the contrasts between the two can readily be seen. The section continues with a treatment of each of the three major steps in the current system: direct appeal to the Oregon Supreme Court, post-conviction trials in Marion County Circuit Court and federal habeas corpus appeals. A few words on executive clemency in Oregon will conclude this section.

Death Penalty Procedure Today in Oregon

The current system envisions ten steps that a person sentenced to death in Oregon may pursue before the state may legally put him to death. These ten steps do not include the conviction and sentence at the county circuit court level.[4] After being convicted of aggravated murder and sentenced to death in the county in which the crime was committed,[5] the defendant may do the following, in the following order:

1. Step 1 is an automatic and direct appeal to the Oregon Supreme Court.[6] This appeal is the only appeal a person cannot waive, the reason being that even if the person wants to be put to death, the state has an interest in ensuring that it is not unwittingly cooperating in and aiding a person's death wish. The state will only put a person to death if the evidence is legally sufficient to permit it. This appeal is concluded as early as three years after commission of the crime and may take 15 or more years to complete.[7]

2. Step 2 is a direct appeal to the United States Supreme Court. This appeal must be made within three months of the Oregon Supreme Court's entry of appellate judgment. Under the leadership of Chief Justice William Rehnquist, the United States Supreme Court has dispatched its agenda fairly quickly. In almost all cases of direct appeal, the United States Supreme Court will deny certiorari within six months of the petition for certiorari. Therefore, Step 2 is usually finished within nine months of the completion of Step 1. Only one Oregon death penalty case in the last twenty years has been granted certiorari by the United States Supreme Court on direct appeal.[8] About half of death row inmates waive this step and proceed immediately to Step 3.

3. Steps 3–6 concern the process called state post-conviction relief. This process begins in the county in which the convicted person lives and is a collateral, rather than direct, attack on the decision of the trial and appellate courts. Step 3 begins by filing a petition in Marion County Circuit Court in which the convicted person (now an inmate at the Oregon State Penitentiary in Salem) attacks the constitutionality of his conviction.[9] Disposition of cases in Step 3 has taken around three to five years, and the Marion County Circuit Court has only disposed of a few of these so far.[10] Statutory authorization for this process is found in ORS 138.510–.687 (1999).

4. Step 4 is an appeal of the result of the defendant's Marion County post-conviction hearing in Step 3 to the Oregon Court of Appeals. That is, a person's post-conviction petition may be dismissed after the three-to-five years, and he is entitled to appeal this dismissal to the court of appeals.[11] Even though Oregon has had a death penalty statute for 15 years, no one has passed through this step as of July 2001. Jesse Pratt's post-conviction case was dismissed in May 1999 and his notice of appeal was then filed with the Oregon Court of Appeals. His case, along with the two other death row inmates whose cases have proceeded furthest to date (Jeffrey Williams and Clinton Cunningham) have not been heard by the appeals court as of July 1, 2001. A late-breaking development in June 2001, to be discussed in Chapter Six, makes it probable that Pratt's case will not be heard at the court of appeals for at least another year or so.

5. Step 5 is an appeal of the Oregon Court of Appeals decision to the Oregon Supreme Court. Because no Oregon inmate has yet made it this far in the process, it isn't clear how long this will take or if the Oregon Supreme Court will give the same detailed level of scrutiny to post-conviction appeals as it does to the automatic and direct appeals. The court may decline to hear the case on post-conviction appeal, though it is hard to conceive that they would refuse to do so, especially for the first few men whose post-conviction appeals come to them.

6. Step 6 is an appeal of the Oregon Supreme Court's decision to the United States Supreme Court. As with direct appeals, state post-conviction appeals to the U.S. Supreme Court are routinely denied, but it buys at least nine months for the person on death row. It is rare for the federal court to hear more than three death penalty cases a year, and those cases are almost always of habeas corpus appeals (Steps 7–9).

7. Steps 7–9 consist of a death row inmate's federal appeals. After he has exhausted all his state challenges, he may bring his claim asserting a denial of federal constitutional rights in a federal forum. The forum for Step 7 is the United States District Court for the District of Oregon, headquartered in Portland. These appeals are referred to as habeas corpus appeals, and must be filed within one year of the exhaustion of a person's state remedies. The new Antiterrorism and Effective Death Penalty Act

of 1996 establishes more rigid timelines for habeas corpus review than had previously been the case, but it has yet to be seen how quickly these cases will actually be processed in Oregon.

8.   Step 8 is an appeal of the U.S. District Court's denial of a person's habeas corpus claim to the United States Court of Appeals for the Ninth Circuit. The Ninth Circuit is the largest of the 13 circuits in the federal court system, and it hears thousands of cases per year. There are approximately 20 judges on the Circuit, though they hear cases in three-judge "panels." The three judges are drawn by a lottery system; one cannot "pick" one's judges.

9.   If the defendant's petition for habeas corpus relief is denied at the Ninth Circuit, he may once again appeal to the United States Supreme Court. Since there are now more than 80 executions per year in the United States and the Supreme Court normally hears two or three death penalty cases per year, he has about a 2% chance that his federal habeas corpus death penalty appeal will be heard by the Supreme Court. The United States Supreme Court heard five death penalty appeals during its October 1999 Term and three during the October 2000 Term. Most significant for Oregon's death penalty, as will be explained below, was the June 4, 2001, decision of the Court to vacate the death sentence of John Paul Penry of Texas because the Texas court had not given adequate consideration to factors that might mitigate Penry's sentence of death. Already, the Court has agreed to hear two death penalty cases for the October 2001 Term, one of which will directly confront the issue of whether executing those with mental retardation violates the Eighth Amendment ban on cruel and unusual punishment.[12]

10.   If that appeal is denied, the defendant has the final remedy of seeking commutation of his sentence from the Governor of Oregon. The commutation power is spelled out in Article V, section 14, of the Oregon Constitution and the particulars of its application are described in ORS 144.640–.670 (1999).

The "Old" System

It is difficult to develop an appreciation of the way that the death penalty trial and appeals process has changed so immensely in Oregon without briefly considering some essential features of the system in place before the passage of the 1984 law reinstating the death penalty.[13] Under the old system, a person was usually convicted within a few months of commission of the death penalty crime.[14] By mid-century, the process usually took about six months. Actually, this part of the process has changed least. When Randy Guzek, currently a death row inmate, was sentenced in March 1988 for the killings of Rod and Lois Houser of Terrebonne, his sentence was handed down only nine months after the June 1987 shooting spree. James Isom, the second person on death row under the 1984 law, was convicted in December 1986 for a March 1986 crime. However, the cases of Michael McDonnell, described in Chapter One, and Scott Harberts, presented in Chapter Eleven, took more than four years from the time of the crime until imposition of a death sentence.

Even though this part of the process has changed the least, it is still astonishing to read death penalty cases from as recently as the 1950s in Oregon where denials of extensions would certainly have been granted in the 1990s. Take the case of Frank Payne, who killed a shop owner during a robbery in January 1951.[15] The crime was committed on January 9 and Payne was apprehended on January 10. The grand jury returned a true bill on January 18 charging him with first degree murder. The presiding judge appointed attorney Maurice Sussman, an experienced attorney, to represent Payne on January 19. Because of his workload, Sussman asked for the appointment of another counsel with him, which was granted on January 23. Trial was set for February 23, 1951.

On February 13 Sussman informed the court that he would pursue an insanity defense for Payne and asked for a continuance until March 12, 1951, to prepare for trial. Sussman submitted an affidavit saying that it took some time to prepare this kind of defense and, with the press of his other activities, he simply could not provide the level of defense that Payne required at such short notice.[16] He was asking for a continuance of 17 days for a crime that had occurred only 33 days earlier. Relying on Oregon Compiled Laws Annotated section 26–905, which left postponement of a trial to the discretion of the court, the judge denied his request. A unanimous Oregon Supreme Court upheld the denial as within the sound discretion of the circuit court judge.[17] Payne would eventually be executed in January 1953.[18]

Even more recently than the Payne case was that of Billy Junior Nunn, who was convicted in August 1956 of the April sexual abuse and murder of 14-year-old Alvin Eacret in Jackson County.[19] An information was filed May 5, 1956, the indictment was returned on May 11 and Nunn was arraigned on May 15. Counsel was appointed shortly thereafter and Nunn pleaded not guilty on May 31, 1956. Trial was set for Tuesday, July 17. On June 28 Nunn, through his attorney, moved for appointment of a psychiatrist to examine Nunn. The order was entered on July 6 approving this request. By July 13, the

report of the psychiatrist had not come back and the defendant's lawyer asked
for a continuance so that the report might be received and studied by the
defense. The request was denied. The report came to the defendant's lawyer
on July 14 and the trial went forward on July 17. The district attorney argued
successfully that the costs of paying for witnesses, many of whom had come in
from California where Nunn was apprehended, argued against granting the
continuance. Again, the Oregon Supreme Court upheld the lower court's decision.

Such rulings, held to be within the discretion of the circuit court judge,
would certainly be overturned today on appeal. These adverse rulings would
not even be made at trial. The Oregon death penalty system today is so solicitous of providing the death penalty defendant every opportunity to make his
case, within reason, that denial of a continuance of 17 days so that trial could
begin six weeks after the crime had been committed would not occur at any
level of Oregon courts today. The earlier image of providing a swift trial and
certain justice, revered for so long, has given way to a system that provides
every opportunity for the defendant to raise issues that might be germane to
his case.

If a person was convicted of first degree murder and sentenced to death
under the old system, he could appeal his conviction to the Oregon Supreme
Court. Before 1955, when the Oregon Legislature provided for automatic
appeal of death penalty sentences, it was up to the defendant whether or not
he would try to appeal.[20] The law controlling appeals to the Oregon Supreme
Court before 1955 went all the way back to the Deady Code of 1864 and had
not been changed since that date. It provided:

> An appeal from a judgment on a conviction stays the execu-
> tion of the judgment, upon filing with the notice of appeal a
> certificate of the judge of the court in which the conviction
> was had, or of a judge of the supreme court, that in his opin-
> ion there is probably cause for the appeal, but not other-
> wise.[21]

Therefore, for an appeal to be considered by the Oregon Supreme Court before 1955, a defendant had to get a certificate from the judge either of the
circuit court or the Supreme Court, stating that there was probable cause for
the appeal.[22]

Of the 58 people who were executed at the Oregon State Penitentiary
from 1903 to 1964, 19 of them did not pursue appeals of their death penalty
convictions to the Oregon Supreme Court.[23] The statistics show that 11 of
the first 24 did not pursue appeals, while only 8 of the last 34 rejected that

course. It became more and more of a given, as the century wore on, that death penalties were normally appealed to the Oregon Supreme Court. However, William Karnes, the last person executed before the automatic appeal statute went into effect in 1955, did not pursue an appeal and went quietly to his death in January 1953.

A person did not stand a very good chance of having his conviction reversed if he actually appealed the sentence of death to the Oregon Supreme Court. Of the 92 sentences of death handed down between 1903 and 1964 in Oregon, 58 were carried out and 23 were commuted by the governors. Of the 11 remaining cases, 2 died in prison awaiting execution, 1 escaped, and 8 had their cases reversed on appeal. Of these eight, none were resentenced to death, though several were resentenced to other terms in prison and one died before his trial could be resumed.[24]

Once an appeal was turned down by the Oregon Supreme Court, the chance for a reversal of the death sentence plummeted. An appeal to the United States Supreme Court could be made, but only one Oregon death penalty case was heard by the Court in the pre-1984 period. That case illustrates both the near futility of appealing to the U.S. Supreme Court but also the possibility of buying time before the sentence is carried out.

It arose out of the conviction late in 1949 of Morris Leland for the August 1949 killing of a 15-year-old girl in Multnomah County.[25] The conviction was affirmed by the Oregon Supreme Court in February 1951. Appeal was taken to the United States Supreme Court, which granted certiorari and heard oral arguments early in 1952. The issue in the case had nothing to do with the facts but the standard with which Oregon law required a defendant to prove an insanity defense in such a trial. Oregon law, unchanged on this issue since the Deady Code, required a person who invoked the insanity defense to prove his insanity beyond a reasonable doubt.[26] By 1952, however, this standard had been relaxed in every other state. Most only required that such a defense be proven by "clear and convincing evidence," a standard far less demanding than beyond reasonable doubt. Oregon was the only jurisdiction that still had this heightened standard. A divided U.S. Supreme Court upheld the standard, even though Justices Felix Frankfurter and Hugo Black thundered in dissent that such a concept of justice in Oregon bordered on the "dark and barbaric."[27] Leland's conviction therefore was upheld. He petitioned the Court for rehearing, but this request was denied in October 1952. With all of his appeals exhausted, he went to his death in January 1953, almost 3.5 years after his crime.

Though Leland's appeals managed to buy him at least two more years of life, he was not able to avoid the ultimate penalty. It was the diligent legal work of Jeannace June Freeman's lawyers from 1962 to 1964 in pursuing every possible avenue of appeal that eventually saved her life. By the time her federal habeas corpus appeal would be heard, Oregon abolished the death penalty and Governor Hatfield commuted her sentence to life imprisonment. She finally walked out of prison in 1985 at age 43. Not only do death penalty cases sometimes "ripen" with age, so that less convincing claims at trial might have more weight in later appeals, but sometimes the death penalty is repealed.

Finally, in the old system a person who had appealed to the United States Supreme Court and was denied did have the possibility of pursuing a federal habeas corpus remedy, but even into the 1940s fewer than 3% of death penalty defendants chose to apply for this remedy. It was granted in so few cases that the remedy really did not appear to be available. Not until the habeas corpus revolution of the late 1950s and 1960s would death penalty defendants try to use this remedy in large numbers.[28] Therefore, under the old system it is fully understandable why the time between imposition of a death sentence and execution in Oregon was, on average, 14.4 months. For almost all defendants it seemed futile to pursue an appeal beyond the Oregon Supreme Court. Many defendants also felt that an appeal to the supreme court was either a waste of time or not economically feasible. If one was sentenced to death, one's most promising remedy would be commutation of the death sentence by the governor. The courts were not a promising venue for relief.

Endnotes

1 See Chapter Two, pages 24–27.

2 "Capital Punishment in Oregon, 1903–64," *Oregon Law Review* 45 (1965), 30–31. Bedau's statistics cover all 92 sentences of death handed down in Oregon in those days. Only 58 of the sentences of death actually led to executions. He does not show statistics that include the time from commission of the crime until execution, but because trials happened very quickly after a murder during most of the early decades of the twentieth century, the 14-month average should only change by a few months when that number is taken into consideration.

3 Though this will not provide a complete history of the development of each of the 10 steps now statutorily provided for a person under a sentence of death, enough of that history will be provided so that one can understand the evolution of death penalty procedure in Oregon during the twentieth century.

4 Those who defend death penalty cases at trial have developed not simply a series of techniques to do their job well but also a mythology or series of stories of great defenses and heroic moves by counsel in these cases. Their goal is simple, to save a person's life, and the emotional and intellectual energy and dedication that goes into that process cannot be gainsaid. This book does not examine the particular trial issues that these counsel often face. For a helpful introduction to some of these issues see *Defending the Death Penalty Case: Tips, Tactics and Practical Advice* (Eugene, OR: Oregon Criminal Defense Lawyers Association, 1998).

5 Unless there is extremely negative pretrial publicity, the trial almost always takes place in the county in which the body of the victim was found. Sometimes it will take place in the county in which the homicide was committed if it differs from the place the body was found. In order to change venue for a trial, one has to show not only that there has been extremely negative pretrial publicity in the county, but that the publicity substantially impairs the defendant from receiving a fair trial in that county. It is a tall order to meet this standard.

6 ORS 163.150(1)(g)(1999) is the statutory authorization.

7 It took only 2 years and 11 months to affirm Clinton Cunningham's October 1991 murder of a woman in Douglas County and 3 years and 8 months to affirm Randall Smith's Washington County murder. His slaying of a Sherwood bank teller was committed in September 1990, and the Oregon Supreme Court affirmed his conviction in May 1994. Michael Hayward's case took only four years and three months from the commission of his crime in Lane County in April 1994 until the affirmation of his conviction by the Oregon Supreme Court in July 1998. Matthew Thompson's case took fewer than five years. On the other hand, as was shown in Chapter One, it has taken nearly 17 years and three juries to try to get Michael McDonnell to the end of Step 1, and there is no end in sight in that case.

8 That case is *State v. Wagner*, 305 Or 115, 752 P2d 1136 (1988) and will be the subject of Chapter Eight. In that case, the Supreme Court granted certiorari on July 3, 1989, and then vacated the decision of the Oregon Supreme Court. Ever since 1988 the U.S. Supreme Court has had almost complete discretion in considering its cases. Its grant of "cert," as it is called, is its way of accepting review of a case. After "cert" is granted, however, the Supreme Court may decide to hear a case at oral argument or do a summary disposition of the case. A summary disposition is an immediate decision, usually because the Court has decided another case recently on the same or similar facts, that gives the lower court instructions to apply the Supreme Court's reasoning on the other case to the case at hand.

9 All death row inmates are housed at the Oregon State Penitentiary in Salem. Though one speaks of it as a "row," there are only about a dozen cells next to each in the first floor of the Disciplinary Segregation Unit ("DSU") in which some are housed (they are single-bunked in Oregon). The rest of the 25 Death Row inmates are scattered throughout the 40 or so units in Administrative Segregation.

10 As will be shown below, the post-conviction relief act was only passed by the Oregon Legislature in 1959. Jeannace June Freeman's post-conviction case in Marion county in 1963 took only two months to dismiss. The first death penalty case since the 1984 statute in which it

was invoked was that of James Isom, who invoked it in 1992. His post-conviction claim was dismissed in 1996. Before he could go to Step 4 in the process he died of cancer in November 1997. The first person who is currently on death row to invoke Step 3 was Jesse Pratt, who began his almost six-year odyssey of post-conviction relief late in 1993. By July 1, 2001, Jesse Pratt, Clinton Cunningham, Jeffrey Williams and Mark Pinnell had completed Step 3. Randall Smith entered post-conviction relief in 1994 but his death sentence was vacated by a Marion County judge early in 2001.

[11]   The appeal is authorized by ORS 138.650.

[12]   The case is *McCarver v. North Carolina* and will probably be scheduled for hearing in October, November or December 2001, with a decision to be rendered by June 2002.

[13]   One of the reasons that death penalty proponents in Oregon so dramatically underestimated the costs of the series of death penalty appeals when the law was being discussed in the House Judiciary Committee in 1983 is that they had only the experience of the early 1960s to consider as well as the changes brought about by the 1959 post-conviction relief act. They thought that appeals would go rather quickly and inexpensively and that people would be executed within a few years of conviction. The cost estimates prepared for that committee are contained in the file on HB 2294 from 1983 in the Oregon State Archives and are laughably low, considering the actual experience of the subsequent 15 years.

[14]   Another case in point is the conviction of attorney James Finch for the November 28, 1908 murder of Ralph Fisher, Secretary of the Oregon State Bar, in Portland. Finch had been suspended from the practice of law a year earlier because of alcohol abuse and mismanagement of client funds, and Fisher had opposed Finch's petition for reinstatement to good standing. The case evoked outrage throughout Portland, and Finch was convicted and sentenced to death on New Year's Eve, just five weeks after the crime. The facts are narrated in *State v. Finch*, 54 Or 482, 103 P 505 (1909) and, more colorfully, in Fred Leeson, *Rose City Justice*, (Portland: Oregon Historical Society, 1998), xi–xii and 80–81. Leeson is incorrect when he says that Finch paid for his crime thirteen months later on the gallows at the Oregon State Penitentiary. Actually, Finch was executed on November 12, 1909, less than one year after the crime. William J. Bowers, *Legal Homicide* (Boston: Northeastern University Press, 1984), 488.

[15]   Facts are described in *State v. Payne*, 195 Or 624, 244 P2d 1025 (1952).

[16]   Sussman was appointed by the court and already had a full load of cases when he was asked to take on Payne's defense.

[17]   195 Or at 633, 244 P2d 1030.

[18]   Bowers, *Op. cit.*, 489.

[19]   *State v. Nunn*, 212 Or 546, 321 P2d 356 (1958).

[20]   *Oregon Laws 1955*, ch. 662, s. 2(1). "When any judgment of death is rendered and no appeal to the Supreme Court has been taken, an appeal to the Supreme Court is automatically taken by the defendant without any action by him or his counsel 65 days after the filing of the judgment."

[21]   Oregon Compiled Laws Annotated, sec. 26–1316 (1940).

[22]   The standard for what constituted probable cause in order for a judge to grant such a request, is never defined in the statute. In practice it worked out that almost anyone who took the effort to collect all the relevant material for appeal, which consisted of a bill of exceptions and the transcript of relevant sections of the trial, together with affidavits and exhibits from the trial, would be granted a certificate of probable cause.

[23]   See the list in Bowers, *op. cit.*, 346–47.

[24]   Tables and statistics are in Bedau, *op. cit.*, 5–6.

[25]   The facts of the case are narrated in the Oregon Supreme Court's decision, *State v. Leland*, 190 Or 598, 227 P2d 785 (1951).

[26]   *Leland v. Oregon*, 343 U.S. 790, 794–95 (1952).

[27]   *Ibid.*, 801 (Frankfurter and Black, JJ., dissenting).

[28]   Bowers, *op. cit.*, 62.

CHAPTER 6

Reflections on Three Aspects of the Present System

Although today there are ten steps that the person sentenced to death in Oregon may take before he can be executed legally, three of those steps are particularly important and merit closer scrutiny: Step 1—automatic appeal before the Oregon Supreme Court, Step 3—post-conviction relief in Marion County Circuit Court, and Step 7—filing a habeas corpus appeal in the United States District Court for the District of Oregon. Because no one has reached Step 7 since the passage of the 1984 statute, I will speak here only of the possible effect of the Antiterrorism and Effective Death Penalty Act of 1996 on habeas corpus death penalty appeals in Oregon. This section concludes with a brief look at Step 10, executive clemency from the Governor of Oregon.

First, a word about the process. After a person is convicted of aggravated murder and sentenced to death in a county circuit court, his case is automatically appealed to the Oregon Supreme Court.[1] Before oral arguments can be scheduled, several things must happen. The most time-consuming aspects of the process are settling the trial transcript and preparating briefs by both sides. The Oregon Rules of Appellate Procedure state that the court reporter must prepare a transcript within 60 days of the reporter's receiving a packet of information from the state court administrator certifying the verdict and giving relevant information about parties and their attorneys.[2] That 60 days may be extended another 30 days to include the transcript of jury selection.

After the transcript is settled, the briefing schedule is then established by the court after a representative of the court confers with the parties. The rules provide for a maximum brief of 100 pages but this is routinely waived in a death penalty case. When one includes various appendices, briefs for both sides may total more than 600 pages. Both sides are usually given between four and six months to write their briefs, with the defendant's attorney (usually the State Public Defender) submitting the first brief. After the state responds, the public defender may write a reply brief. This process can take anywhere from one to five years. The reason for a longer period is often because of the press of workload in one or both offices.[3]

Oral arguments are then scheduled and decisions are usually handed down between 2 and 18 months afterwards. Because of Measure 40, the opinion to remand Michael McDonnell's case for a third consideration by a Douglas County jury occurred three years and five months after oral argument.[4] Each case has its own pace, however, and few comments beyond those made in Chapter One can be made about the flow of the cases.

Automatic Appeal Before the Oregon Supreme Court

When the case reaches oral argument, counsel for the convicted man makes arguments that usually fall into four or five categories. Counsel may argue that the court below erred in certain pretrial motions usually with respect to evidence. Counsel may also object to the jurors who were actually selected, arguing that the court erred in allowing prejudiced jurors on the panel. Counsel may further argue that the judge made certain rulings during trial that prejudiced the defendant. In several cases the Oregon Supreme Court has wrestled with the issue of how prior crimes or bad acts of the defendant may be brought to the jury's attention. In addition, counsel can challenge the instructions given to the jury, that they are insufficient as a matter of law or that they unduly prejudice the client. Finally, counsel can challenge the kind of evidence permitted or excluded in the sentencing phase of an aggravated murder trial. The Oregon Supreme Court requires that the defendant's attorney "preserve" the lower court's errors for appeal by objecting to them in a timely fashion at trial. Normally a brief for the convicted man (the appellant's brief) will include everywhere from five to forty assignments of error made in the defendant's trial at the circuit court.

The Oregon Supreme Court needs to determine if these errors were in fact made by the lower court and, if they were made, whether the errors were "harmless" or "harmful." If the errors were harmful, that is if they prejudiced the defendant's ability to receive a fair trial, the supreme court has to decide whether the case needs to be completely retried or if only the sentencing phase of the trial needs to be repeated. One of the issues of immense importance after the *Penry* decision in 1989 was whether the implications of the United

States Supreme Court decision should lead to new trials for all men on death row or only to new sentencing hearings.[5]

A few citations from some cases of men on death row in Oregon today may illustrate the points made above. Cesar Barone was convicted in January 1995 of the October 1992 slaying of nurse midwife Martha Bryant in Washington County.[6] At trial, his counsel objected to the seating of a juror who admitted during his examination that he could think of no situations where the death penalty was inappropriate when one committed an especially brutal murder.[7] Despite this admission, the Oregon Supreme Court rejected Barone's challenge to the juror because the juror also said that he would follow the instructions of the court in sentencing a person.

Barone was later convicted in December 1995, in a separate trial, of the murders of three other women in the Portland area from 1991 to 1993.[8] On appeal, his lawyer pointed out to the Oregon Supreme Court that the judge in the Washington County trial, Michael J. McElligott, forgot to swear in the jury before trial and, as a matter of fact, did not do so until he realized near the end of the trial that he hadn't. Most attorneys and judges would probably recognize this as a major gaffe, equivalent to a minister's forgetting to pray in a religious service or a teacher's forgetting to show up to the classroom to teach a class, but the Oregon Supreme Court decided that this oversight did not affect Barone's right to an impartial jury.[9]

Objections of a different nature were made by the public defender on behalf of Clinton Cunningham. Cunningham was convicted in October 1992 for the October 1991 aggravated murder of Shannon Faith off Highway 38 near Elkton.[10] At the sentencing phase of his trial, Cunningham's attorney asked that the state be required to produce statewide data in which the defendant, like Cunningham, was convicted of at least one count of murder and at least one count of first degree rape or attempted rape and received a sentence less than death. The purpose of this proportionality data was to determine if others had committed the same kind of crime but received a sentence less than death. If so, Cunningham's attorney would argue that the death sentence was inappropriate in this instance. On appeal, the Oregon Supreme Court held that proportionality data may be appropriately considered only for the *county* in which the person was convicted. Since Douglas County supplied this information, there was no error.

Cunningham's attorney also objected to the jury instructions given at the close of his trial. He argued that the jury should have been instructed not only on the crimes of aggravated murder, intentional murder and first degree manslaughter but also on second degree manslaughter. Though this may appear at first glance to be a legal quibble, Cunningham's attorney was thinking that if the jury is given instructions on less severe crimes, they may be inclined to convict on a less severe crime. Under Oregon law such an instruction may be given only if a rational jury could have found him guilty of the crime but innocent of the more serious offense. The difference between first and second degree manslaughter has to do with whether the slaying was done with a "reckless" state of mind (second degree) or "under circumstances manifesting extreme indifference to the value of human life" (first degree). The trial court's decision not to instruct on second degree manslaughter was upheld by the Oregon Supreme Court because of the nature and severity of the wounds inflicted on the victim.

An objection that led the supreme court to overturn the trial jury's judgment of conviction and remand for new trial happened in the case of Jesse Pratt, convicted in February 1988 of the June 1986 slaying of Carrie Love near Klamath Falls.[11] Pratt operated a long-haul trucking service in Seattle and wanted Love to accompany him to Los Angeles to set up an office there. Love went along and her body was found a few days later. At trial, the prosecution introduced evidence of Pratt's abduction and sexual abuse of another woman in 1980. Relying on the distinction between prior crimes' evidence in order to show the defendant's "bad character" and prior crimes' evidence to show defendant's motive or plan in committing a crime, the court held that the prosecutor introduced the evidence of Pratt's earlier crime for the former purpose. Therefore, it remanded the case for a new trial. In 1993, the court affirmed Pratt's conviction after the prosecution dropped the evidence of prior crimes and relied this time on the testimony of a jailhouse informant regarding Pratt's crime.[12]

Though many of the issues affirmed or reversed on appeal are fairly technical in scope, two decisions of the Oregon Supreme Court have touched legal issues of more signal importance, such as the psychotherapist-client privilege and the constitutional rule invalidating *ex post facto* criminal laws. The former came up in one of the trials of Robert Langley and the latter in the recently remanded decision in the *McDonnell* case.

Robert Langley was convicted in Marion County in June 1989 of the April 1988 slaying of Larry Rockenbrandt in a garage at the Oregon State Hospital and also in Marion County in December 1989 for the December 1987 slaying of Ann Gray in Salem.[13] Though both cases resulted in convictions of aggravated murder, the former case on remand did not lead to reimposition of the sentence of death. One piece of evidence introduced at the trial for Gray's murder over defendant's objection were notebooks that Langley had written as part of his group therapy project while being held at the Oregon State Hospital in Salem. The documents in question were Langley's "daily journal" and "life history," the latter of which described the reasons for his criminal activity. The state contended on appeal that the psychotherapist-patient privilege did not apply because Langley was not really a patient and the treatment team for whom Langley prepared the reports were not psychotherapists.[14]

The Oregon Supreme Court allowed the documents into evidence but on different grounds than those urged by the state. The court held that because other documents from Langley's treatment were admitted at trial—his "treatment contract" and a "self assessment"—Langley had waived the privilege as to the other documents.[15] The supreme court reasoned that because Langley had written all these documents as part of his treatment program and because his counsel had not objected to the introduction of other documents written while he was in this program, innocuous as they were, he could not object to the introduction of these more incriminating documents.

A final example of the procedure of Step 1, from the recently decided case of Michael McDonnell, probes the murky and difficult area of *ex post facto* laws and their applicability in the criminal context.[16] We met Michael McDonnell in Chapter One, and the facts of his case do not need repetition. Before the Oregon Supreme Court remanded his case in 1992 for a new sentencing trial, the Oregon Legislature changed the sentencing law for a death penalty case both in the 1989 and 1991 legislative sessions.[17] These changes required a judge on remand for a new penalty phase hearing to instruct the jury that the convicted man could be given one of three kinds of sentences: life imprisonment, life imprisonment without the possibility of parole ("true life"), or the death penalty. Before the passage of the 1989 law permitting the true-life sentencing option, Oregon juries had only the other two sentencing options open to them in a case of aggravated murder.

Those convicted of aggravated murder before the summer of 1989, therefore, could only receive a sentence of life imprisonment or death. The issue in the latest *McDonnell* case had to do with the sentencing options open to a judge on remand after 1991 for an aggravated murder committed before the summer of 1989. When the case was remanded to Douglas County, both the state and the defendant wanted the jury to have the three options to consider, since a section of the 1991 law provided: "The provisions of this section are procedural and shall apply to any defendant sentenced to death after December 6, 1984."[18] The trial judge, however, refused these requests. Relying on another case decided in 1993 by the Oregon Supreme Court in which the court held that the sentencing options *at the time of the crime* were the ones to be applied, the judge only instructed the jury on the two options available at that time.

To make matters more complicated, McDonnell had also executed an agreement on remand in which he waived any constitutional *ex post facto* objection that might have been open to him. That is, he was saying that he wanted the jury to have the three sentencing options open to them as a result of the 1989 and 1991 laws, and that he would not bring up any *ex post facto* objection if this was done.[19] On appeal, the Oregon Supreme Court held that the trial judge had erred in only instructing the jury on the two sentencing options available at the time of the crime.[20] The court further held that McDonnell was within his rights in waiving any *ex post facto* objection that might be raised to the applicability of the new law. Thus, the case was remanded for yet another sentencing trial, where the judge, no doubt, will instruct the jury on all three options.[21]

Once the supreme court affirms the conviction of a death sentence, the convicted person may ask for reconsideration of the court's opinion within 21 days of the decision.[22] Requests for reconsideration are routinely denied but in one of the Langley cases reconsideration was granted and a new decision was not handed down until November 1993, 16 months after the original decision.[23] Cases then move on to the next steps of the process.

Post-Conviction Relief

Though the average length of time between committing an aggravated murder and having one's conviction affirmed in the Oregon Supreme Court is a very significant change in Oregon's death penalty jurisprudence in the twentieth century, the most significant change is the availability of post-conviction relief. Post-conviction relief adds four new steps to the process (Steps 3–6) and adds years, perhaps even a decade, to Oregon death penalty appeals. Twelve death row inmates whose convictions have been affirmed by the Oregon Supreme Court are now in either Step 2, 3, or 4 of the process. A few comments on the length of the process will then be followed with an exposition of the law authorizing this process and conclude with the kinds of claims brought up in one post-conviction case, that of Clinton Cunningham, dismissed in August 1999.[24]

Thirteen death row inmates have had their convictions affirmed by the Oregon Supreme Court by July 1, 2001 (Barone, Cunningham, Hayward, Lotches, McNeely, Montez, Pinnell, Pratt, Reyes-Camarena, Simonsen, Smith, Thompson and Williams), but one of these 13, Randall Smith, had his sentence of death vacated during his post-conviction relief hearing in 2001.[25] Of the remaining 12 who are currently on death row, about half of them then appeal to the United States Supreme Court after their conviction is affirmed in Oregon and about half go directly to post-conviction relief. Direct appeal to the U.S. Supreme Court normally buys a person another four to nine months. For example, Michael McNeely's conviction was affirmed in Oregon in August 2000, his petition for certiorari was denied by the U.S. Supreme Court in December 2000 and he entered post-conviction relief in Marion County in April 2001. Ernest Lotches has appealed his December 2000 affirmance by the Oregon Supreme Court and, to date, his petition for certiorari has not yet been denied.[26]

A few of the remaining 10 men have not proceeded very far in the post-conviction process. Reyes-Camarena only entered the post-conviction system in 2001 and Cesar Barone and David Simonsen in 2000.[27] Matthew Thompson entered post-conviction in July 1999 and his case is scheduled for a status conference late in July 2001. There is no indication of when his hearing will be. The two still in Step 3 whose cases have proceeded furthest are Michael Hayward and Marco Montez. Hayward entered the system on October 28, 1998, and after several extensions to file his petition, a pretrial conference has been set for September 2001. Montez entered the system in September 1997 and his post-conviction hearing, originally scheduled for February 2000, has now been moved to the end of July 2001. He has also joined the mandamus proceeding (to be discussed in the consideration of Dallas Ray Stevens' case in Chapter Eleven) attacking the method of selecting jurors in death penalty cases, that has been heard but not decided by the supreme court as of July 1, 2001. It is unclear at this point to what extent a favorable ruling in the supreme court on the mandamus issue might affect Montez's post-conviction relief hearing in Marion County.

The other four men have had their post-conviction petitions dismissed and have moved along to Step 4. Jesse Pratt was the first to enter this step, with his post-conviction petition having been dismissed in July 1999. Clinton Cunningham followed soon after when his post-conviction petition was dismissed in August 1999 and Jeffrey Williams entered post-conviction later in 1999. Mark Pinnell entered Step 4 early in 2001.

A significant development for the case of Pratt occurred in late June 2001. It will probably not affect either Clinton Cunningham or Jeffrey Williams. Mark Pinnell's case is still too far away from hearing to be immediately affected. The development had to do with the length of brief that the court of appeals would allow to be filed on behalf of Pratt.

Pratt's attorney Eric Cumfer moved in late 2000 to file an extended brief in the case. The Oregon Rules of Appellate Procedure would only allow a 50-page brief in a case like this. In January 2001, the court decided that he could file a 100-page brief on Pratt's behalf. Not content with that length, Cumfer moved the court to reconsider its decision, and in February 2001 the court decided it would allow a 150-page brief. Not content with that length, Cumfer then filed a petition for review in the Oregon Supreme Court in March contending that the 150-page limitation violated the rights of his client. Cumfer was joined in this petition by a brief submitted by Michael Curtis on behalf of the Oregon Criminal Defense Lawyers Association. Rather surprisingly, to some observers, the supreme court agreed to hear the case. Though the court may decide to forego oral arguments and issue a per curiam decision on the issue, if it requires briefing and oral arguments the case will probably not be heard and decided until 2002 or 2003 at the earliest. In the meantime, Pratt's case before the court of appeals is stayed.

Cumfer is also co-counsel for Clinton Cunningham but it is doubtful whether the same issue will arise in his case. Counsel for Jeffrey Williams, however, has not chosen this route. His motion for an extended brief was granted, and he filed his 63-page opening brief in his case on May 3, 2001. The Department of Justice now has until late summer to file its brief in response. Both the Williams and Cunningham cases will probably be heard by the court of appeals late in 2001, while the Pratt case will take longer to get a hearing.

Because five men completed Step 3 by July 1, 2001 (Cunningham, Pinnell, Pratt and Williams' petitions were dismissed while Smith's death sentence was vacated), one can start to estimate how long Step 3 might typically last. Williams' case moved along with greatest speed, and it was dismissed in August 1999—only 2.5 years after he filed for post-conviction relief. Randall Smith's moved the slowest. He entered the system in September 1994 and, as indicated above, his sentence of death was vacated in March 2001 because the judge determined that Smith's trial attorney rendered ineffective assistance, in violation of the U.S. Constitution, by not putting on witnesses in defense of Smith in the penalty phase of his trial. Mark Pinnell's case took more than six years until his petition was dismissed. The average time to complete Step 3 for the five men who completed it was five years. In contrast, the cases of two men who are nearest to completing Step 3 at the present (Hayward and Montez) have averaged 3.5 years. At this point it is safe to conclude that the average post-conviction case in Marion County will take between 4–5 years to complete, with 2.5 years being the shortest time and more than 6 years being the longest time.

Authority for Step 3 is to be found in the Post-Conviction Hearing Act passed by the Oregon Legislature in 1959.[28] The purpose of the act was to satisfy the requirement set down by the United States Supreme Court that states needed to furnish state prisoners "some clearly defined method by which they may raise claims of denial of federal rights."[29] States chose different methods to accomplish this, with Oregon choosing to do so through the 1959 statute.

The grounds on which relief must be predicated are spelled out in the original and current law. Though four grounds are listed in ORS 138.530, the only ground that has been used so far is the first. The petitioner must establish:

> A substantial denial in the proceedings resulting in the petitioner's conviction, or in the appellate review thereof, of petitioner's rights under the Constitution of the United States, or under the Constitution of the State of Oregon, or both, and which denial rendered the conviction void.[30]

As will be shown in the consideration below of Clinton Cunningham's post-conviction plea, the most significant constitutional violation asserted is the Sixth Amendment right to counsel. Most post-conviction attorneys spend the better part of their time trying to dredge up examples of inadequate assistance of counsel from the trial and appellate transcripts and briefs. Due process violations, under the Fifth and Fourteenth Amendments to the United States Constitution and Article I, sections 1, 10 and 20, of the Oregon Constitution are also frequently alleged.

The scope of constitutional violations that can be brought up in post-conviction relief, however, is narrowly circumscribed by the law. The statute also provides that:

> No ground for relief may be asserted by petitioner in a petition for relief under ORS 138.510 to 138.680 unless such ground was not asserted and could not reasonably have been asserted in the direct appellate review proceeding.[31]

It is clear, therefore, that post-conviction relief is not simply a second "bite" of the proverbial apple, a secret and sneaky way to bring up in another forum the same issues rejected once before by the Oregon Supreme Court.

An inmate applies for post-conviction relief in Marion County because, as the statute provides, two copies of the petition must be filed with the clerk of the circuit court for the county in which the inmate is imprisoned.[32] If the Marion County Circuit Court determines that the hearing can be "more expeditiously" conducted in the county in which the petitioner was convicted, it may order the petitioner's case to be transferred to that county.[33]

One of the provisions of the post-conviction statute that has changed a few times since 1959 is how long a petitioner has to file his petition. When the statute was passed in 1959 the intended beneficiaries of the act were non-death penalty people. There were thousands of them and no death row inmates in 1959.[34] Therefore, the bill passed by the 1959 legislature provided no timeframe within which such a petition must be filed. The reasoning was that since the person was imprisoned and could only benefit from the act if he invoked it, his delay only hurt him. If he never invoked the act, the system was no worse off than before.

The presence of death row inmates after 1984 who might use the avenue of post-conviction appeals led to two changes in the statute. In 1989 the time for pursuing post-conviction relief was limited to 120 days after conviction; in 1993 that time was extended to two years.[35] The current statute requires that a post-conviction petition be filed within two years of the final disposition of the case on direct appeal.[36]

In 1991 the Legislative Assembly passed a law requiring a person sentenced to death to seek a stay of execution within 90 days of his death sentence being affirmed by the state supreme court. If the prisoner was not going to pursue post-conviction, why should the state have to wait two years before discovering that? Under this provision, to obtain a stay of execution a death penalty defendant's first petition for post-conviction relief had to be filed within 90 days after direct appeal is final.[37] This filing acted as a signal to the state that the defendant was going to pursue the full scope of post-conviction relief available to him. The statute also provided that extensions to file the final petition may be granted if defendant shows that "progress is being made in the preparation of the petition."[38]

This provision was modified by the 1999 Legislative Assembly to permit a stay of execution to be sought anytime during the two-year period for filing for post-conviction relief.[39] Once post-conviction is timely filed and all materials are submitted to the judge assigned to the case, the hearing is somewhat anticlimactic. Even though the underlying case is a criminal case, post-conviction relief is called a civil hearing and does not include a jury. Only the judge hears the evidence. In addition, since the major purpose of the hearing is to evaluate the extent of error in the previous trial and appeal, it is primarily a "paper" hearing. Witnesses are sometimes called and testimony is sometimes given, but the focus of the hearing is the presentation and evaluation of written material submitted to the judge. This makes the post-conviction hearing more like an appeal than a trial. Thus, post-conviction hearings in Marion County are a hybrid: they concern a criminal defendant but are civil cases; they seem to be a trial but look more like an appeal. The standard of proof is preponderance of the evidence, the usual standard in civil cases.[40]

Relief that may be granted includes "release, new trial, modification of sentence, and such other relief as may be proper and just."[41]

It almost goes without saying that the court may also dismiss the prisoner's petition.

The process may be illustrated through a brief consideration of the post-conviction petition of Clinton Cunningham.[42] Cunningham's case was the quickest of any current death row inmate to be affirmed by the Oregon Supreme Court. He was convicted of the October 1991 murder of Shannon Faith in October 1992, and the Oregon Supreme Court affirmed the conviction in September 1994.[43] He appealed directly to the United States Supreme Court and his petition was denied on March 6, 1995. In accordance with the Post-Conviction Hearing Act, he filed for an automatic stay of execution on May 3, 1995. His post-conviction case was underway.

The first few months of post-conviction relief usually see a flurry of activity as the petitioner files the automatic stay, files a petition of indigency coupled with an affidavit of indigency, receives court-appointed counsel, usually asks for replacement counsel, asks that the judge assigned be recused and asks a few more times for recusal of a new judge or reappointment of a new attorney.[44] The court usually grants many of these motions. After the initial dust had cleared, Cunningham had a court-appointed attorney, Kenneth Hadley, and a judge, Judge Pamela Abernethy. As it actually turned out, Cunningham's hearing was held in 1999 before Senior Judge Erstgaard because Judge Abernethy was on medical leave at the time caring for her mother. Nevertheless, the preliminary jockeying took about three to four months.

The heart of the process, and the reason it has taken as many as 5.5 years in a few cases, is the filing of the prisoner's petition. By April 1996, a first petition had been filed and a status conference was scheduled to see how things were going. The post-conviction hearing was then scheduled for December 1996. The defendant's attorney then wished to amend the petition and permission was granted. The hearing was set over until 1997. In May 1997 Cunningham wrote a letter to Judge Abernethy from the Oregon State Penitentiary saying that he wanted a new attorney because he did not feel counsel understood his case or was spending the time on it that it deserved. Because the process was already two years along, the judge denied Cunningham's request.

Lest it appear that excessive delays are already creeping into the system, two points should be clarified. First, the attorneys who take on post-conviction defense work are attorneys who already have their plates fairly full with other cases. Death penalty cases are arguably very important to them but must be integrated into their other work. Second, the number of attorneys statewide who handle post-conviction death penalty cases is less than a dozen. These attorneys are usually not the same attorneys who argue death penalty cases at trial, because the whole purpose of post-conviction relief is to show the inadequacy of trial counsel. Also, the director of Indigent Defense Services at the state court administrator's office has established criteria of competence and experience that these post-conviction attorneys must meet before they can be named.[45] At this point, these two factors contribute largely to the pace of post-conviction death penalty cases in Marion County.

After Cunningham's request for new counsel was denied, his counsel made a series of motions: to gain access to juror questionnaires (granted), to have Cunningham take a polygraph test (granted), to submit Cunningham to a complex neurocognitive exam to help determine his mental condition (denied) and to request funds for a Canadian investigator (granted). The last motion was driven by counsel's attempt to show that the murdered woman, Shannon Faith, a native of British Columbia, lived a life of prostitution before she came to Oregon and that some of the bruises found on her body could have been the result of encounters with other men than Cunningham. At trial, former Multnomah County Medical Examiner William Brady had testified that some of the bruises also could have resulted from "enthusiastic (thus consensual) sexual activity." If counsel could establish this point, he could perhaps argue that jury instructions in the trial were too limited.

As information came in from these various sources, counsel asked for and received permission to amend the petition yet again. Finally, on August 19, 1998, the sixth amended petition was submitted and a hearing was scheduled for March 5, 1999. The hearing was held before Judge Erstgaard and led ultimately to the dismissal of Cunningham's case. After the hearing, however, counsel requested permission to amend the petition yet again. In May 1999, three years after filing his first petition, petitioner's counsel filed his seventh (and final) amended petition. The state, which had been filing responses along the way, filed its response within ten days of the petitioner.

Cunningham's petition ended up being 42 pages in length and alleged 25 errors in the conduct of the trial and two in the appellate proceedings. In legal language, these allegations of error consisted of alleged violations of petitioner's Sixth Amendment right to counsel under the Federal Constitution, along with a Fourteenth Amendment claim, and a violation of Article I, section 11, of the Oregon Constitution. In addition, Cunningham's attorney alleged six due process violations of the Fourteenth Amendment of the Federal Constitution and Article I, sections 1, 10 and 20, of the Oregon Constitution. The Department of Justice's response, prepared by Assistant Attorney General Kathleen Cegla, was 52 pages in length, with 10 pages of supplementary exhibits. Cunningham's attorney then filed a reply brief.

In order to get a flavor of the allegations, a few should be mentioned. Cunningham alleged that his trial attorney, Mark Hendershott, failed to file a motion to suppress Cunningham's illegally obtained confession that was, according to the petition, coerced. He further alleged that his trial counsel failed to request a hearing to determine whether keeping Cunningham in leg irons during the trial was necessary. Hendershott had failed, the petition claimed, to secure a DNA test of pink tissue found between the decedent's legs in order to help determine if the sexual activity with Cunningham was consensual. The trial attorney failed to impeach the witness for the prosecution, Dr. Cochran, who testified about Cunningham's future dangerousness, but who himself was having "licensing and reputation" problems at the time of the trial. Petitioner's allegation would then be that the prosecution witness was attempting to curry favor with the prosecution by testifying against Cunningham in hopes of straightening out his professional difficulties. The allegations go on and on.

On August 18, 1999, Judge Erstgaard issued his findings of fact and conclusions of law.[46] The 63 findings of fact attempt to refute the claims made by Cunningham's attorney. For example, the court was not convinced that Cunningham's case was prejudiced by his trial attorney's failure to cross-examine Dr. Cochran about the investigation the Board of Psychological Examiners was conducting on him. The court was not convinced by the evidence submitted that the victim was in fact a prostitute. The court found that even if someone other than Cunningham had had sexual intercourse with Shannon Faith close to the time she was killed, Cunningham failed to establish that such evidence would have been relevant to any issue in his criminal trial. The court concluded, therefore, that "petitioner did not prove any of his claims by a preponderance of the evidence."[47]

Cunningham's case took four years and three months to conclude. It took less time than the cases of Pinnell, Pratt and Smith but longer than that of Jeffrey Williams. From the perspective of the time taken to complete the process, Cunningham's petition was average. He now proceeds to Step 4 of the process, appeal of the dismissal of his post-conviction petition before the Oregon Court of Appeals.

Federal Habeas Corpus Appeals

Even though Latin instruction dropped out of the curriculum of Oregon public high schools more than 20 years ago, the two Latin words that all death penalty prisoners know are "habeas corpus." They might not know what the words mean, but they know that if they are granted habeas corpus relief they may not have to face the death penalty.

This is not the place to review the history of the writ of habeas corpus or even to discuss its ebb and flow in the jurisprudence of the United States Supreme Court in the last 40 years.[48] Suffice it to say that the writ is of longstanding importance in criminal law and acts as a directive to a state official, usually the superintendent of the facility where the inmate is housed, requiring him or her to hand over the body ("habeas corpus" literally means, "you have the body"—of the prisoner) to the court to determine if the person is being imprisoned in violation of the United States Constitution.

Though the writ of habeas corpus is mentioned in the United States Constitution, it was applied at first exclusively to federal prisoners and only later, in the late nineteenth century, to state prisoners.[49] Its broad use by state prisoners was invoked more and more in the 1960s and 1970s, though significant erosion of its scope has taken place in the last few decades. The most significant law relating to habeas corpus and death penalty appeals is the Antiterrorism and Effective Death Penalty Act of 1996 (AEDPA).[50] A few comments on this law and its possible effect in Oregon will suffice for this section.[51]

AEDPA was passed in the wake of the bombing of the Murrah Federal Building in Oklahoma City in April 1995 and was intended to express Congress' outrage at the seemingly growing number of senseless acts of terrorist violence on American soil. In addition to sections deterring terrorism, the act also reflects Congress' attempt to revise and restrict habeas corpus appeals in death penalty cases. As Senator Orrin Hatch (R-Utah), chairman of the Senate Judiciary Committee, said:

> At long last, after more than a decade of effort, we're about to curb these endless, frivolous, costly appeals of death sentences, and as so many of the people standing here with us today know, habeas corpus reform is the only substantive provision in this bill that will directly affect the Oklahoma City bombing case.[52]

The major thrust of AEDPA as it relates to death penalty cases is to accomplish two things. The first is to provide an expedited federal habeas corpus appeals process for states that qualify for and opt in to Chapter 154. The second is to provide restrictions on bringing successive petitions within certain time limits in for prisoners in states whose appeals fall under Chapter 153. The Chapter 154 provisions, codified at 28 U.S.C. sections 2261–2266, are completely new, while the Chapter 153 restrictions are scattered throughout the existing habeas corpus law in 28 U.S.C. sections 2241–2255. The Chapter 154 provisions are easier to grasp and will be presented first.

The Chapter 154 provisions arose out of a commission appointed by Chief Justice William Rehnquist in 1988 and chaired by retired Supreme Court Justice Lewis Powell to study the problem of delay in death penalty habeas corpus appeals and to propose legislative changes to streamline the process.[53] The goal of these provisions was to balance fairness with finality in death penalty cases by offering states an expedited, death penalty review process if the state qualified under the act and "opted in" to the statute. The act provides, in Chapter 154:

> This chapter is applicable if a State establishes a statute, rule of its court of last resort, or by another agency authorized by State law, a mechanism for the appointment, compensation, and payment of reasonable litigation expenses of competent counsel in State post-conviction proceedings brought by indigent prisoners whose capital convictions and sentences have been upheld on direct appeal to the court of last resort in the State or have otherwise become final for State law purposes. The rule of court or statute must provide standards of competency for the appointment of such counsel.[54]

In other words, in order to qualify for the provisions of Chapter 154 the state must have a mechanism for appointing counsel for all post-conviction death penalty appeals, must assure that these counsel are competent, and must pay them fairly. Because the availability of mandatory post-conviction counsel for indigent death penalty defendants is not mandated by law or Supreme Court decision, the Powell Committee felt that states would jump at the trade-off suggested. "You, states, supply the adequate counsel and, as a reward, we, Congress, will provide you a more expedited process."

That more expedited process is spelled out in the following sections. The case must be filed in the district court within 180 days after the completion of post-conviction relief, and the district court must render its decision not later than 180 days after the date on which the application is filed. A district court may grant an additional 30-day delay if it finds that the ends of justice served by allowing the delay outweigh the interests of the public and the applicant in a speedy disposition of the application.[55]

If the case is then appealed to the court of appeals, the court has 120 days to render a decision after the date on which the reply brief is filed. Again, a 30-day "justice" extension is permitted.[56] Other provisions cover applications for reconsideration or mandamus relief, but their language emphasizes an expeditious process.

A state qualifies and opts in to Chapter 154 by asserting in a habeas corpus appeal by a state prisoner that it will be applying the provisions of Chapter 154.[57] The prisoner then challenges that decision, and the federal district court where the prison is located makes a determination on whether the state has properly opted in to the benefits of the act. By 2001 more than 20 states have tried to opt in to the benefits of the act, but no federal district or circuit court has found the state process sufficiently demanding to support the state's action. The usual problem courts find is that state provisions to assess attorney competency and grant sufficient compensation are scattered throughout statutes, court decisions and court rules, and therefore do not constitute a systematic approach to the issue. Therefore, even though Chapter 154 is on the books and provides a way to expedite the death penalty process, no state currently qualifies for Chapter 154 benefits.[58] This was certainly not what the drafters of the law envisioned.

Changes in the federal habeas corpus statute in death penalty cases, where the state either does not qualify or opt in to Chapter 154 benefits, are governed by the traditional habeas corpus statute and fortified by new provisions in AEDPA which limit the time for filing such a petition, limit successive petitions and limit the kind of evidence that may be introduced in a federal habeas corpus death penalty case. Now, a final issue regarding the retroactivity of Chapter 153 to currently pending death penalty cases needs mentioning.[59]

Chapter 153 now provides, in part: "A one-year period of limitation shall apply to an application for a writ of habeas corpus by a person in custody pursuant to a judgment of a state court." Though the rules are unclear of when the clock begins and whether the one year includes the time in which a person is pursuing his appeal to the United States Supreme Court (Step 6), the purpose of the section is to limit the timeframe for habeas corpus appeals. The previous version of the statute had no timelimit within which an appeal had to be brought.

Second, the nature of the evidence that may be introduced in federal court has changed.[60] After providing that a state court's determinations of a factual issue be presumed correct, the law provides that if a person has failed to develop the claim in state court, a new evidentiary hearing should be granted. It should be granted only if the claim relies on: 1) a new rule of constitutional law, made retroactive to cases on collateral review by the Supreme Court that was previously unavailable; or 2) a factual predicate that could not have been previously discovered through the exercise of due diligence.[61] In addition to the difficulty in understanding the language of 1), this new provision eliminates the discretion a federal court had to conduct an evidentiary hearing.

Third, the act cuts back significantly on successive habeas corpus petitions. Such a petition will only be permitted if the applicant shows that the claim relies on a new rule of constitutional law made retroactive to cases on collateral review by the Supreme Court or whether the factual predicate for the claim could not have been discovered previously by the exercise of due diligence.[62] This tightens the procedure significantly for those who file a habeas corpus petition in death penalty cases. Unlike the state post-conviction process, where Cunningham's lawyer had been permitted to file seven amended petitions, one has the impression that the new habeas corpus law would only permit the first petition and requires the attorney to say all he or she has to say in that petition.

Chapter 154 of the act was clear that its provisions would apply to all cases pending on or after the date of enactment.[63] But the Chapter 153 provisions offered no guidance about their application to pending cases. This was litigated within one year of the act's passage. The Seventh Circuit held that Chapter 153 applied to pending cases; but on review the United States Supreme Court, by a 5–4 vote, reversed and held that in a non-capital case the provisions of 153 do not apply to a pending case.[64] The case at issue was from Wisconsin, which does not have a death penalty, even though the crime was one that would have provoked the death penalty in other jurisdictions. Left undecided was whether the new provisions of Chapter 153 apply to a pending capital case of a prisoner whose state has not qualified or opted in to Chapter 154 benefits.

State Clemency Process

This chapter concludes with a few words about Step 10, the statutory process permitting the governor of Oregon to grant a reprieve, commutation or pardon of a convicted criminal.[65] In states authorizing the death penalty, there are five statutory schemes for the Governor to commute a death sentence. In 14 states the Governor has sole authority to commute the sentence. In nine states the Governor must have a recommendation of clemency from the state parole board before commuting the sentence. In nine states the Governor must consult the state parole board but is not bound by their recommendations. In three states the parole board makes the decision, and in three states the board makes the decision but the Governor is a member of the board.[66]

Oregon is one of 14 states in which the governor has sole power to issue commutations, reprieves or pardons of convicted criminals. The language of the statute is unequivocal:

> Upon such conditions and with such restrictions and limita-
> tions as the governor thinks proper, the governor may grant
> reprieves, commutations and pardons, after convictions, for
> all crimes and may remit, after judgment therefor, all penal-
> ties and forfeitures.[67]

Copies of the application for commutation must be sent to various people,
and then those people shall provide the governor such information relating to
the case as the governor desires, but the material sent may not exclude statements by the victim or the victim's family, photos of the victim or the autopsy
report.[68] Following receipt of the application for pardon or commutation, the
Governor does not grant the application for at least 30 days, and if the Governor hasn't granted the application within 180 days the application lapses.[69]
Though the statute is not explicit on the matter, presumably the condemned
inmate only gets one chance to ask for commutation by the Governor after he
has exhausted all his appeals.[70]

If the Governor decides to grant a reprieve, commutation or pardon, he
or she reports to the next session of the legislature not only who was pardoned
or commuted, but the reasons for it. As with the victims' rights provisions
earlier mentioned, if the Governor decides to pardon or commute the sentence, he or she must also report the statements by the victim or the victim's
immediate family, photos of the victim and the autopsy report, if applicable.[71]
If all provisions of law are complied with and no commutation is forthcoming, a condemned defendant may finally—legally—be put to death in Oregon.

Endnotes

1   The appeal is made under the authority of ORS 163.150(1)(g)(1999).
2   *Oregon Rules of Appellate Procedure* 12.10(3)–(5).
3   For example, the briefs for both Alberto Reyes-Camarena, convicted by a Douglas County jury and sentenced to death in January 1997, and Michael McNeely, convicted by a Multnomah County jury and sentenced to death in October 1994, were withdrawn by the public defender after a personnel change in the office. The court permitted the public defender to refile the briefs. Reyes-Camarena's conviction was upheld by the Oregon Supreme Court in July 2000 and McNeely's in August 2000. The case that took the longest to date to get a hearing on automatic appeal after county conviction was that of Ernest Lotches. He was sentenced to death by a Multnomah County jury in June 1993 for an August 1992 aggravated murder. After numerous procedural wrangles and delays in filing his briefs, his case was heard by the court in March 2000 and his conviction was affirmed on one of three grounds in December 2000. The length of time for Lotches to get through Step 1, however, pales in comparison to the pre-*Penry* defendants, several of whom have not completed Step 1 even though their crimes took place well over a decade ago.
4   Oral argument in May 1996, decision in October 1999.
5   See the discussion in Chapter Nine. There were also some who argued, and this will be the thesis of Chapter Ten, that the effect of the *Penry* decision was actually to invalidate the Oregon death penalty statute, and that the Oregon Legislature did not pass a constitutional death penalty statute until 1991.
6   The Oregon Supreme Court decision, which recites some of the facts of the case, is at *State v. Barone*, 328 Or 68, 969 P2d 1013 (1998).
7   *Ibid.* 75, 969 P2d 1020.
8   *State v. Barone*, 329 Or 210, 986 P2d 5 (1999). Barone is a native of Fort Lauderdale, Florida, which he left in the 1980s after a troubled past that included the normal array of minor crimes as well as the suspicion of murder of his neighbor, a retired school teacher, in 1979. Florida was planning to try Barone on this case in 1997 but it decided to put off the case until after 2001. There is some thought that Florida may never extradite Barone from Oregon for a trial since he is already under the sentence of death in Oregon.
9   *Ibid.* This issue will no doubt be a major issue in state post-conviction proceedings.
10   *State v. Cunningham*, 320 Or 47, 880 P2d 431 (1994).
11   309 Or 205, 785 P2d 350 (1990).
12   *State v. Pratt*, 316 Or 561, 853 P2d 827 (1993).
13   Facts of the cases can be found in *State v. Langley*, 314 Or 247, 839 P2d 692 (1992) (Gray) and *State v. Langley*, 314 Or 511, 840 P2d 691 (1992) (Rockenbrandt).
14   *State v. Langley*, 314 Or 261, 839 P2d 702. The psychotherapist-patient privilege is set out in Oregon Evidence Code 504(2), which provides: "A patient has a privilege to refuse to disclose and to prevent any other person from disclosing confidential communications made for the purposes of diagnosis or treatment of the patient's mental or emotional condition among the patient, the patient's psychotherapist or persons who are participating in the diagnosis or treatment under the direction of the psychotherapist, including members of the patient's family."
15   *State v. Langley*, 314 Or 266, 839 P2d 704.
16   *State v. McDonnell*, 329 Or 375, 987 P2d 486 (1999). McDonnell has now been removed from death row because of this decision and is in general population at the Oregon State Penitentiary. He will remain there until the Douglas County jury again determines which sentence he should receive.
17   Or Laws 1989, ch. 720, secs. 1–2 and Or Laws 1991, ch 885, sec. 2. These changes were to ORS 163.150. Also see the Appendix for changes in the death penalty statute.
18   ORS 163.150(5)(e)(1993).

19   The *ex post facto* clauses of the Oregon and United States Constitutions prevent the passage of criminal laws and application of them to pending cases if the results would be *more severe* than the results under the statutory scheme at the time of the crime. Article I, section 21, of the Oregon Constitution, provides, in part: "No *ex-post facto* law...shall ever be passed ...." Article I, section 10, of the United States Constitution provides, in part: "No State shall...pass any...*ex post facto* law."

20   Opinion at page 6.

21   The latest McDonnell opinion is deeply unsatisfying to this author for two reasons. First, the court never said whether the laws passed by the 1989 and 1991 legislatures were, in fact, *ex post facto* laws. If they were not, then the discussion of whether one can waive one's *ex post facto* rights is somewhat irrelevant. But, if these laws were *ex post facto* laws, then the court needed to take a moment to explain how this was the case. If McDonnell felt and his lawyers agreed that the new law was an *advantage* to him in that it provided the jury with yet a third option for sentencing, how then is the law an *ex post facto* law? The difficulty in characterizing the new law is that it is neither better nor worse necessarily than the previous law. It gives an "in-between" option. In order for the decision to make sense, however, one must assume that the 1989 and 1991 laws were *ex post facto* laws. The court needed to show this was the case. The second problem with the opinion is that it assumes that the effect of *ex post facto* laws can be waived by a defendant. That is, it assumes that the law attaches to the person rather than to the entire criminal justice system. If it attaches to the person only, the person can certainly waive it. If, however, the law is something that is a fundamental rule regarding the operation of the criminal justice system, it cannot be waived simply at the decision of one of the parties. The court's reasoning on this issue, contained in the opinion at pages 7–9, is muddled and unclear. At oral argument in the Langley case on October 13, 1999, more than one of the justices said that the ruling in *McDonnell* "announces a new rule of law." In other words, they were reversing their earlier decision. This new rule of law was also used to vacate the sentences of death of Robert Langley and Dayton Leroy Rogers in 2000. Both of them, whose crimes go back to the 1980s, will now receive yet another penalty phase trial in their local circuit courts. Most observers believe that this rule of law will also be applied to the case of Randy Guzek, convicted in March 1988 for a June 1987 aggravated murder. That is, his case, to be argued for the third time to the Oregon Supreme Court sometime in the near future, will probably be remanded once again to Deschutes County where it began more than 14 years ago.

22   *Oregon Rules of Appellate Procedure* 9.25.

23   *State v. Langley,* 318 Or 28, 861 P2d 1012 (1993). The reconsideration had to do with how many sentencing options should have been available to Langley on conviction. The conclusion in 1993 was squarely in opposition to the conclusion in 1999. Yet, there was still some wiggle room for the state in Langley's appeal on October 13, 1999, when it argued it was permissible to give Langley only two sentencing options because of the "law of the case" doctrine. That doctrine says that if a particular court is given particular instructions on a particular defendant, the appellate court will uphold the court's decision on those instructions even if the appellate court has changed its mind on applicable law in the intervening years. This ongoing debacle in the Oregon Supreme Court today is one of the costly effects of the delays in pre-*Penry* cases.

24   Details of each person's case may be found by consulting the Oregon Judicial Information Network, a computer program available in any county courthouse in Oregon. The Network lists the name of the offender and all the entries made in the file of such a person. It is not unusual for a death penalty post-conviction case to have more than 100 entries of actions in the case. Case files are public documents and can be inspected at the Marion County Circuit Court.

25   As of this writing, Randall Smith is still officially on death row, but will be removed shortly pending the results of a new penalty phase hearing in his case in Washington County. That is why I list him as one of the 13 above, even though he is not in Steps 2, 3, or 4 of the process any longer.

26 A rather technical though noteworthy point is that even though Lotches' conviction was upheld by the Oregon Supreme Court on December 29, 2000, the appellate judgment in the case, which officially closes the case, was not entered until February 2, 2001. The defendant then has 90 days from the entry of the appellate judgment to file a petition for certiorari to the U.S. Supreme Court. That petition was duly filed on May 7, 2001. Lest one think that May 7 is more than 90 days after February 2, one might take the time to count the days. February only has 28 days, and there are the additional days of the final weekend, since May 7 was a Monday. Even though cases may take twenty years to work through the system, some lawyers patiently count and recount every day, so as to maximize the time for his or her client. In contrast, it is interesting to note that McNeely's lawyer filed the petition for certiorari with the U.S. Supreme Court on October 12, 2000 even though the decision was handed down on August 3 and appellate judgment in that case was only entered on October 5. The U.S. Supreme Court denied certiorari on December 11, 2000.

27 When I say that a person "entered the system," I mean, in the first instance that he invokes the post-conviction statute which gives a stay of his sentence of death until the conclusion of post-conviction relief. This automatic stay is provided for in ORS 138.685(1999).

28 Or. Laws 1959, ch. 636, ORS 138.510–.680 (1959). For a description of the original act with explanations of its provisions, see Jack G. Collins and Carl R. Neil, "The Oregon Postconviction-Hearing Act," *Oregon Law Review* 39 (1960), 337–67.

29 *Young v. Ragan,* 337 U.S. 235 (1948). Quoted and discussed in Collins and Neil, *op. cit.,* 337.

30 ORS 138.530(1)(a)(1999). In light of the argument in Chapters Nine and Ten, one wonders if some death row inmates might bring their claim also under ORS 138.530(1)(c)(1999), which provides, "Sentence in excess of, or otherwise not in accordance with, the sentence authorized by law for the crime of which petitioner was convicted; or unconstitutionality of such sentence."

31 ORS 138.550(2)(1999).

32 ORS 138.560(1)(1999).

33 ORS 138.560(4)(1999). Post-conviction relief for some of Gregory Wilson's crimes, discussed in Chapter Eleven, will probably be sought in Multnomah County where his aggravated murder was committed. His case and that of Grant Charboneau represent the most procedurally complex cases of anyone sentenced to death in Oregon since 1984.

34 As shown in Chapter Three, Governor Robert Holmes had commuted all the sentences of death before he left the office of Governor in January 1959.

35 Or Laws 1989, ch. 1053, sec 18; Or Laws 1993, ch. 517, sec. 1.

36 ORS 138.510(2)(a)–(b)(1999).

37 Or Laws 1991, ch. 885, sec. 3, codified at ORS 138.685(1999).

38 *Ibid.* The uncertainty created by this last phrase has been problematic in Marion County because it does not suggest that there is any time within which such a petition *must* be filed. As a result, extensions to file these petitions are legion and have led to post-conviction processes exceeding five years.

39 As a practical matter, if the defendant intends to pursue all ten steps, in order to take advantage of a newly passed federal law discussed below, he must file his post-conviction petition within one year of his death sentence being affirmed. 28 USC section 2244(d)(2).

40 ORS 138.620(2)(1999).

41 ORS 138.520(1999).

42 Case No. 95C-11416 in the Marion County Circuit Court. The bulky file includes all motions and rulings during the four years that this case was open. In the following discussion, I am relying on the Findings of Fact and Conclusions of Law of Senior Judge Duane Erstgaard, dated 18 August 1999 and entered on 26 August 1999.

43 *State v. Cunningham,* 320 Or 471, 880 P2d 431 (1994).

44 The specifics in Cunningham's case may be followed by reading his 1995 case in the Oregon Judicial Information Network and following the 100 or so entries in his case.

45   Interview with Ann Christian, director of the Indigent Defense Services Division in the state court administrator's office, 5 October 1999.
46   The attorney for the victorious side actually draws up the "Findings of Fact and Conclusions of Law" for the judge's signature.
47   Conclusion of Law 14, "Findings of Fact and Conclusions of Law," p. 18.
48   A brief introduction to these questions may be found in Stephen B. Bright, "Is Fairness Irrelevant?: The Evisceration of Federal Habeas Corpus Review and Limits on the Ability of State Courts to Protect Fundamental Rights," *Washington & Lee Law Review* 54 (1997), 1–30. The United States Supreme Court case which brought about a "Copernican" shift in habeas corpus thinking is *Fay v. Noia,* 372 U.S. 391 (1963). Unlike the situation of Copernicus, however, the Supreme Court later overruled its decision in *Fay v. Noia* in *Keeney v. Tamayo-Reyes,* 504 U.S. 1 (1992).
49   Deborah L. Stahlkopf, "A Dark Day for Habeas Corpus: Successive Petitions under the Anti-terrorism and Effective Death Penalty Act of 1996," *Arizona Law Review* 40 (1998), 1115–1136.
50   Pub. L. No. 104–132, 110 Stat. 1214 (amending 28 U.S.C. sections 2241–2255 and adding 28 U.S.C. sections, 2261–2266 (Supp. 1996)). Citations to the statute in the following discussion will be either to the section of AEDPA (Sections 102–108), chapter of AEDPA (either Chapter 153, traditional habeas corpus petitions, or Chapter 154, the new or expedited death penalty provisions under 28 U.S.C. sections 2261– 2266) or the section in the current law where the citation can be found (28 U.S.C. sections 2241–2266).
51   Because no one in Oregon has progressed beyond Step 4 of his appeals, many of the questions relating to the applicability of the new law in Oregon have not yet been answered. The most important question, discussed below, is whether Oregon will qualify as a "Chapter 154" jurisdiction and thus have available to it the more expedited process of federal death penalty appeals than is available to a non-qualifying, or Chapter 153, jurisdiction.
52   Quoted in Stahlkopf, *op. cit.,* 1115.
53   The process is described by Alexander Rundlet, "Opting for Death: State Responses to the AEDPA's Opt-in Provisions and the Need for a Right to Post-conviction Counsel," *University of Pennsylvania Journal of Constitutional Law* 1 (1999), 661–718.
54   28 U.S.C. s 2261(b)(Supp. 1996).
55   28 U.S.C. s 2266(b)(1)(A)–(C)(Supp. 1996).
56   28 U.S.C. s 2266(c)(Supp. 1996)
57   The only case to reach the United States Supreme Court so far regarding a state's attempt to opt in to Chapter 154 of AEDPA is *Calderon v. Ashmus,* 118 S. Ct. 1694 (1998). In that case, the State of California tried to opt in to Chapter 154's benefits. A prisoner, on behalf of all the death penalty prisoners similarly situated, protested the action. Both the District Court and the Ninth Circuit Court of Appeals forbade California from claiming those benefits, but the United States Supreme Court threw out the case because it was not yet ripe for consideration.
58   A survey of the cases on the issue is in Rundlet, *op. cit.,* note 165. Oregon does not have to join this issue until it has a case that is reaching Step 7 in the process. Not much attention has yet been given to the process it might use in qualifying for Chapter 154 benefits or even if it wants to try to qualify for them.
59   The most complete exposition of the new habeas corpus provisions of AEDPA is Marshall J. Hartman and Jeannette Nyden, "Habeas Corpus and the New Federalism after the Anti-terrorism and Effective Death Penalty Act of 1996," *John Marshall Law Review* 30 (1997), 337–387.
60   Hartman and Nyden also discuss at length the problem of the degree of deference a federal court should grant to findings of the state court under the new act. *Ibid.,* 353–370.
61   28 U.S.C. s 2254(e)(2)(Supp. 1996).
62   28 U.S.C. s 2244(b)(2)(Supp. 1996).
63   Section 107(c) of the act.

64   *Lindh v. Murphy,* 521 U.S. 320 (1997) reversing *Lindh v. Murphy,* 96 F3d 856 (7th Cir. 1996).
65   The governor's power to do this goes all the way back to the Deady Code, General Laws, ch. 33, sec. 333, p. 499. It is presently codified at ORS 144.640–.670(1999).
66   The states which have these statutory schemes are listed in the Death Penalty Information Center's Web page, www.deathpenaltyinfo.org. Texas, the state with by far the largest number of executions since they began again in 1977, has a statute of the second type, where the Governor must abide by the decision of the parole board. Even though more than 100 executions happened under the governorship of George W. Bush in Texas, his power to commute was far different than the Governor of Oregon.
67   ORS 144.640(1999).
68   ORS 144.650(3)(1999).
69   ORS 144.650(4)(1999).
70   The statute does not restrict an applicant from appealing for pardon or commutation to the final stage before his execution. The usual practice is that an outgoing Governor will be deluged by commutation or pardon applications and may deny or grant some. Commutation or pardon is put here at Step 10 because there is no doubt that it can and will be sought at this stage of the process.
71   See ORS 144.660(1999).

Part III
Law

CHAPTER 7

The Development
of Mitigating Circumstances
in the United States Supreme
Court's Jurisprudence,
1976 to 1987

While Oregon was waging its particular battle with the death penalty from 1964 to 1984 (Chapters Three and Four), and while it was developing its new process in death penalty cases (Chapters Five and Six), the fate of capital punishment nationwide also went through a metamorphosis. Figures for the number of executions in America from 1930 to 1967 show a gradual but distinct decline in application of capital punishment in America. The average number of people executed from 1930 to 1934 was 155; the average number executed from 1960 to 1964 was only 36.[1] By 1967 only two people were executed nationwide, and from 1968 to 1976 none. It appeared to many people as if the death penalty was indeed a "relic of barbarism" that had, once and for all, been consigned to the ash heap of history.

This is not the place to tell the story of the challenge to state death penalty statutes which bore fruit finally before the United States Supreme Court in *Furman v. Georgia*.[2] The purpose of this chapter is to explain how the Supreme Court refined its approach to death penalty cases, from the Court's

115

holding in three cases in 1976 that the death penalty was not per se unconstitutional to its focus on the subject of mitigating circumstances in a series of cases between 1976 and 1987. This chapter will show that in those eleven years the Supreme Court established that a death penalty statute would only pass constitutional muster if it provided explicitly for jury consideration of all circumstances that might mitigate a sentence of death.[3] In addition, in order for such a statute to be applied constitutionally, jury instructions in the sentencing phase of a capital trial must explicitly provide that jurors consider all evidence in mitigation before sentencing a convicted person to death.

To accomplish these aims, this chapter will first discuss the evolution of the Supreme Court's death penalty jurisprudence from the *Furman* case in 1972 to the five cases it handed down on July 2, 1976.[4] Because the major outlines of contemporary death penalty jurisprudence were hammered out in those four years, care will be taken to describe the types of death penalty statutes upheld and rejected by the United States Supreme Court. The chapter will then discuss how the Court refined its approach to the death penalty in the following decade by its choice to focus on how evidence in mitigation of a sentence of death was allowed in the state death penalty statutes and jury instructions.[5] The chapter will conclude with the assertion that any death penalty statute that would pass constitutional muster in 1988 must have explicitly provided for full consideration of circumstances which could mitigate a sentence of death.[6]

From *Furman* to *Gregg* and Their Companions

In 1972 the United States Supreme Court held in *Furman* that current capital punishment statutes were unconstitutional because they provided such unlimited discretion for juries in sentencing a person to death that no meaningful basis existed to distinguish the few cases in which death was imposed from the many in which it was not.[7] To use some of the phrases that came out in the nine separate opinions in the *Furman* case, the death penalty statutes allowed for "untrammeled discretion," "standardless sentencing," or "random," "arbitrary" or "discriminatory" results.[8] Victims were "capriciously selected" through a "freakish" system. Justice Potter Stewart seemed to sum up the opinion of the majority when he said that "[if] any basis can be discerned for the selection of those few sentenced to die it is the constitutionally impermissible basis of race."[9]

In so holding, the Court was referring to the phenomenon that had evolved during the nineteenth and twentieth centuries to replace mandatory death penalty sentences, which provided that anyone convicted of first degree murder would automatically be sentenced to death, with discretionary death penalty sentences, which left the sentence of death or life imprisonment up to the jury. [10] In short, the Court was telling the states that their experiments with unlimited jury discretion were unsuccessful. The Court did not hold, however, that the death penalty violated the Eighth Amendment prohibition against cruel and unusual punishment; the most that could be inferred from its decision was that the current state statutes needed to be changed.

The states went back to work. As indicated briefly in Chapter Four, 35 states revised their death penalty statutes to limit juror discretion in death penalty cases. Several states chose to eliminate juror discretion altogether and returned to mandatory death penalties if guilt of a particular crime was proven beyond reasonable doubt. An example of this type of statute was North Carolina's. After the *Furman* decision, North Carolina rewrote its murder statute, making only the most minor verbal changes. Its pre-1972 statute had the following:

> A murder which shall be perpetrated by means of poison, lying in wait, imprisonment, starving, torture, or by any other kind of willful, deliberate and premeditated killing, or which shall be committed in the perpetration or attempt to perpetrate any arson, rape, robbery, burglary or other felony, shall be deemed to be murder in the first degree and shall be punished with death: Provided, if at the time of rendering its verdict in open court, the jury shall so recommend the punishment shall be imprisonment for life in the State's prison, and the court shall so instruct the jury. [11]

The post-*Furman* statute was changed by eliminating the "Provided" clause, so that the penalty for a murder described in the statute would be death. No juror discretion was permitted. It was a return to the old system of mandatory death penalties upon conviction of a certain offense.

Most states, however, used the Model Penal Code (MPC) as a model to rewrite their capital punishment statutes. [12] The key features of the MPC as it related to capital punishment were to provide a bifurcated trial process and the consideration of aggravating and mitigating circumstances in the sentencing phase of a capital punishment trial. The bifurcated trial, in the first phase of which guilt was determined and the second phase of which penalty was assessed, was developed as a means of eliminating confusion in the presentation of evidence to jurors and weighing of evidence by jurors. If the jury had only one question to consider at a time (Is defendant guilty of a capital offense? Which sentence does defendant deserve?), the jurors could work more dispassionately and fairly.

The purpose of presenting aggravating and mitigating circumstances in the penalty phase of a capital punishment trial was to allow for maximum consideration of individual circumstances before sentencing a particular defendant to death. The twin pillars of the MPC approach, therefore, were to channel or guide the discretion of the jury but to provide for the consideration of individualized attention. This approach seemed to proponents to answer the Supreme Court's criticism of unlimited jury discretion while, at the same time, providing an opportunity to weigh aggravating and mitigating circumstances, rather than return to the specter of mandatory death sentences.

Florida and Georgia were among the many states developing MPC-type death penalty statutes. Georgia's statute was an example of the "aggravating only" type of statute in that it listed ten aggravating and no mitigating circumstances.[13] If the jury finds at least one aggravating circumstance it may, but need not, recommend death. The judge must sentence the individual to death if the jury so recommends but may not do so if the jury recommends otherwise. Some of the aggravating circumstances follow the MPC guidelines fairly closely, such as the aggravating factor of felony murder, murder-for-hire, previous conviction of another violent felony or an especially heinous murder.[14]

The Florida statute was an MPC-type statute but provided for a weighing process of aggravating versus mitigating circumstances. It lists eight aggravating and seven mitigating circumstances, the former taken almost word for word from the MPC's eight aggravating factors.[15] The seven mitigating factors, including the factors that the defendant has no significant history of prior criminal activity, the commission of the crime under the influence of extreme mental or emotional disturbance, the age of the defendant, and the diminished capacity of the defendant, are derived from the eight MPC factors.[16] Under Florida law if a jury finds an aggravating circumstance, death is presumed to be the proper sentence unless one or more mitigating circumstances are also found and judged to outweigh the aggravating circumstances.

The final approach, which Texas alone pursued in the mid-1970s, has been called a "structured discretion" capital punishment statute because for a murder to qualify as a capital offense, the jury's discretion is "structured" at both ends of the process.[17] It is structured at the "front end" of the process because the murder must be committed in one of five circumstances or against a protected person in order to merit the death penalty. The murder must be committed either against a peace officer or fireman in the line of duty, or it must be a felony murder, a murder-for-hire, a murder while escaping from a penal institution or a murder while in a penal institution.[18]

Structured discretion also has a "back-end" requirement in that it obliges the jury, in a case where one of the circumstances just mentioned is present, to conduct a separate sentencing hearing to determine whether death is the appropriate punishment. The three questions which the jury must answer unanimously in order to sentence a person to death, which Oregon copied, are:

1.   Whether the conduct of the defendant that caused the death of the deceased was committed deliberately and with the reasonable expectation that the death of the deceased or another would result;
2.   Whether there is a probability that the defendant would commit criminal acts of violence that would constitute a continuing threat to society; and
3.   If raised by the evidence, whether the conduct of the defendant in killing the deceased was unreasonable in response to the provocation, if any, by the deceased.[19]

On July 2, 1976, the United States Supreme Court handed down more capital punishment decisions—five—than on any date in its history, and held that North Carolina's and Louisiana's mandatory death penalty statutes were unconstitutional but that Georgia and Florida's MPC-type statutes and Texas' structured-discretion statute were constitutional.[20] Georgia's statute was upheld in *Gregg* because the bifurcated trial, the additional opportunity for the jury to hear aggravation or mitigation evidence, and the automatic review of each sentence by the Georgia Supreme Court to determine whether the punishment was proportionate to the crime prevented the arbitrary and freakish imposition of the death penalty that had led to the *Furman* decision.[21]

Florida's statute was upheld in *Proffitt* for a similar reason. It was in the *Jurek* (TX) and *Woodson* (NC) decisions, however, that the Court began to focus on juror consideration of mitigating circumstances in death penalty deliberations. In *Woodson* the Court overturned North Carolina's mandatory death penalty statute as an example of an archaic statute that America had long ago abandoned.[22] The Court was not satisfied with providing just one reason for the constitutional deficiency of North Carolina's statute, however. It also held:

> A third constitutional shortcoming of the North Carolina statute is its failure to allow the particularized consideration of relevant aspects of the character and record of each convicted defendant before the imposition upon him of a sentence of death.[23]

This phrase, "particularized consideration of relevant aspects of the character of and record of each convicted defendant," will recur as a refrain over the next dozen or so years in Supreme Court jurisprudence. The Court went on:

> A process that accords no significance to relevant facets of the character and record of the individual offender or the circumstances of the particular offense excludes from consideration in fixing the ultimate punishment of death the possibility of compassionate or mitigating factors stemming from the diverse frailties of humankind.[24]

Perhaps struck by the unusual phraseology of its final four words, the Court kept playing the humanistic card.

> Consideration of both the offender and the offense in order to arrive at a just and appropriate sentence has been viewed as a progressive and humanizing development.... While the prevailing practice of individualizing sentencing determinations generally reflects simply enlightened policy rather than a constitutional imperative, we believe that in capital cases the fundamental respect for humanity underlying the Eighth Amendment, see *Trop v. Dulles,* 356 U.S., at 100, requires consideration of the character and record of the individual offender and the circumstances of the particular offense as a constitutionally indispensable part of inflicting the penalty of death.[25]

A general humanistic concern for the diverse frailties of human nature has now become a constitutional imperative. Full consideration of the offender and the offense are now constitutionally mandated. It will take the Supreme Court more than a decade before it more completely develops its understanding of what this full consideration would entail.

Even though the mandatory death penalty statute struck down in *Woodson* provided the context for the Supreme Court to wax eloquent on the need to consider all aspects in mitigation of a defendant's character and crime, the *Jurek* decision gave the Court the opportunity to uphold the Texas statute that would become the prototype for Oregon's.[26] The Supreme Court held that Texas' system for imposing capital punishment narrowed the scope of its laws relating to capital punishment and therefore narrowed the class of death-eligible felons.[27] Texas' action in narrowing the category of murders for which a death sentence may be imposed serves much the same function as a list of statutory aggravating circumstances.

> Thus, in essence, the Texas statute requires that the jury find the existence of a statutory aggravating circumstance before the death penalty may be imposed.[28]

But, the Court went on to say, a system which allowed the jury to consider only aggravating circumstances would fall short of providing the individualized sentencing required under *Woodson*.[29] In order to meet the requirements of the Eighth and Fourteenth Amendments, a capital-sentencing scheme must allow the sentencing authority to consider mitigating circumstances. The Texas statute does not explicitly speak of mitigating circumstances. Therefore, the Court needed to determine whether the enumerated questions allow consideration of particularized mitigating factors.[30]

Though there is no language in the three questions of the Texas statute that would seemingly allow or require consideration of mitigating circumstances, the Texas Court of Criminal Appeals had held that it would interpret the second question (on future dangerousness) to allow a defendant to bring to the jury's attention whatever mitigating circumstances he may be able to show.[31] In the only case where the Texas Court of Criminal Appeals upheld a death sentence, it permitted the jury to consider defendant's prior convictions as well as his prior attempts to rehabilitate himself, his mental duress and the testimony of psychiatrists regarding his potential for future dangerousness. The Supreme Court concluded:

> It thus appears that, as in Georgia and Florida, the Texas capital-sentencing procedure guides and focuses the jury's objective consideration of the particularized circumstances of the individual offense and the individual offender before it can impose a sentence of death.[32]

Therefore, by the summer of 1976 the U.S. Supreme Court had not only held that the death penalty could be constitutional under certain circumstances, but that there needed to be a full consideration of relevant circumstances mitigating the defendant's guilt in the sentencing phase of the trial. Two types of MPC statutes were upheld: those requiring consideration of statutory aggravating circumstances and non-statutory mitigating and aggravating circumstances (Georgia), and those requiring the jury to weigh aggravating and mitigating factors before making a death penalty determination (Florida). The Texas structured-discretion statute was also upheld, with the proviso that mitigating measures had to be considered in the sentencing phase, especially when considering the question of future dangerousness. The Supreme Court did not reflect extensively, however, on the scope of what mitigating circumstances might mean. Their major task in the 1976 decisions was to determine the larger question of whether the statutes met constitutional muster. Detailed consideration of what constituted mitigating circumstances would be left for the next decade.

From *Lockett* (1978) to *Hitchcock* (1987)

Over the next decade, the United States Supreme Court honed its understanding of the scope of mitigating circumstances that could be presented on behalf of a defendant to a sentencing jury. In *Lockett v. Ohio* the defendant, Sandra Lockett, was convicted of aggravated murder with specifications, in this case a crime somewhat like felony aggravated murder in other jurisdictions, and she was sentenced to death.[33] The Ohio capital punishment statute under which she was sentenced had undergone considerable change in the years preceding her sentence. Before *Furman* the statute permitted broad discretionary jury sentences, as did most jurisdictions.

In the months preceding the *Furman* decision, however, the Ohio House of Representatives passed a bill that abandoned the practice of unbridled sentencing discretion and instructed the sentencer to consider a full list of aggravating and mitigating circumstances.[34] After *Furman* was handed down in June 1972 condemning the practice of unlimited jury discretion, the Ohio Legislature changed course again because it thought that permitting the sentencing jury to consider a full range of aggravating and mitigating circumstances would resurrect unlimited jury discretion. Thus, they passed a revised law which listed seven statutory aggravating circumstances and only three mitigating circumstances that a jury had to consider.

According to the revised Ohio statute, once a defendant was found guilty of aggravated murder with at least one of the seven specified aggravating circumstances, the death penalty must be imposed unless, considering the "nature and circumstances of the offense and the history, character, and condition of the offender," the sentencing judge determined, by a preponderance of the evidence, that one of the following three circumstances applied:

1.   The victim of the offense induced or facilitated it.
2.   The offense would not have been committed except for duress or coercion.
3.   The offense was the product of the offender's mental deficiency.[35]

Despite the fact that the Ohio Legislature had limited the relevant mitigating circumstances to comply with its reading of *Furman*, the U.S. Supreme Court held that they had violated *Furman* by unduly contracting the range of mitigating circumstances which may be considered by the sentencer. The Court suggested, by way of example, that the sentencing jury might have wanted to take into account the comparatively minor role that Lockett played in the offense.

Ohio's confusion about what the Supreme Court required by way of individualized consideration was partially created by the Supreme Court itself. It had condemned unlimited jury discretion in *Furman* as leading to "freakish" results. But its decisions in *Woodson* and to a lesser extent in *Jurek* could be read to require full jury discretion in considering mitigating circumstances on behalf of the defendant. The hand that appeared to take away discretion in 1972 had given it back, only in a different form, in 1976. The Supreme Court itself confessed its responsibility for the confusion:

> The signals from this Court have not, however, been always easy to decipher…we have an obligation to reconcile previously differing views in order to provide that guidance.[36]

In trying to clarify the confusion created, the Court reiterated the important holding from *Woodson* that a sentencing process must permit the jury to consider the "character and record of the individual offender and the circumstances of the particular offense as a constitutionally indispensable part of the process of inflicting the penalty of death."[37] Full opportunity must be given the sentencer to consider the full range of relevant information relating to the individual and his or her offense.[38] In this connection, the Court made a crucial distinction between capital and non-capital cases. In the former, because of the stakes involved, the full consideration of relevant mitigating circumstances was a constitutional requirement.

The scope of what constituted relevant mitigating circumstances was explored further in *Eddings v. Oklahoma*.[39] The significance of *Eddings* is that it was the first case in which the Court applied its now predictable clause, "character and record of the individual offender and the circumstances of the particular offense," to events not specifically associated with the crime in question. That is, the assumption behind the *Lockett* decision was that mitigating circumstances referred only to things that mitigated the guilt *at the time of* the crime. Now, in *Eddings*, the Court held that relevant mitigating circumstances could reach to any aspect of the defendant's upbringing.

The particular facts of *Eddings* were no doubt of importance in the Supreme Court's willingness to extend its understanding of relevant mitigating circumstances. Eddings was a 16-year-old resident of Missouri when he and some friends were stopped by the Oklahoma Highway Patrol while driving erratically in Oklahoma. When the officer approached their vehicle, Eddings shot and killed him. Eddings entered a plea of nolo contendere and was sentenced to death by the court.

At his sentencing hearing, Eddings presented evidence of his troubled youth. Other witnesses testified to his emotionally disturbed state because of his upbringing. A psychiatrist testified that he thought Eddings could be rehabilitated by intensive therapy over a 15 to 20-year period. The judge, however, decided that because of the language of the U.S. Supreme Court quoted above, he was only permitted to consider evidence of mitigation present at the time of the crime. Therefore, the only evidence of mitigation he allowed was the fact of Eddings' youth at the time of the crime. This piece of mitigating evidence did not outweigh the aggravating circumstances present. The Oklahoma Court of Criminal Appeals affirmed this decision.

If the facts of *Woodson* provided the Court an opportunity to wax eloquent on humane justice, the facts of *Eddings* gave Justice Lewis Powell, with his extensive background in school law and youth issues, an opportunity to lionize the time of youth. The trial judge had only considered Eddings' youth as a "chronological fact." But to Powell,

> Youth is more than a chronological fact. It is a time and condition of life when a person may be most susceptible to influence and to psychological damage. Our history is replete with laws and judicial recognition that minors, especially in their earlier years, generally are less mature and responsible than adults. . . . In this case, Eddings was not a normal 16-year-old; he had been deprived of the care, concern, and parental attention that children deserve.[40]

In true Ciceronian style Powell was preparing for his peroration, in which he would once and for all extend the meaning of relevant mitigating circumstances to envelop perhaps everything in a person's past. He was not trying to suggest that Eddings had no responsibility for the shooting. He was trying to say,

> that just as the chronological age of a minor is itself a relevant mitigating factor of great weight, so must the background and mental and emotional development of a youthful defendant be duly considered in sentencing.[41]

The then recently appointed Justice Sandra Day O'Connor added a forceful concurrence in which she emphasized how the Court had gone "to extraordinary measures" to ensure that a sentenced prisoner will be accorded process that will guarantee, "as much as is humanly possible," that the sentence was not imposed out of "whim, passion, prejudice, or mistake."[42] In all but the rarest circumstances, the rule of *Lockett* required that juries in capital cases not be precluded from considering any aspect of a defendant's character or record and any of the circumstances of the offense.

The bemused and somewhat chagrined dissenters could only complain that in its ruling the Court had violated one of its cardinal rules: not to decide a question that was not presented on the petition for certiorari.[43] Nevertheless, the engine of "mitigating circumstances" had gathered steam and now included anything from a defendant's past.

This jurisprudence was extended even further in the next case to consider mitigating circumstances, *Skipper v. South Carolina*.[44] The major contribution of the *Skipper* case was to extend the temporal scope for considering mitigating circumstances to the time *after* the crime had been committed and while the convicted person was in custody before trial and sentencing. Skipper was convicted in a South Carolina trial court of capital murder and rape and sentenced to death. At his sentencing hearing, Skipper presented mitigating evidence of the difficult circumstances of his upbringing, which was permitted under the rule articluated in *Eddings*. He also tried to introduce testimony of two jailers and one regular visitor to his cell to the effect that he had made a "good adjustment" during his time spent in jail.[45] The state court ruled that such evidence was irrelevant and hence inadmissible. The South Carolina Supreme Court affirmed.

Writing for a unanimous United States Supreme Court, Justice Byron White reiterated the now familiar standard that any relevant mitigating evidence must be permitted if it related to any aspect of the defendant's character or record or any circumstances of the offense.[46] White read the word "mitigating" very broadly, however. If any inferences were mitigating "in the sense that they might serve as a basis for a sentence less than death," they were permissible.[47] Whatever distinction the Court had been trying to maintain between mitigating evidence and relevant mitigating evidence was eradicated by that line; now a defendant would have full scope to present anything that might help him escape the sentence of death.[48]

With this clarification made, the result was a foregone conclusion. Testimony of jailers and visitors might be helpful in reducing Skipper's sentence; therefore, it was admissible as mitigating evidence in a capital sentencing process. The Supreme Court held that the distinction between past circumstances and future good conduct was elusive at best. A defendant's disposition to make a well-behaved and peaceful adjustment to prison life is "by its nature" relevant to the sentencing determination. Because the state was permitted to introduce evidence of the defendant's potential future dangerousness, why shouldn't defendant be able to introduce evidence regarding his potential future peaceableness?

The dramatic extension of the scope of mitigating circumstances in a capital sentencing trial in Supreme Court jurisprudence by 1986 can best be expressed by utilizing a metaphor derived from property law. Common law property ownership posited that a person's ownership interest in a parcel of land extended *a caelo ad infernos,* or literally "from heaven to hell." Property interest extended vertically up and down forever. Likewise, in developing its mitigating circumstances jurisprudence, the Court extended the reach of these circumstances horizontally, *ab initio usque hodie,* or literally from the beginning until today (the day of sentencing). Everything in that "space of time" is potentially admissible for mitigation purposes.

Finally, in 1987 the Court handed down *Hitchcock v. Dugger.*[49] The significance of this brief opinion is its focus not on the Court-defined nature of mitigating circumstances but on the requirements for a state statute to meet constitutional standards on mitigating circumstances. We saw in *Lockett* that Ohio's law requiring a jury to consider only three mitigating circumstances violated the constitutional requirement for sentencing juries to conduct a fully individualized sentencing process. In *Hitchcock* the Supreme Court unanimously held that, even though Florida law permitted the jury to hear evidence "as to any matter that the court deem[s] relevant to sentence," and even though the jury could consider the seven mitigating circumstances derived from Model Penal Code proposed statute, the jury was also required to consider "nonstatutory" mitigating factors.[50]

Hitchcock murdered a 13-year-old girl in 1976 and was sentenced to death. After exhausting his direct and post-conviction appeals, he sought habeas corpus relief in the federal courts. He claimed that the jury and judge were precluded by Florida statute from considering some of the evidence of mitigating circumstances before them. Because of its relevance to our consideration of Oregon's death penalty statute in the next chapter, more extensive detail is required at this point.

Florida, like Oregon, had a statute permitting the trier of fact in a sentencing hearing to hear evidence "as to any matter that the court deem[s] relevant to sentence." After it heard this evidence, the trier of fact was to consider whether sufficient mitigating circumstances as enumerated in the next section of the statute would outweigh the aggravating circumstances also found in the statute.[51] If the mitigating circumstances outweighed the aggravating circumstances, a lesser sentence than death would be imposed.

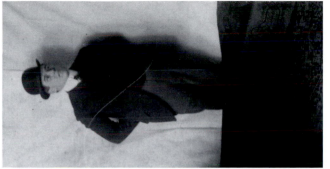

Jack Wade, convicted murderer of James Morrow, stands in jail cell in basement of courthouse; hung January 1902, Portland.
Photo courtesy of Oregon Historical Society, CN 019407/0351P084.

William Dalton, convicted murderer of James Morrow, seventh man to hang from gallows at old courthouse, Portland, January 1902.
Photo courtesy of Oregon Historical Society, CN 021551/0353P105.

Claude Branton hanging in Eugene, 1899. Wm. W. Withers, Sheriff at right.
Photo courtesy of the Oregon Historical Society, OrHi 23665/#361-L.

Old Multnomah County Courthouse taken from 4th and Main looking northwest; ca. 1900. J.F. Ford photo. Courtesy of the Oregon Historical Society, OrHi 46594/ #1781.

Invitation to the execution of George Smith, 1903. Copied from the Oregon Historical Society's Ethnology Collection. Mss 1521, Ethnology Collection.

Mr. ~~Jefferson Myers~~

You are respectfully invited to be present at the Execution, as provided by law, of

George Smith
(Colored)

on Friday, June 5, 1903, at the hour of 6:30 A. M., within the enclosure of the Jail Yard, Multnomah County, Oregon.

Sheriff.

This Card is Not Transferable, and Must be Presented at the Door

George Smith (colored) murdered his white wife, Annie Smith, by shooting her through the breast, on the 11d of August, 1901. He was tried, convicted and sentenced to be hanged on the 19th day of December, 1901. He took an appeal from this decision to the Supreme Court, where the opinion of the lower Court was affirmed. He was then sentenced to be executed on Friday, June 5, 1903.

Invitation to the execution of James A. Finch, 1909. Finch was the only attorney ever executed in Oregon's history. Copied from the Oregon Historical Society's Justice Collection. Mss 1519, Justice Collection.

OREGON STATE PENITENTIARY
C. W. JAMES, SUPERINTENDENT

Salem, Oregon, Nov 8/09

Mr J d Griffin

You are hereby invited to be present and witness the Execution of

JAMES A. FINCH

On Friday, the 12th day of November, 1909,

at the hour of 12:30 p. m., within the enclosure of the Execution Chamber, of the Oregon State Penitentiary, at Salem, Oregon.

SUPERINTENDENT OREGON STATE PENITENTIARY

James A. Finch was convicted of the crime of murder in the first degree for the killing of Ralph B. Fisher in Multnomah County, Oregon. Convicted December 30, 1908.

NOT TRANSFERABLE.   PRESENT THIS CARD FOR ADMITTANCE.

Oswald West, 1910.
Photo courtesy of the Oregon Historical
Society, OrHi 6425/#1110.

William
Lamb,
Oregon's
official
hangman,
executed 14 in
Oregon, also
worked for the
Philippine
Constabulary,
ca. 1930.
Photo courtesy
of the Oregon
Historical
Society, CN
014064/
0097D001.

Neil Hart and Jim Owens,
handcuffed together
after their capture.
Both were later convicted
and hung; ca. 1935.
Photo courtesy of the Oregon
Historical Society, CN
009556/0318P223.

*Flanked by guards, Wayne
Long walks to auto to take
him to the gas chamber,
convicted of murder;
August 8, 1952.
Photo courtesy of the
Oregon Historical Society,
CN 012234/0093P411.*

*Mark Hatfield, 1955.
Photo courtesy of the
Oregon Historical Society,
OrHi 83427/#479-A.*

Even though the statutory mitigating factors were much more extensive than the Ohio list, the Supreme Court held this list inadequate because the interpretation of this statute by the Florida Supreme Court prohibited the jury and judge from considering mitigating circumstances not specifically enumerated in the statute.[52] That is, the Florida Supreme Court considered this list an exhaustive list of mitigating measures. As a result, the United States Supreme Court, writing through Justice Scalia, held:

> We think it could not be clearer that the advisory jury was instructed not to consider, and the sentencing judge refused to consider, evidence of nonstatutory mitigating circumstances, and that the proceedings therefore did not comport with the requirements of *Skipper, Eddings,* and *Lockett.*[53]

In order for the Florida statute and procedure to have passed constitutional muster there needed to be a process that included not just statutory but also nonstatutory mitigating circumstances.

Conclusion

In the evolving jurisprudence of the United States Supreme Court regarding mitigating circumstances in capital sentencing trials, three things ought to be clear. First, by the mid-1980s the Court had collapsed the distinction between any mitigating evidence that may be *presented* to the jury and relevant mitigating evidence that must be *considered* by the jury. This distinction was made in the cases from 1976 to 1982, but the *Skipper* case eliminated it as unworkable.

Second, as a result, relevant mitigating evidence can include anything from a person's past or even evidence from a time after the crime which the defendant might want to use to convince the jury that a sentence less than death was justified. The Court has rejected the notion that the mitigating evidence must relate temporally to the crime (such as diminished capacity, duress, being in a lesser role during the commission of the crime) or must even relate to the crime in any easily observable way. Information from a person's upbringing and nurture is permissible. If a petitioner wants to put on evidence that he had the habit of inhaling gasoline as a youth and that his mind wandered as a result, he ought to be able to do so.[54] A premium is placed, therefore, on creative advocacy.

Third, and most significant, the U.S. Supreme Court made some crucial observations about the kind of statute that would be held constitutional under its new and expansive reading of mitigating circumstances emerging from the *Woodson* line of cases. In order for a statute to be safely constitutional, it needed to provide three things: 1) a general statement at the beginning in which all evidence or all relevant evidence would be considered by a sentencing jury, 2) a specific list of statutory aggravating and mitigating factors, or in Texas' case, a list of statutory questions which a jury has to answer unanimously and, finally, 3) a catch-all provision, supported by jury instructions, which would enable juries to consider non-statutory as well as statutory mitigating circumstances before applying the death penalty.

The "catch-all" portion of the statute and instructions was especially required by the *Hitchcock* case. It was not enough that the statute articulated seven very precise mitigating factors the jury had to take into consideration. The statute also needed to include a way for factors beyond those listed, factors which the Court called "non-statutory factors," to be included in jury consideration. The Court did not explicitly say how the statute ought to provide for these non-statutory factors, but a reasonable extrapolation from *Hitchcock* would be that, in addition to several specific mitigating factors, there should be a final factor requiring the jury to consider "any other or any combination of the foregoing" factors which might lead to an imposition of a sentence less than death. This would force the jury not simply to look at various categories of mitigation that have been refined over more than 30 years, but would allow for the development of law and human understanding in the future. Its very open-ended quality would give the kind of finality and certainty to the process that the Supreme Court has said should characterize modern death penalty jurisprudence.

It is not enough, however, for the statute to include a catch-all mitigating factor at the end of the list of statutory factors. The jury must also be instructed that it may take into consideration as broad an array of factors as the (rewritten) statute permits. In other words, the deficiency in the Florida court's instruction in *Hitchcock* was that it interpreted the seven mitigating factors as an exhaustive list. The U.S. Supreme Court never reached the question of whether a process would have been constitutional had the court instructed the jury to consider any and every factor in mitigation, but the statute had only listed seven specified factors. The Court held only that the interpretation of the seven factors as exhaustive violated constitutional requirements. The safest course, therefore, would be for a statute to have the catch-all factor at the end of the list of mitigating factors and for the judge to be required to instruct the jury as broadly as the statute was written. The evolving jurisprudence of the United States Supreme Court on mitigating measures from 1976 to 1987 would seem to demand no less.

Endnotes

1   William J. Bowers, *Legal Homicide* (Boston: Northeastern University Press, 1984), 25–26.

2   408 U.S. 238 (1972). The story has been told often and well. Bowers covers highlights of it, pages 25–41. Bowers seems at a loss to explain the reasons for America's changed mood with respect to the death penalty. "This abandonment of executions in America has not been adequately explained from a historical standpoint," 40. The brief explanation given in Chapter Three attempts to fill this gap.

3   "Mitigating circumstances" refers to the whole panoply of factors that might serve to soften or mitigate the convicted person's sentence from the sentence of death.

4   The five cases were *Gregg v. Georgia*, 428 U.S. 153; *Proffitt v. Florida*, 428 U.S. 242; *Jurek v. Texas*, 428 U.S. 262; *Woodson v. North Carolina*, 428 U.S. 280 and *Roberts v. Louisiana*, 428 U.S. 325. In these cases the Supreme Court considered death penalty statutes in five states that had rewritten their statutes in the wake of *Furman v. Georgia*. Three of the statutes were upheld (Georgia, Florida and Texas) and two were struck down (North Carolina and Louisiana). In fact 35 states had rewritten their statutes between 1972 and 1976. These decisions established the broad parameters for constitutional acceptability of any death penalty statute. Some of this discussion expands on that in Chapter Four.

5   The four decisions from 1978 to 1987 that refined these parameters and focused largely on how explicitly the statute provided for jury consideration of all mitigating circumstances before it sentenced a person to death are *Lockett v. Ohio*, 438 U.S. 586 (1978), *Eddings v. Oklahoma*, 455 U.S. 104 (1982), *Skipper v. South Carolina*, 476 U.S. 1 (1986) and *Hitchcock v. Dugger*, 481 U.S. 393 (1987).

6   This conclusion will provide the background necessary to understand the Oregon Supreme Court's first consideration of the constitutionality of Oregon's 1984 statute in 1988. That decision, *State v. Wagner*, 305 Or. 115, 752 P2d 1136 (1988), will be the focus of Chapter Eight.

7   *Furman v. Georgia*, 408 U.S. 238 (1972).

8   One can go to almost any of the authors who were in the majority (Douglas, Brennan, Marshall, White, Stewart) to find these phrases.

9   *Furman v. Georgia*, 408 U.S. at 309–310.

10   A helpful chart showing the movement from mandatory to discretionary capital punishment for murder by jurisdiction is in Bowers, *op. cit.,* 11. As the notes at the bottom of Bowers' chart indicate, the situation was a bit more complicated than the statement above, but the general statement is correct.

11   *North Carolina General Statutes*, 14–17(1969), quoted in *Woodson v. North Carolina*, 428 U.S. at 286, n. 4.

12   Model Penal Code (Philadelphia: American Law Institute, 1962). Provisions for murder and the death penalty are included in MPC 210.2–210.6

13   The text of *Georgia Code Annotated*, 27–2534.1 (Supp. 1975) is provided in *Gregg v. Georgia*, 428 U.S. 166, n. 9.

14   See, for example, the MPC's list of aggravating factors at MPC 210.6(3). While the MPC provides eight aggravating factors, the Georgia statute provides ten. Georgia also includes a murder of a judicial officer (Factor 5) or a peace officer, corrections employee or fireman while engaged in the performance of his official duties (Factor 8). The MPC list of aggravating factors focuses only on the type of crime committed and not the person against whom the crime is committed. When Oregon wrote its aggravated murder statute in 1977, it provided for more severe punishment if one *either* committed a particularly heinous crime or committed a murder of a *protected* person. By coordinating the aggravated murder statute and the new death penalty statute, Oregon's 1984 death penalty statute provided that the death penalty might be appropriate if óne committed either a particularly heinous crime or if one killed a protected person.

[15] The Florida statute does not list one of the MPC factors (factor 3): "At the time the murder was committed the defendant also committed another murder." It provides one factor (factor seven) that is absent from the MPC: "The capital felony was committed to disrupt or hinder the lawful exercise of any governmental function or the enforcement of laws." *Florida Statutes Annotated*, 921.141 (1974). A possible reason for Florida's exclusion of MPC Factor 3 is that Factor 3 and 4 seem to overlap. Factor 3 provides: "At the time the murder was committed the defendant also committed another murder." Factor 4 provides: "The defendant knowingly created a great risk of death to many persons." Some might contend that Factor 4 includes Factor 3.

[16] MPC 210.6(4).

[17] Bowers uses this term to describe Texas' statute in *Legal Homicide*, 197.

[18] Texas Penal Code, Article 1257, s 19.02(b)(1)–(5)(effective January 1, 1974), quoted in *Jurek v. Texas,* 428 U.S. 265, n. 1.

[19] *Ibid.*, Article 37.071(a).

[20] For the citations in the five cases, see Note 4 above.

[21] *Gregg v. Georgia,* 428 U.S. 162–206.

[22] 428 U.S. 298.

[23] *Ibid.*, 303.

[24] *Ibid.*, 304.

[25] *Ibid.*

[26] Comments in the House State Government Operations Committee minutes during the 1977 Legislative Assembly on HB 2321 suggested not simply that the Texas statute was used as a basis for the Oregon law, but that as early as July 1976 the drafting process for the Oregon law commenced. Legislative Counsel, which is responsible for drafting all bills that are considered by the Oregon Legislature, submitted its original bill draft in December 1976. See HB 2321, Original Bill Files, 1977 Oregon Legislative Assembly.

[27] *Jurek v. Texas,* 428 U.S. 268.

[28] *Ibid.*, 271.

[29] Even though the Georgia statute upheld by the Supreme Court in *Gregg v. Georgia* seems to permit only a consideration of aggravating factors, it also includes language to allow the consideration of other nonstatutory aggravating and mitigating circumstances. Though the scope of the mitigating circumstances is not delineated in Georgia's statute, the text provides that the jury must consider "any mitigating circumstances or aggravating circumstances otherwise authorized by law…" *Gregg v. Georgia,* 428 U.S. 164.

[30] The Court's reference to "allowing" consideration of particularized mitigating factors will be picked up by the Oregon Supreme Court in 1988–1990 as it tried to determine the proper scope of Oregon's capital punishment law.

[31] *Ibid.*, quoting *Jurek v. Texas,* 522 SW2d 939–40 (1975).

[32] *Jurek v. Texas,* 428 U.S. 2743–74.

[33] *Lockett v. Ohio,* 438 U.S. 586 (1978).

[34] Thus, it was an MPC-type statute. See the discussion in *Lockett v. Ohio,* 438 U.S. 600, n. 7.

[35] *Ibid.*, 607.

[36] *Ibid.*, 602.

[37] *Woodson v. North Carolina,* 428 U.S. 305.

[38] Footnote 12 of the opinion presented a bit of a caveat, however, when it said: "Nothing in this opinion limits the traditional authority of a court to exclude, as irrelevant, evidence not bearing on the defendant's character, prior record, or the circumstances of his offense." 438 U.S. 695, n.12.

[39] 455 U.S. 104 (1982).

[40] *Ibid.*, 116.

[41] *Ibid.* Powell's words only reach the "youthful" defendant, but the flow of his argument would naturally include far more than just the youthful defendant. If upbringing and personal

background is relevant for a youth, on what legal basis can it be said not to be relevant for an adult? One need not quote Wordsworth about the child being the father to the man to recognize that Powell's argument now makes it constitutionally impermissible to exclude any evidence regarding the person's upbringing and background from the sentencing jury's mitigation consideration.

42   455 U.S. 118.

43   The petition for certiorari only asked for consideration of whether the Eighth and Fourteenth Amendments to the U.S. Constitution prohibited the imposition of a death sentence on an offender because he was 16 years old at the time of the offense. *Ibid.*, 120.

44   476 U.S. 1 (1986).

45   476 U.S. 2.

46   *Ibid.*, 4. The unanimity of the Court on the judgment should not be confused, however, with its split on the subject of the admissibility of Skipper's prison behavior after the crime as relevant mitigating evidence. Only six justices concurred in that part of the opinion. The three justices concurring in the judgment alone (Powell, Burger and Rehnquist) would have remanded because the petitioner was not allowed to rebut evidence and argument used against him. *Ibid.*, 9. They disagreed with the Court's expansive reading of relevant mitigating circumstances and said that while factors relating to someone's emotional history may bear directly on his crime, "[t]hat simply cannot be said of the defendant's behavior in prison following his arrest. Society's interest in retribution can hardly be lessened by the knowledge that a brutal murderer, for self-interested reasons, has been a model of deportment in prison while awaiting trial or sentence." *Ibid.*, 14.

47   *Ibid.*, 4–5.

48   The Court tried one last-ditch effort in a footnote to maintain the distinction between mitigating evidence (not all of which was relevant and thus admissible) and relevant mitigating evidence (admissible) when it said, "We do not hold that all facets of the defendant's ability to adjust to prison life must be treated as relevant and potentially mitigating. For example, we have no quarrel with the statement of the Supreme Court of South Carolina that 'how often [the defendant] will take a shower' is irrelevant to the sentencing determination." The absurdity of the example proves the point: the distinction between mitigating evidence and relevant mitigating evidence has collapsed. *Ibid.*, 7, n. 2.

49   481 U.S. 393 (1987).

50   *Ibid.*, 397–98. The Florida law quoted is Fla. Stat. s. 921.141(1)(1975), quoted in *Ibid.*, 395.

51   *Florida Statutes Annotated*, 921.141(6) lists the mitigating circumstances while 921.141(5) provides the aggravating circumstances. The mitigating circumstances include no prior significant criminal history, extreme mental or emotional disturbance in committing the crime, victim participation in crime, defendant's being merely an accomplice in the crime, defendant's acting under duress, the limited ability of the defendant to appreciate the criminality of his conduct and the age of the defendant. Quoted in 481 U.S. 396, n.3.

52   See 481 U.S. 396 for brief discussion of a relevant Florida case, *Cooper v. State*, 336 So2d 1133 (Fla. 1976).

53   481 U.S. 398–99.

54   This was one of the pieces of information which Hitchcock presented before the jury in his case. 481 U.S. 397.

CHAPTER 8

Wagner I (1988)

We saw in the previous chapter that 1976 was a turning point in the modern U.S. Supreme Court's death penalty jurisprudence. From 1972 to 1976 the Court struggled with the question of what kind of state death penalty statute would pass constitutional muster. Because the Court had previously held in 1972 that the death penalty was unconstitutional as applied because juries were given excessive discretion in sentencing people to death, there was some doubt whether the Court would find *any* state capital punishment constitutional. When five death penalty cases made their way to the Supreme Court in 1976, the focus of the Court's consideration was, in the words of Oregon Supreme Court Justice Michael Gillette, on the "constitutional permissibility of a particular statutory method of creating a class of death-eligible defendants."[1]

On July 2, 1976, the Court answered that question by upholding two types of MPC death penalty statutes and Texas' guided-discretion statute. Once the Court decided that various death penalty statutes were generally constitutional, it began to focus on particular issues raised by the precise wording of several state statutes. The Court's jurisprudence of mitigating circumstances then began to evolve in a dynamic fashion. By 1987 the Court held, among other things, that evidence from the convicted person's youth, his upbringing, and even his post-arrest behavior in jail was relevant for the jury to consider in mitigation of the death penalty. Capital punishment statutes and the jury instructions in capital cases should explicitly provide for full consideration of mitigating measures.

This broad understanding of mitigating circumstances in 1987 stood in some contrast to the rather parsimonious view of mitigating circumstances in the Court's 1976 decision in *Jurek*. The Texas capital punishment statute upheld in *Jurek* never mentioned that the jury was to consider evidence in mitigation as it answered the three sentencing questions.[2] The U.S. Supreme Court was convinced, however, that it was the practice of Texas courts to give instructions on mitigation even though the statute did not explicitly provide for them.

In 1976 a state death penalty statute was constitutional if it *implied* that mitigating circumstances had to be considered by the jury. An explicit mention in the statute of jury consideration of mitigating circumstances was not required. In addition, it was sufficient if juries actually considered mitigating circumstances with respect to only one of the three statutory questions of the Texas scheme. There was no requirement that circumstances in mitigation *beyond* the information gained by the three questions be considered in 1976. Even though the Court said in *Jurek* that all evidence of mitigating circumstances could be brought before the jury, the Court really was not fully aware of the contours of this statement in 1976. By emphasizing the constitutionality of various capital punishment schemes, the Court did not give the matter of mitigating circumstances much thought in 1976. It simply had not thought through the questions which *Lockett*, *Eddings*, *Skipper* and *Hitchcock* would raise in the next decade.

The expansion of the concept of mitigating circumstances would become one of the most significant developments in the U.S. Supreme Court's death penalty jurisprudence over the next decade. By the time it issued the *Lockett*, *Eddings*, *Skipper* and *Hitchcock* opinions, the Supreme Court was much more clear on the need for explicit statutory provision for mitigating circumstances and full jury instructions on the breadth of those circumstances.

The *most* that one could say about *Jurek*, therefore, after *Lockett*, *Eddings*, *Skipper* and *Hitchcock*, is that it was not fully inconsistent with the later cases. If one wanted to get the Supreme Court's best thinking on mitigating circumstances in 1988, however, one would not consult *Jurek*. In a word, by 1988 *Jurek* was out-of-date. Not unconstitutional, necessarily. Not necessarily a bad decision. Not a strong decision, however. Just out-of-date. It would be like trying to prosecute a case of racial discrimination in 2000 solely on pre-1964 laws. It is not impossible, but it is a bit irrelevant. Why should one look to *Jurek* when there are four more recent, complete and focused decisions on the specific issue of mitigating circumstances?

Turning to Oregon

One must understand this evolving and dynamic mitigating circumstances jurisprudence of the U.S. Supreme Court, this "odyssey" if you will, in order to put the 1988 *Wagner* decision of the Oregon Supreme Court in context.[3] The 1988 *Wagner* decision is significant because it was the first decision of the Oregon Supreme Court regarding the constitutionality of the 1984 death penalty law. What will be astonishing to note is that in upholding Oregon's 1984 capital punishment statute in *Wagner*, a majority of the justices of the Oregon Supreme Court ignored the national legal developments on mitigating circumstances between 1978 and 1987. In fact, a majority of the court in *Wagner I* simply refused to go any further than *Jurek* in its consideration of mitigating circumstances. The primary concern of the court in its first look at Oregon's capital punishment statute was to determine whether or not it was constitutional. In order to answer that question, the court looked almost exclusively to the *Jurek* decision.

Instead of asking the more precise question of the scope of mitigating circumstances that a jury must consider and whether Oregon law permitted that scope, the Oregon court focused on a bewildering variety of challenges to the law's constitutionality.[4] Though *Wagner I* is a very long opinion its structure and argument are easy to discerrn: *Jurek* has not explicitly been overrruled; *Jurek* is therefore still good law; the Oregon law is based on the Texas statute upheld in *Jurek;* therefore, the Oregon statute is constitutional. Q.E.D.[5] The dyamism of mitigating circumstances jurisprudence in the U.S. Supreme Court had been replaced by a scholastic syllogism in Oregon.

Facts and Argument in *Wagner I*

On June 26, 1985, Jeffrey Wagner beat and strangled Jeri Koenig to death in Linn County.[6] Koenig was scheduled to testify against Wagner at a subsequent trial, and so Wagner was charged with aggravated murder for violating a portion of the Oregon statute making killing of a juror or witness in a criminal proceeding an aggravating circumstance to the crime.

Wagner was indicted on July 3, arraigned on July 10 and granted until July 22, 1985, to enter a plea. On July 22 he appeared with counsel, entered a plea of not guilty and reserved the right until September 1 to demur and enter a defense of mental disease. Shortly thereafter, however, Wagner moved the court for an order to represent himself, with co-counsel present for the purpose of answering questions Wagner might have about legal issues. After defendant insisted that this was his right and desire, the court approved his request early in 1986.

On February 10, the day the case was to go to trial, Wagner informed the court that he would be changing his plea from not guilty to guilty of aggravated murder. The court was taken aback and explained to Wagner, over the course of the next two weeks, that he was foregoing rights and courting risks by such a confession. Nevertheless the court permitted Wagner so to plead. The sentencing part of the trial was then immediately scheduled.

Jury selection lasted several days and the state presented its case in chief from February 20–25. Wagner, however, put on no defense, and made no opening statement. At the conclusion of the sentencing hearing, the jury was instructed on the following three statutory issues:

1. Whether the conduct of the defendant that caused the death of the deceased was committed deliberately and with the reasonable expectation that death of the deceased or another would result;

2. Whether there is a probability that the defendant would commit criminal acts of violence that would constitute a continuing threat to society. In determining this issue, the court shall instruct the jury to consider any mitigating circumstances offered in evidence, including, but not limited to, the defendant's age, the extent and severity of the defendant's prior criminal conduct and the extent of the mental and emotional pressure under which the defendant was acting at the time the offense was committed; and

3. If raised by the evidence, whether the conduct of the defendant in killing the deceased was unreasonable in response to the provocation, if any, by the deceased.[7]

A unanimous jury answered all these questions affirmatively, and Wagner was sentenced to death. The case came to the Oregon Supreme Court on automatic and direct appeal, as provided in the statute.[8] The case, however, bristled with legal difficulties. First, there was a host of issues surrounding Wagner's desire not to be represented by counsel. Was it legal or ethical for a state to condemn a person to death who wanted to represent himself and then, when he had the chance, refused to do so? Would the state unwittingly be cooperating with a person who might have a death wish? This concern was heightened during the sentencing proceeding, as Wagner refused to put on witnesses to support him or to make an opening statement.

Was Wagner's plea to a charge of aggravated murder admissible when he could be opening himself up to the sentence of death by such a plea? That is, a defendant usually pleads guilty to a crime if there is some assurance that the *worst* scenario envisioned under the law will not be visited upon one. By pleading guilty in this circumstance, Wagner was actually increasing his danger. In addition, did the Oregon Constitution permit a plea of guilt to aggravated murder or could one only be convicted of such a heinous crime after a jury weighed all the evidence?

There were additional legal issues concerned more with the Oregon statute than the particular facts of the Wagner case. Was Oregon's statute still constitutional in view of the fact that the U.S. Supreme Court had developed its more supple understanding of mitigating circumstances from 1978 to 1987 and Oregon's law only seemed to permit consideration of mitigating circumstances in connection with a defendant's future dangerousness? Was the statute vague in defining a number of crucial terms? Did the statute violate Article I, section 15, of the Oregon Constitution by permitting punishment for crime that was not based on principles of reformation? Did Article I, section 40, of the Oregon Constitution, which purported to blunt the effect of sections 15 and 16 of the same article, actually do so or was it ineffective in its attempt to do so? Did the statute sufficiently narrow the class of death-eligible people to meet Supreme Court standards? The questions never seemed to stop.

Perhaps because of the gravity of the issue, the irregularity of the procedure in Wagner's case and the scores of legal questions provoked by the new law, the Oregon Supreme Court's decision, including two dissenting opinions, was 120 pages in length. It is the longest decision the Oregon court has issued in the years since 1988, and may very well be the longest decision the court has ever issued. The majority opinion, supported by five justices, tried to answer all of the questions thrown at it. The court held that dispensing with a jury trial in a capital case did not violate the Oregon Constitution.[9] It held that sections 15 and 16 of Article I were overridden by Article I, section 40, passed by the voters in 1984. It held further that this constitutional overriding did not violate the equal protection clause of the Fourteenth Amendment. It held that the Oregon death penalty scheme, based on Texas' constitutionally acceptable scheme, was likewise constitutional. The statute sufficiently narrowed the class of death-eligible defendants and was not vague in its crucial terms. In a long explanation, the court held that the procedural developments in Wagner's case did not violate various Oregon statutes.

The court also devoted several pages to a consideration of whether Oregon's statute allowed the jury to consider all evidence that might mitigate a defendant's sentence of death.[10] Rather than examining the section where the three questions quoted above were listed, the majority opinion quoted the section giving a series of general pieces of advice to the court on how to proceed in the sentencing phase. It is worth quoting the entire subsection, because the court focused on a few words in it as justifying its holding that the statute permitted full consideration of all mitigating factors:

> Upon a finding that the defendant is guilty of aggravated murder, the court shall conduct a separate sentencing proceeding to determine whether the defendant shall be sentenced to life imprisonment or death. The proceeding shall be conducted in the trial court before the trial jury as soon as practicable. If the defendant has pleaded guilty, the sentencing proceeding shall be conducted before a jury impaneled for that purpose. *In the proceeding, evidence may be presented as to any matter that the court deems relevant to sentence*; however, neither the state nor the defendant shall be allowed to introduce repetitive evidence that has previously been offered and received during the trial on the issue of guilt. The court shall instruct the jury that all evidence previously offered and received may be considered for purposes of the sentencing hearing. This subsection shall not be construed to authorize the introduction of any evidence secured in violation of the Constitution of the United States or of the State of Oregon. The state and the defendant or the counsel of the defendant shall be permitted to present arguments for or against a sentence of death (emphasis supplied).[11]

The words quoted are general instructions to the court. They emphasize, in the context of the subsection, that all kinds of evidence, except illegally secured and cumulative evidence, may be presented in the sentencing hearing. The specific issues to be submitted to the jury, referred to above as the three questions, are then listed in the next subsection. The statute moves from general instructions to specific commands in these two subsections. The only place where mitigating circumstances are explicitly mentioned in the Oregon statute is in connection with question 2 in subsection 2. According to the U.S. Supreme Court's jurisprudence, especially in *Eddings, Skipper* and *Hitchcock*, such a statute would need to be much more explicit in mentioning the full range of mitigating circumstances in order to meet constitutional muster. In addition, general instructions, such as those in subsection 1, will not save a statute that does not explicitly recognize the full scope of mitigating circumstances.

Nevertheless, the Oregon Supreme Court held in *Wagner I* that the general instructions of subsection 1 permit the consideration of all mitigating circumstances, and that the specific instructions of subsection 2 cannot be held to contradict that determination. Only one quotation is needed to show that the majority of the court completely misconstrued the U.S. Supreme Court's evolving jurisprudence of mitigating circumstances. The Oregon court quoted the italicized section of the statute:

> In the [sentencing] proceeding, evidence may be presented as to any matter that the court deems relevant to sentence.[12]

The court then went on to say:

> Even if the statute were silent, obviously, either defendant or the state would have the right to introduce any evidence relevant to the resolution of all or any of the three questions which frame the jury's resolution of the three issues.[13]

That is, the Oregon Supreme Court was saying two things about this general instruction on admissibility of evidence at the sentencing proceeding: 1) it permits the introduction of any and all evidence in mitigation, and 2) even if the provision from the statute just quoted was *not* there, a person could still present evidence of mitigation with respect to the three questions. In other words, the actual statutory authorization for the supreme court to bring forth evidence in mitigation is so unimportant that even if the generic words of 163.150(1) were not there, such evidence could be brought forth. Rather than following the U.S. Supreme Court, which had been moving towards *explicit* statutory authorization and *explicit* jury instructions so that *all* evidence that might mitigate a sentence of death may be presented, the court was saying that it was completely unimportant if mention of mitigating circumstances was made at all. An attorney can always present any relevant evidence he or she wants to present, the court reasoned, so why should one care if an explicit statutory authorization is present? Since you can *always* present mitigating circumstances, you do not need a statute to say that you can.

Using this strained logic, the Oregon Supreme Court then went on to find that the part of the statute authorizing consideration of mitigating circumstances for purposes of determining future dangerousness applied not simply to question 2 but to *all three questions.*

> We construe the statute to mean that a defendant shall be permitted to introduce any competent evidence relevant to mitigation on any of the three issues.[14]

Since one can find full consideration of mitigating circumstances in the few words of 163.150(1) and can even find them when no words are present, it is not surprising that the supreme court can find them in questions 1 and 3 where no mention of them is made. Mitigating circumstances can be presented by defense attorney whether or not they are mentioned in the statute. Statutory authorization is simply unimportant.

After making this terribly inauspicious beginning, the court went on to find that the U.S. Supreme Court cases decided between 1978 and 1987 dealing with mitigating circumstances actually do not affect this conclusion. The sole concern of the Oregon court was to raise the question of whether *Lockett, Eddings, Skipper* or *Hitchcock* overruled *Jurek*. No attempt was made to understand the gradually increasing scope and importance of mitigating evidence in the U.S. Supreme Court's cases.

Therefore, the Oregon Supreme Court came to the following. *Jurek* is good law because it has not been explicitly overruled. *Jurek* has some language that the Texas courts interpreted to authorize consideration of mitigating evidence for all three statutory questions. The Oregon statute was based on Texas' law. Oregon's statute permitting consideration of mitigating circumstances for question 2 can be construed to permit consideration of mitigating circumstances for all three questions. Therefore, Oregon's law passes constitutional muster.[15]

The Dissenters Speak

It is no surprise that the two justices of the Oregon Supreme Court most conversant in issues of federal constitutional law, Justice Hans Linde and Justice Michael Gillette, vigorously dissented. Their dissenting opinions take up nearly 50 pages in the *Oregon Reports*.[16] While Justice Gillette's dissent focuses almost completely on the court's misconstrual of the U.S. Supreme Court's evolving jurisprudence of mitigation in capital sentencing proceedings, Justice Linde's dissent is a more far-reaching examination of accuracy standards in capital cases, the language of Oregon's capital punishment statute, state constitutional provisions, law review articles on Texas' statute, as well as the U.S. Supreme Court's developing jurisprudence of capital sentencing mitigation. Both dissenting opinions are fully researched, accurately presented, and eloquently written. As subsequent events would show, they were also largely correct.[17] Yet they differ from each other in a crucial way that will be significant when the Oregon Supreme Court considered the issue again in *Wagner II* early in 1990. Only the briefest contours of that emerging disagreement between the dissenters will be described here.

First, the agreement between the dissenters. Both felt that the majority had erred in reading the Oregon statute so broadly. They each thought that the Supreme Court's evolving jurisprudence of mitigating circumstances had been ignored by their colleagues. Both dissenting justices felt that the Oregon capital punishment statute as it was passed in 1984 had significant deficiencies to it. They differed on what to do about these shortcomings.

For Justice Gillette, the statutory deficiency could be corrected by a vigorous jury instruction that told the jury explicitly to consider all evidence that might be used to mitigate a death sentence for a convicted aggravated murderer. He opined:

> This court could so construe the statute as to permit the admission of all mitigating evidence and to require an instruction to the jury delineating the scope of the jury's authority to reprieve an otherwise death-eligible defendant on the basis of that evidence.[18]

What might be the shape of that particular instruction? Justice Gillette went on:

> One solution perhaps would be to instruct the jury that, even if it concludes that all three statutory questions should be answered "yes," it nonetheless should answer one of them "no" unless it unanimously concludes that the mitigating evidence does not call for a lesser penalty. A second alternative might have the jury answer a fourth, constitutionally required question after the three statutory ones: After considering all the mitigating evidence, does the jury still unanimously conclude that the prisoner should be put to death, rather than spared?[19]

This was the first judicial reference to a "fourth" question, which would occupy the attention of the Oregon Department of Justice, the Oregon Legislature and the Oregon Supreme Court from June 1989 to June 1991.

Justice Gillette, therefore, believed that the statute was inadequate not because of the insufficiency of the statutory language but because the language was construed by sentencing judges in too narrow a fashion. What seemed to be needed would be not only an effort by the Oregon Supreme Court to construe the statute broadly but also a coordinate effort by local circuit courts to broaden the questions to juries to include all possible evidence in mitigation in a capital sentencing proceeding.

There is a deep unclarity that runs through this suggestion, however, an unclarity that is significant enough to mention at this point because it will be at the heart of an even more confused decision, *Wagner II,* in January 1990, when the Oregon Supreme Court both did and did not uphold Oregon's capital punishment statute.[20] Did Justice Gillette believe in 1988 that the Oregon statute was inadequate or only that the jury instructions in capital cases were inadequate? The energy and power of the first 14 pages of his dissent is based on the notion that Oregon is behind the times in its death penalty jurisprudence, that the Oregon Supreme Court has fully misunderstood the mitigation requirements of the U.S. Supreme Court, and that the Oregon statute is inadequate.[21]

But then, his tone seemed to change. The Oregon statutory scheme is not unconstitutional on its face. Perhaps all it needs is the addition of one or the other of the two approaches quoted above. Is the suggestion that Justice Gillette is giving a suggestion for statutory change or only a jury-instruction change? If he is suggesting a statutory change, then he cannot be correct when he says that the Oregon law is adequate ("not unconstitutional on its face"). But, if he is only suggesting a jury instruction change, why does he seem to have so many problems with the statute? What is the role of a supreme court justice in giving advice, in a dissent no less, to circuit court judges on how they are to conduct sentencing proceedings in capital cases? Should anyone take it seriously? And why does he put his suggestion as a "fourth question" which is an obvious reference to the statutory questions that must be put to a jury? Is he suggesting a statutory change? If the statute is adequate, why dissent? He ultimately seems to acquiesce in the majority's tortured attempt to explain the breadth of the statute, but wants to make sure that trial courts instruct juries in a constitutionally proper manner. Hence, he dissents.

Justice Linde's dissent not only commends Justice Gillette for showing how the court was basically asking and answering the wrong question with respect to mitigating circumstances, but also strikes out in a different direction. Justice Linde would consider the statute inadequate because it cannot, by its terms, permit the consideration of mitigating factors for any question but the second. In addition, it does not permit a jury instruction that is broader than the language of the statute itself. In his own words:

> It is difficult if not impossible to insert the broad consideration of "mitigating aspects of the defendant's character" and other mitigating circumstances as demanded by the "rule in *Lockett"* even into the Texas statute. But in Oregon, the sponsors of ORS 163.150(2)(b) foreclosed any such judicial manipulation by expressly tying "mitigating circumstances" to

the second issue that the jury is told to answer "yes" or "no," the specific issue of danger to society from a defendant's probable criminal acts of violence. While agreeing with most of Justice Gillette's dissent, 305 Or at 210, I see no room in the statute for a court to instruct the jury to answer different or additional questions.[22]

What to do? Justice Linde went on:

It might well be a service to invalidate this statute now. That would give the state an appeal to the Supreme Court or let the sponsors of another death penalty measure start over.[23]

Thus, on the one side one had a majority of five justices, whose reasoning and decision were diametrically opposed to the developing jurisprudence of the United States Supreme Court. On the other side were the court's two most scholarly justices unsuccessfully imploring their colleagues to recognize their clear error. Lives were, literally, at stake. In this situation, Justice Gillette took the unusual and courageous step in his dissent of asking the U.S. Supreme Court to consider this case on direct review. As was shown in Chapter Five, the United States Supreme Court almost never grants certiorari on direct review of a death penalty case from a state. Perhaps, Justice Gillette thought, the impossible might happen. The situation in Oregon, in his and Justice Linde's minds, was so serious that it required a U.S. Supreme Court response to the problem. Nothing less would do.

As this story unfolds, we will see that the impossible occurred. The United States Supreme Court would accept jurisdiction in Wagner's direct appeal and would vacate the decision of the Oregon Supreme Court. But that did not happen until July 3, 1989. Before reaching that date, two other crucial events for Oregon's death penalty occurred in 1989: the handing down of yet another U.S. Supreme Court decision on mitigating measures on June 26, and conclusion of the 1989 Oregon Legislative Assembly five days later, where the results of the June 26 Supreme Court decision were hurriedly adopted into the Oregon statute. Both of these events would complicate the issue yet further and call the legitimacy of the Oregon Supreme Court's decision in *Wagner I* further into question.

Endnotes

1   *State v. Wagner,* 305 Or 115, 229, 752 P2d 1136 (1988) (Gillette, J., dissenting).
2   Questions relating to deliberateness of the murder, future dangerousness of the offender, and evidence of provocation by the victim.
3   *State v. Wagner,* 395 Or 115, 222, 752 P2d 1136 (1988) (Gillette, J., dissenting). This decision will also be referred to in the text as *Wagner I.*
4   Many of these challenges are mentioned in the next section of this chapter.
5   Q.E.D. stands for *quod erat demonstrandum* and can be translated, "the very thing which was to be demonstrated," and means that the concluding statement was exactly what one was trying to prove from the beginning.
6   *Wagner,* at 117. The facts of the case are derived from the following pages of the case.
7   ORS 163.150(2)(a)–(c)(1985).
8   ORS 163.150(6)(1985).
9   305 Or 134–35.
10   *Ibid.,* 156–67.
11   ORS 163.150(1)(1985).
12   ORS 163.150(1), quoted in 305 Or 156.
13   *Ibid.*
14   *Ibid.,* 156–57.
15   Most of the court's opinion from page 159–167 is a series of long quotations from other cases, with almost no analysis. One gets the impression that the issue of mitigating circumstances was really not the issue that the majority wanted to deal with. The tight logic, completely devoid of any concern for legal development, is all that the court seemed to want to consider.
16   *Ibid.,* 188–237.
17   See Chapters Nine and Ten.
18   *State v. Wagner,* 232.
19   *Ibid.,* 233.
20   That opinion is even more tortured than *Wagner I* and will be the subject of Chapter Ten. *State v. Wagner,* 309 Or 5, 786 P2d 93 (1990). What makes these cases so poignant, however, is that the strained reasoning of the Oregon Supreme Court is the basis on which at least ten men may be facing the sentence of death in Oregon. I say "did and did not uphold" Oregon's capital punishment scheme because the court said that the Oregon statute was constitutional but then proceeded to change it in the decision.
21   *State v. Wagner,* 305 Or 219–233.
22   *Ibid.*
23   *Ibid.,* 207.

CHAPTER 9

A Most Hectic Week,
June 26 to July 1, 1989

On October 25, 1979, a moderately retarded John Paul Penry raped, beat and stabbed Pamela Carpenter to death in Livingston, Texas. Before she died, she was able to describe her assailant to authorities, and they apprehended Penry shortly thereafter. Penry was on parole from prison at the time for an earlier rape conviction. He confessed to the crime against Carpenter and was charged with capital murder.[1]

At a pretrial competency hearing in 1980 psychiatrists testified that Penry had an IQ of 50–63, a score which indicates mild or moderate retardation. One clinical psychologist testified that Penry had the mental age of a 6 1/2-year-old and a social maturity of a 9 or 10-year-old. A particularly unfortunate aspect to Penry's retardation was that he probably would be unable to learn from his past mistakes. No one was quite sure into which category of mental retardation to place him. The learned psychologists and psychiatrists really could go no farther than a designation which most lay people would have instinctively accorded to Penry: "borderline."

The jury found Penry competent to stand trial. At trial the defense sought to show that Penry suffered from an organic brain disorder, that he had been repeatedly abused as a child and that he was not able to appreciate the wrongfulness of his conduct or to conform his conduct to the law.[2] The state, in contrast, put its own psychiatrists on the stand to testify that, even though Penry was a person of extremely limited mental ability and seemed unable to learn from his mistakes, he knew the difference between right and wrong. He was, therefore, legally sane at the time of the murder. The jury did not accept the defense theory of insanity and convicted Penry of capital murder. At the sentencing hearing, the jury unanimously answered Texas' three statutory questions affirmatively and Penry was sentenced to death. The Texas Court of Criminal Appeals affirmed this decision.[3]

Penry then filed for habeas corpus relief in the federal district court, which also affirmed his conviction and sentence. The Court of Appeals for the Fifth Circuit affirmed the decision of the district court but noted that it found considerable merit in Penry's claim that the jury was not able, under Texas' capital sentencing procedure, to consider and apply all of his mitigating circumstances in coming to their decision.[4] Although it had rejected Penry's earlier claim on direct appeal, the United States Supreme Court granted certiorari to hear Penry's habeas corpus claim.

On June 26, 1989, the United States Supreme Court reversed the Fifth Circuit and held that Texas' three statutory questions in a capital punishment sentencing proceeding did not permit the jury to take into consideration all evidence in mitigation of a sentence of death for Penry.[5] The Supreme Court did not actually reach the question of whether Texas' death penalty statute was unconstitutional because it was only asked to consider whether the three statutory questions *in Penry's case* permitted jury consideration of all evidence in mitigation of the death penalty for Penry. Nevertheless, the Supreme Court's holding strongly suggested that Texas' three questions did *not* meet constitutional muster. Certainly the four dissenters in the case understood the majority's opinion to hold as much.[6]

Penry's major point was that the mitigating evidence of his mental retardation and childhood abuse had relevance to his moral capacity beyond the scope of the three questions (which the Supreme Court called the "special issues"), and that the jury was not permitted to give its "reasoned moral response" to all the evidence.[7] The Supreme Court agreed. It agreed with this assessment despite the fact that the Texas statute, which Oregon copied, has an explicit statement permitting jury consideration of all relevant evidence in a capital sentencing proceeding. The statute provided:

> The [sentencing] proceeding shall be conducted in the trial
> court before the trial jury as soon as practicable. In the pro-
> ceeding, evidence may be presented as to any matter that the
> court deems relevant to sentence.[8]

The Court held that just because the trial court was instructed by the first part of the statute (the general instructions) to allow any relevant evidence to be presented to the jury, this did not mean that all evidence of mitigation was

permitted by these words. Rather, the three statutory questions or special issues in a Texas-type capital sentencing statute had to provide for consideration
of all evidence in mitigation of a death sentence.[9]

The Supreme Court then went on to show how each of the three questions in Texas' capital sentencing procedure did not permit full jury consideration of Penry's mitigation evidence. Let us hear the words of the Court itself:

> The first special issue asks whether the defendant acted "de-
> liberately and with the reasonable expectation that the death
> of the deceased...would result." Neither the Texas Legisla-
> ture nor the Texas Court of Criminal Appeals have defined
> the term "deliberately."... Assuming that the jurors in this
> case understood "deliberately" to mean more than that Penry
> was guilty of "intentionally" committing murder, those ju-
> rors may still have been unable to give effect to Penry's miti-
> gating evidence in answering the first special issue.[10]

How so? The Court reasoned that a rational juror could have found, in
the light of testimony given at trial, that Penry killed Pamela Carpenter to
escape detection for his crime. This would mean that the murder was committed "deliberately," or more than simply "intentionally." The jury could have
unanimously found on this evidence alone that Penry killed Carpenter deliberately. Therefore, a reasonable jury could have unanimously answered the
first question affirmatively. There is no requirement in the statute that the
jury "weigh" any possible mitigating evidence in answering the question of
deliberateness. But a rational juror, if given the chance, could also have found
that because of his mental defect Penry was unable to control his impulses or
to evaluate the consequences of his actions. But since deliberateness was already determined by examining the reason for his crime, the jury may not
have had an opportunity to give its "reasoned moral response" to the evidence
of his mental condition.

The second special question asks:

> [w]hether there is a probability that the defendant would
> commit criminal acts of violence that would constitute a con-
> tinuing threat to society.[11]

The mitigation evidence concerning Penry's mental retardation suggested that
one effect of his retardation was that Penry was unable to learn from his mistakes. Thus, in all probability, if he was released in the future he would injure
others. Even in a prison context the prosecutor argued that he could hurt

doctors, nurses or other professionals that worked in the prison. A rational juror could have answered the second question affirmatively without even considering the "two-edged sword" of his mental retardation: that the same characteristic that enhanced the probability of his future dangerousness argu-ably mitigated his blameworthiness for the crime. The Court concluded:

> The second special issue, therefore, did not provide a vehicle for the jury to give mitigating effect to Penry's evidence of mental retardation and childhood abuse.[12]

> The third special issue asks:

> whether the conduct of the defendant in killing the deceased was unreasonable in response to the provocation, if any, by the deceased.[13]

Penry confessed at trial that he stabbed the victim after her struggle ended and she was lying in a helpless condition. Had he testified that he killed her only as a result of a struggle, he might have been found less culpable. But a confession to the slaying of a "helpless" person would have provided the jury with enough information to answer special issue three affirmatively. But, ar-gued the Court:

> A juror who believed Penry lacked the moral culpability to be sentenced to death could not express that view in answer-ing the third special issue if she also concluded that Penry's action was not a reasonable response to provocation.[14]

The prosecutor, in summing up his case, reminded the jurors that they had taken an oath to uphold that law and that they must follow the instruc-tions they were given in answering the special issues. In other words, if the jury could answer each one of the special issues affirmatively they must sen-tence the defendant to death. The Supreme Court concluded:

> In light of the prosecutor's argument, and in the absence of appropriate jury instructions, a reasonable juror could well have believed that there was no vehicle for expressing the view that Penry did not deserve to be sentenced to death based upon his mitigating evidence.[15]

Or in words that were seemingly more dear to Justice O'Connor than the traditional test of juror consideration of evidence "relevant to a defendant's character or record or the circumstances of the offense," she concluded that the jury was not permitted to express its "reasoned moral response" to the evidence in mitigation of a capital sentence for Penry.

Despite the fact that the majority only emphasized the inadequacy of jury instructions in Penry's case, the dissenters knew that the majority's decision had implications for the constitutionality of the statute. If the three questions of the Texas statute were inadequate in Penry's case to allow a jury's "reasoned moral response" to evidence in mitigation of a sentence of death, it was probably inadequate in other cases as well. The statute, therefore, was infirm. Its cramped words simply did not allow the full consideration of mitigating circumstances. So, the dissenters wrote:

> The Texas system upheld in *Jurek* was precisely the same one the Court finds unacceptable today, which structures the jury's discretion through three questions relating to the defendant's personal culpability for the crime, his future dangerousness, and the reasonableness of his response to any provocation by the victim. In holding this scheme unconstitutionally limits the jury's discretion to consider the mitigating evidence of Penry's mental retardation and abused childhood, the Court today entirely disregards one of the two lines of our concern....[16]

The majority and the dissenters apparently disagreed on the precise scope of the majority's holding. The majority contended that its conclusion was not inconsistent with *Jurek* because Penry's case was only an "as applied" challenge to the statute. The dissent, however, argued that the majority was, in essence, overruling *Jurek*. Whatever conclusions one draws from reading the *Penry* case, the case signaled to Texas and any other state which had a Texas-like capital sentencing statute, that three special issues or three questions were simply not enough. In order for a state to be safe it needed either to have some kind of a "fourth" question, which Justice Michael Gillette predicted, or it needed to have a statement which said that all evidence of mitigating circumstances was relevant for jury consideration with respect to the three special issues and however many other issues might arise.[17]

Oregon's Response

As mentioned above, Oregon was the only state that followed Texas in its capital sentencing procedure. The invalidation of the Texas statute or just the invalidation of the procedure as it related to Penry, depending on how one read the *Penry* decision, therefore would only have implications in Texas and

Oregon. But rather than take the time to study the results of the *Penry* decision and come to some kind of agreement on its implications for Oregon, the
Oregon Legislature, at the behest of the Oregon Department of Justice, immediately amended the Oregon capital punishment statute in a major way.
This was done before members of the House or Senate Judiciary Committees
even had time to read the *Penry* decision.[18] It is to a consideration of those
crucial days, June 28– July 1, 1989, that we now turn.

The decision of the United States Supreme Court caused immediate and
immense waves in Oregon. Within two days of the decision the state court
administrator, on behalf of the Oregon Supreme Court, wrote to parties involved in upcoming death penalty oral arguments, asking them for their responses to four questions provoked by the *Penry* decision. Within three days
of the *Penry* decision, the Oregon Department of Justice approached the 1989
Oregon Legislature in its waning days with all the firepower it could muster to
request several changes in Oregon's capital sentencing statute. The central
change was the addition of a "fourth question" or a fourth issue to submit to
the jury that would allow consideration of mitigating circumstances beyond
the reach and scope of the first three questions or issues. Within a week, Oregon's
statute was redrafted to reflect the philosophy and approach of the Department of Justice.

Before going through the history of this most tumultuous week, the basic
philosophy and approach of the Oregon Department of Justice (DOJ) in the
wake of the *Penry* decision should be explained. The philosophy, at its heart,
was based on contradictory assertions that could not be examined closely by
either the DOJ or the legislature because the DOJ decided that speed was
absolutely of the essence. The first assertion or guiding principle of the DOJ
in approaching the Legislature was that the *Penry* decision did not invalidate
the Texas statute. The statute upheld in *Jurek*, therefore, was still good law.
Because Oregon's statute was based on Texas, Oregon's capital sentencing procedure was therefore still valid. The second assertion is that the statute *had* to
be changed immediately to reflect what the U.S. Supreme Court held to be a
constitutionally necessary fourth question. So, the DOJ was going to argue
that the Oregon statute was constitutional but it *had* to be changed. Immediately.

The DOJ would argue the validity of Oregon's capital sentencing law at
the same time as the constitutional necessity of immediately changing it. This
contradiction will underlie not simply the legislative debate and approval, but
the subsequent Oregon Supreme Court decision, *Wagner II,* which seemed to
uphold but also expand Oregon's death penalty statute.

The Oregon Supreme Court Responds—June 28, 1989

The first major ripple caused by the *Penry* decision was in the Oregon Supreme Court. Seven death penalty oral arguments had been scheduled for the next few months, and the court wanted counsel on both sides to answer four questions which it felt were provoked by the *Penry* decision. On June 28, 1989, the state court administrator, at the behest of the court, sent a letter to the public defender, the solicitor general's office and three attorneys in private practice,[19] asking them to answer four questions within fourteen days.[20] Because the four questions would eventually frame the inquiry of the Oregon Supreme Court when it handed down *State v. Wagner* (*Wagner II*) in January 1990, some care should be taken here to review those questions.

First, the court requested an answer to the question, "Under *Penry v. Lynaugh*…is the Oregon statute, ORS 163.150(1)(b), facially unconstitutional?" At first glance the question appears to be a good one. Before a court can decide whether a statute requires a change or whether a change meets constitutional muster, it might want to consider whether the statute itself is constitutional. "Facial" constitutionality is to be contrasted with "as applied" constitutionality. To be facially constitutional means that the words themselves, without regard to how the statute is applied, are constitutional. "As applied" constitutionality refers to whether the statute is constitutional in a particular instance. A facially constitutional statute might be applied in an unconstitutional manner. So, the supreme court wanted to know from counsel if, in their judgment, *Penry* invalidated the words of the Oregon statute.

Upon second glance, however, the question entangled the DOJ, the legislature and the Oregon Supreme Court itself in a morass of huge proportions. The United States Supreme Court could not even agree if the *Penry* decision said *anything* about the constitutionality of the Texas statute, much less whether the Texas statute was unconstitutional. Five justices in the majority held that Penry's case required a fourth question to be asked of the jury. Four dissenters said that this was tantamount to holding that the fourth question was constitutionally required. Therefore, the dissenters argued, the majority was really invalidating the Texas statute. The majority did not explicitly say whether they were doing that.

The problem with the Oregon Supreme Court's first question to counsel is that the question would only rehearse an unsatisfactory debate that was not resolved explicitly by the U.S. Supreme Court and could not be resolved quickly in Oregon. It also placed the DOJ in an untenable position and led to its contradictory approach to the legislature the next day. In response to the first question, the DOJ needed to argue that the Oregon capital sentencing statute was constitutional even after *Penry* because if it argued any other way it would be admitting that almost two dozen men were sentenced to death under an unconstitutional law. In view of the fact that Oregon's voters had so emphatically approved the death penalty, the DOJ was loath to find any reason why the statute was unconstitutional. This comes out most clearly in the testimony of Attorney General David Frohnmayer on June 29, and the letter sent by Deputy Attorney General James Mountain to the chairs of the House and Senate Judiciary Committees on July 1, 1989.[21]

A better question and one calculated to extricate the state from rather than plunge the state into an insoluble morass, would have been, "Does the *Penry* decision require Oregon to include a fourth statutory issue or question or some other way to make sure that all mitigating circumstances are considered in ORS 163.150?" Both sides would have answered affirmatively, though the DOJ might have wanted to argue that the fourth question might not be required in all instances. The uncertainty of whether four questions were required in all instances will be at the heart of the utterly opaque first three words of the statutory change introduced by the DOJ on June 29.[22] If the court had rephrased the question to the legislature as to whether *Penry* required four questions in the statute, then they could move quickly to the issue of remedy. What do we do with the 22 cases in which this was not done? Do we retry the men? Only resentence them? Limit their sentence to life imprisonment?

An unpromising first question from the Oregon Supreme Court then leaves out the logical second question. Their second question was, "If the answer to question 1 is no" (meaning that the statute *is* constitutional; one should not get confused by the double negatives), "does the Oregon statutory scheme permit a fourth question?" A better second question would have been, if one accepts the propriety of the unhelpful first question, "If the answer is yes" (and the statute therefore is unconstitutional), "what is the remedy?" That is, the Oregon Supreme Court either did not consider that the statute could possibly be unconstitutional or it assumed that if it were found unconstitutional, everyone would naturally agree on the remedy. The only problem with that scenario is that the remedy is not readily apparent. Should all death row inmates be retried again under the 1984 statute without the death penalty as an alternative? Retry them under the predecessor statute? Realizing that if you retry them under the 1984 statute without the possibility of a death penalty the *only* penalty left is life imprisonment, forgo a trial and sentence them all to life imprisonment? Remand the cases with instructions to the circuit court to sentence them all to life imprisonment?

Instead, the second question the court propounded was, "If the answer to question 1 is no, does the Oregon statutory scheme permit a fourth question?" It is a strange question, but in this question one can already see the contours of the decision the court will reach in *Wagner II* in January 1990. The court would then argue that the statute is constitutional and that it permits a fourth question. By doing this, the court was hoping to "preserve" the death penalty statute by holding that the unmodified statute (pre-1989) was flexible enough to stretch and accommodate another question. In other words, by these first two questions the court was tipping its hand on how it was inclined to handle the issue already.

But the second question is not a good one. What does it mean to ask if the Oregon statutory scheme permits a fourth question? How can three issues or three questions permit a fourth? And, if they permit a fourth question, why don't they permit six or eight or 43 questions? It is almost as if the supreme court was trying to create out of the pre-1989 statute a law that already included a fourth issue so that any new statute explicitly written to include a fourth issue could be said to be entirely consistent with the preceding statute. In this way Oregon would have a "floating" death penalty statute that was always constitutional. What this second question shows more than anything is that the Oregon Supreme Court may not have wanted to face the possible implications of considering its death penalty statute inadequate.

The third question is the "as applied" question: "If the answer to question 2 is yes (meaning that the statute allows a fourth question), was there evidence proffered or received in this case which required that a fourth question be asked?" In other words, the court was making a distinction between cases in which three questions might suffice and cases where three questions might not suffice. In some cases, like that of Penry, all evidence of mitigation might not be permitted in the three statutory questions. In this situation, one would be required to ask a fourth question. On the other hand, in some cases a fourth question might not be needed. So, the court wanted to know whether each particular case would have required a fourth question. The distinction between cases that require three and those that require four questions will entangle the legislature the next day.

Finally, the supreme court asks about the remedy. "If the answers to questions 2 and 3 above are yes, what is the remedy? That is, is the defendant entitled to a new trial on both the guilt and penalty phases, or only on the penalty phase? May this court reverse only on the penalty phase, leaving the option of a sentence of life imprisonment?" This is a good question, because it forces consideration of what the court must do in response to *Penry.*[23]

At the Oregon Legislature—June 29 to July 1, 1989

With the legislative leaders only dimly aware of this background, the DOJ approached the Senate Judiciary Committee on Thursday, June 29, to ask for some statutory changes. But the DOJ would approach the legislature burdened with the contradiction described above. Because of the infelicitous first question of the Oregon Supreme Court on June 28, the DOJ had to testify to the legislature that the statute was constitutional. But, one might ask, if the statute is constitutional, why approach the committee? And why with so much urgency? And why with a remark by the attorney general and a follow-up letter from the deputy attorney general suggesting that a statutory change was constitutionally required?[24]

In any case, the biggest guns the DOJ could muster, Attorney General David Frohnmayer and Solicitor General Virginia Linder, appeared before the committee at 1:30 p.m. on Thursday, June 29.[25] Deputy Attorney General James Mountain would follow up this visit with a July 1 letter requesting the changes. David Frohnmayer was known to the committee. He had been a distinguished legislator in the 1970s and 1980s and had already served eight years as attorney general. His brilliance, low-key manner, fluency in speech, experience and general affability gave him an air of credibility before the legislature. Virginia Linder was several years his junior but matched her boss in fluency, intelligence and personableness. An impressive duo would present the changes.

The committee had only 15 minutes to hear and consider the changes, 13 of which were spent in presentations by Frohnmayer and Linder. The committee then would take 15 minutes later in the day, without Frohnmayer or Linder or anyone from the DOJ present, to discuss the suggested changes and vote on them. In his opening remarks, Frohnmayer said that the *Penry* case, in which the Texas scheme was held facially constitutional, had implications for pending Oregon cases.[26] In addition, he recognized that the committee just the day before had also passed a massive change to ORS 163.150, authorizing the penalty of life imprisonment without the possibility of parole for convicted aggravated murderers.[27] He was asking for another three changes in the statute because the U.S. Supreme Court, in the *Penry* decision, "has suggested that a fourth factor may be constitutionally required."[28] He pledged to be available to the committee for the balance of the legislative session because of the importance of the issue.

Virginia Linder then spelled out the specific language of the changes. Space only permits a discussion of the first change.[29] Because the change may be constitutionally required, according to the DOJ, the DOJ suggested a fourth question that would oblige the court to submit the following issue to the jury:

> If constitutionally required, whether the defendant's charac-
> ter or background, or the circumstances of the offense suffi-
> ciently reduce the defendant's moral culpability or blame-
> worthiness for the crime such that a sentence other than death
> should be imposed.[30]

Solicitor General Linder gave very few comments about this wording. All she said, in a fairly convoluted sentence, was that the United States Supreme Court required a fourth question to be submitted to juries where the constitution requires some other factor relating to a defendant's background, character or circumstances of the offense which might mitigate against a sentence of death when these three characteristics were not presented in the three statutory is-sues.[31] One does not have confidence in listening to the tape that she was altogether clear on what the point was. Certainly the committee was not.

The committee had time for only a question or two and then adjourned. It met again later in the day, at 4:15 p.m., to give a more complete (15-minute) consideration of the issue. Neither Attorney General Frohnmayer nor Solici-tor General Linder was present. Marion County District Attorney Dale Penn would handle questions. By the time the committee met, the wording of the fourth question had been changed. Now it read,

> If constitutionally required, considering the extent to which
> the defendant's character or background, or circumstances
> of the offense may reduce the defendant's moral culpability
> or blameworthiness for the crime, should a sentence of death
> be imposed?[32]

Senator Bob Shoemaker expressed his obvious frustration with the word-ing of the revised proposal. How, he wanted to know, could a jury possibly understand this question? How does one parse it? He stated that he had no objection to the idea behind it, but that the language of the proposal was less than clear.[33]

Committee Chair Joyce Cohen interrupted Senator Shoemaker with some impatience. She knew that the language was not crystal clear but this was what the United States Supreme Court required, and she was not about to change the statute "just for the sake of English."[34]

With this inauspicious beginning, the chair asked District Attorney Penn to comment. He was a member of the committee hastily called by the attor-ney general to put together wording for the statute in the wake of the *Penry* ruling. He admitted to Senator Shoemaker that the language was confusing but that it was what was required in light of the "Penway" ruling. It might have inspired the committee with less than full confidence when the resident expert on the statute mispronounced the case name that provoked the statutory change, and when the chair of the committee was reluctant to change the statute just for the sake of English. In any case, the proposed language passed the committee unanimously and was sent on to a conference committee.

At a conference committee meeting on July 1, new language for the fourth question was approved. The fourth question as it would be codified now read:

> If constitutionally required, considering the extent to which the defendant's character and background, and the circumstances of the offense may reduce the defendant's moral culpability or blameworthiness for the crime, whether a sentence of death be imposed.[35]

Though this language did not address the concerns raised by Senator Shoemaker, there was no further discussion of the fourth issue in the Conference Committee on HB 2250. Representative Tom Mason, who was probably the only legislator to read the *Penry* decision, had other complaints about the proposed statute. His concern was with a proposed subsection 3 in which people who were sentenced to death under the old law would only be subject to resentencing if their cases were remanded by the Oregon Supreme Court. He was clearly troubled because he felt that the better remedy was a full retrial. But partly because of the case made by Virginia Linder about the cost savings involved with only a resentencing process, Mason reluctantly went along and voted for the change.[36]

One of the reasons that some of Mason's concerns were allayed was that he had consulted several times with Deputy Attorney General James Mountain in the intervening days. On July 1, Deputy Mountain wrote a letter to Senator Cohen and Representative Mason explaining once again the DOJ's rationale for seeking these statutory changes. In the letter he reiterated the DOJ's approach to the Oregon capital punishment statute—that it was facially constitutional.[37] He went on, however, to say that an additional procedure was constitutionally required in certain death penalty cases. Hence the language of the statute. He nowhere explains the word "certain," nor does he explain how a law which is facially constitutional requires additional language in order to meet constitutional requirements.

He went on to explain, in two revealing sentences, what really motivated the DOJ's concern:

> If the Oregon Supreme Court disagrees with our assessment of the facial constitutionality of the scheme, the amendments

will preserve the statute for future cases. The Department
believes that the death penalty laws should be preserved out
of respect for the people's overwhelming choice to establish a
constitutional death penalty scheme in Oregon.[38]

The heart of Deputy Mountain's case was that the DOJ wanted to "preserve"
the capital punishment statute. It wanted to preserve the statute out of respect
for the people of Oregon, who voted overwhelmingly to have such a statute.
But respect for the people and the constitutionality of a statute are not necessarily the same thing. People might desire a particular penalty for a crime, and
they might overwhelmingly vote to pass a law providing for such, but if the
United States Supreme Court says that such a penalty is unconstitutional, all
the respect in the world for the people of Oregon should not affect the law's
constitutionality. Indeed, respect for the people of Oregon was not even mentioned in the 1981 decision overturning the 1978 capital punishment statute
which had also passed by an overwhelming margin. Respect can influence
preservation of a law only if the law itself is constitutional in the first place.

Second, he said that even if the Oregon Supreme Court disagreed with
their assessment, the amendments "preserve" the statute. Presumably he meant
that if the supreme court says that the capital punishment law was unconstitutional, the good will or good effort of the legislature to update the law should
make it valid in future cases. This is tantamount to an admission by the DOJ
that if the Oregon Supreme Court found the law unconstitutional, the 22
people then on death row would have to be removed and resentenced, presumably, to life imprisonment.

The full contours of the DOJ's approach are now visible. They worked
out their approach under the constraints of the four questions propounded by
the Oregon Supreme Court through the state court administrator on June 28,
1989. The fundamental contradiction in the DOJ's position was that Oregon's
capital punishment statute was constitutional but had to be changed to reflect
a new constitutional requirement imposed by the U.S. Supreme Court in
Penry. If the Oregon Supreme Court disagreed with this assessment, the 22
men on death row would probably have to be resentenced to life imprisonment. However, since the DOJ believed the old statute to be constitutional
and because the statutory changes in 1989 were in accord with the requirements of *Penry*, the capital punishment statute would continue to be constitutional at the date of the passage of the amendments by the Oregon Legislature.[39] One therefore had a continually effective and constitutional statute,
despite the constitutional inadequacy of the original statute. Standing behind
the entire process, however, was "respect" for the people of Oregon. Respect,

according to the DOJ, should probably have something to do with finding the original statute constitutional.

Yet the fundamental contradiction cannot be overlooked or dismissed. It can be expressed once again as follows: Why is there so much urgency to make a change which is constitutionally required if the statute being changed is facially constitutional? If the change is constitutionally required, this must mean that the statute changed must be deficient without the change. If the statute is deficient without the change, then why not admit it? Perhaps the "respect" for the people of Oregon is more like a "fear" of what might happen if the legal authorities declare, for a second time, that the capital punishment law is unconstitutional. If the change in the law is not required, however, why should the attorney general's office have approached the subject with so much force and seriousness in their words and actions? The committee chairs acted as if they had no choice but to pass the measure. The U.S. Supreme Court had said so. They had to act. It was with this level of uncertainty and with this pressure for action that the DOJ answered the Oregon Supreme Court's questions and urged the compliant legislature to make desired changes. The Department of Justice, albeit in a contradictory fashion, had weighed in on the issue.

Endnotes

1　　*Penry v. Lynaugh*, 492 U.S. 302 (1989). An issue also discussed by the Court at length in the decision was whether the Eighth Amendment prohibition against the infliction of cruel and unusual punishment prohibited the execution of a mentally retarded person. The Court passed down no per se rule on the subject in this case. Each case was to be considered on its own merits.

2　　*Ibid.*, 309. These last two characteristics are what a defendant had to show traditionally to prove a defense of insanity.

3　　*Penry v. State*, 691 SW2d 636 (1985).

4　　*Penry v. Lynaugh*, 832 F2d 915 (1987).

5　　*Penry v. Lynaugh*, 492 U.S. at 322.

6　　*Ibid.*, 354 (Scalia, J., concurring in part and dissenting in part).

7　　*Ibid.*, 322. The phrase "reasoned moral response" is derived from *California v. Brown*, 479 U.S. at 545 (O'Connor, J., concurring). Justice O'Connor authored the majority opinion in *Penry*.

8　　*Vernon's Texas Statutes Annotated*, Code of Criminal Procedure, Art. 37.071(a) (West 1981).

9　　*Penry v. Lynaugh*, 492 U.S. at 315.

10　　*Ibid.*, 322.

11　　*Vernon's Texas Statutes Annotated*, Code of Criminal Procedure, Art. 37.071(b)(2) (West 1981).

12　　*Ibid.*, 324.

13　　*Vernon's Texas Statutes Annotated*, Code of Criminal Procedure, Art. 37.071((b)(3) (West 1981).

14　　492 U.S. 324.

15　　*Ibid.*, 326.

16　　492 U.S. 354 (Scalia, J., concurring in part and dissenting in part).

17　　The *Penry* case has had an interesting history. In 1989 the Court remanded the case to the Texas court because the jury instructions and deliberations at the original trial provided no meaningful vehicle for a reasoned moral response to Penry's mitigating evidence. A Texas jury resentenced him to death in 1990, a decision that was upheld by other appellate courts. The Supreme Court decided to hear the case again, and on June 4, 2001, remanded the case once again to Texas because the sentencing procedure in 1990 also provided an inadequate vehicle for the jury to make a reasoned moral choice on Penry's mitigating evidence. Inasmuch as Oregon's death penalty statute is derived from the Texas statute, it seems that the most recent *Penry* decision could result in a deluge of Oregon cases exploring whether juries in fact were given an adequate "vehicle" through the statute and jury instructions to give a "reasoned moral consideration" to all of a defendant's mitigating circumstances. Since there is already a cadre of Oregon lawyers who believe that the present Oregon death penalty statute is unconstitutional because it does not provide this vehicle, the recent *Penry* decision ought to add more fuel to their flame.

18　　The tapes of the committee debate on the issue reveal, in addition to the committee comments, personal asides that never make it into the committee minutes kept in the Oregon State Archives. One member of the House Judiciary Committee, an attorney, confessed to not having even looked at the case and asked the chair how he could have done so in "one hour." It can be safely said that no one on the Senate Judiciary Committee had even looked at, much less studied, the *Penry* decision by the time they adopted significant changes in Oregon's capital sentencing statute.

19　　One of the three attorneys was Philip Margolin, who has since left private practice to become a best-selling author of Oregon-based murder mysteries.

20　　Letter from Cecile Lyon, Supreme Court Administrator, June 28, 1989. In the exhibit file for HB 2250, 1989 Legislative Session, Oregon State Archives.

21   Attorney General Frohnmayer's testimony on June 29 is on Tape 255, Side A, Senate Judiciary Committee, 1989 Oregon Legislative Assembly, Oregon State Archives. Deputy Attorney General Mountain's letter is in the exhibit file for HB2250, 1989 Legislative Assembly, Oregon State Archives.

22   The statutory change suggested by the DOJ on June 29 would place a fourth question in the statute, but would not require that it be asked in every instance. It would only be asked "If constitutionally required." This three-word phrase raises questions that even skilled constitutional law specialists have a hard time articulating. Among them are: Does this mean that in some instances a fourth question might not be required? What are those instances? Can you spell them out with such specificity that a jury could easily understand them? If so, then why not spell them out in the statute? If not, then are you relying on circuit court judges to know the contours of all the possible exceptions before they can properly instruct a jury? And, then, what is a jury to do? If the experts think there is a distinction between some cases which may require a fourth question and some that may not but cannot explain this distinction very clearly, how is a jury to understand what that distinction is? And, since those three words are the first three words in the new statute, that means that they need to be answered before one can even go to the next fifty words of the question. If you can't answer this first question, how can you possibly expect a jury to answer the entire question? These are some of the issues that would be provoked by the phrase, "If constitutionally required."

23   It is not very clear what the last question of question 4 means. Does it mean that the court is considering the option of invalidating their death sentences so that the only option open to juries on resentencing would be life imprisonment?

24   The DOJ faced a genuine conundrum as a result of the *Penry* decision. It only had *Wagner I* and *Penry* for guidance. *Wagner I* held that the statute was constitutional while *Penry* called that claim into question. Before July 3, 1989, when the U.S. Supreme Court vacated *Wagner I*, the DOJ could be forgiven for trying to play both sides of the debate. Everyone, really, was groping in the dark.

25   Minutes of the meeting can be found in Senate Judiciary Committee Minutes, HB 2250, 1989 Legislative Assembly.

26   The attorney general's reference to the "facial" constitutionality of the Texas statute, upheld in *Penry*, was merely an aside in his remarks. No one could have picked up from his passing comment that this was the most important issue (question 1) for the Oregon Supreme Court. Perhaps if he had emphasized the constitutionality of the Oregon law, someone might have wanted to ask him about the urgency of his appearance in the waning days of the legislative session.

27   This bill, HB 3303, received a "Do Pass" recommendation from the committee on June 27 and would be passed by the full Senate on June 29. Or Laws 1989, ch. 720.

28   What does it mean that something "may" be required? It is or it isn't, right? Because Attorney General Frohnmayer urged the change, one can infer that he believed it was required. But this, of course, opens up the contradiction explored above.

29   The second change proposed, which would remove all the words relating to mitigation which were in the second question directed to the jury, ORS 163.150(1)(b)(B) and place them in a separate subsection (c) was described by Ms. Linder as "housekeeping." She meant by that word that the Oregon Supreme Court in *Wagner I* had construed the 1984 statute, which only explicitly tied mitigating circumstances to the second question or issue, to apply mitigating circumstances to all three issues. Therefore, by putting consideration of mitigating circumstances in a separate section, subsection (c), the legislature would be codifying what the court had decided in 1988. The third change was a fairly major one, and would result in the addition of 163.150(3)(1989) to the statute. That section represented the DOJ's answer to question 4 of the state court administrator's June 28, 1989 letter. The DOJ would want all cases decided under the 1984 statute before the *Penry* decision to be remanded for sentencing only, not for a new trial. The 1984 statute only allowed sentencing before the same jury which had convicted

the aggravated murderer. Therefore, a new section of law was needed to allow a new sentencing jury to either give a sentence of death or life imprisonment on remand. The reason that this section became section (3) of the law (ORS 163.150(3)(1989)) is that the legislature on June 29 had passed a long section (2) of the statute, allowing the sentence of life imprisonment without the possibility of parole. This was only to be applied to people whose trials began after the effective date of the act (July 19, 1989). Or Laws 1989, Ch. 720, sec.2, codified as ORS 163.150(2)(1989). These changes, taken together, represent massive changes in the structure of Oregon's death penalty statute.

30 This was the proposal given to the committee at 1: 30 p.m. that day. It differs from the one finally approved. Text may be found in the Original Bill Files, HB 2250–3, 6/29/89 Proposed Amendments, Oregon State Archives.

31 I have tried to be fair to her statement. She was obviously reading a prepared text. It is not clear that she was the one who had prepared the text. She was trying to capture more than ten years of United States Supreme Court precedents in this one, overlong sentence. Again, after reading this sentence, she went right on to discuss the second change that the DOJ was presenting on that date with scarcely a pause for breath.

32 There is no draft in the Original Bill files that has this language. But in the Senate Judiciary Committee Minutes, Senator Bob Shoemaker read the version of the fourth question before him in asking his question of Mr. Penn. The text that he read is what is cited here.

33 Tape 256, Side A, Senate Judiciary Committee, 1989 Legislative Assembly, Oregon State Archives. While Senator Shoemaker did not take apart the sentence phrase by phrase, he could not really get beyond the first three words without wondering what a jury was being asked to do. The words "If constitutionally required" are filled with so much unclarity that any juror who would be doing his or her job would be obliged to confess that he or she did not know what to do. The DOJ used these words, apparently, because it read the *Penry* case to require a fourth question in Penry's circumstances. The DOJ inferred, perhaps from a 1988 Texas capital punishment case in which the U.S. Supreme Court upheld Texas' procedure in that instance without mentioning a fourth question, that there were some cases based on Texas law that only required three questions and others that required four. Therefore, the constitution might not require four questions in every case. Hence the phrase, "If constitutionally required." Of course, no one seemed to know in the legislative hearing why those words were there but they seem to suggest such gravity and seriousness that an explanation of what they mean should have been required. The other Texas case decided by the United States Supreme Court was *Franklin v. Lynaugh,* 487 U.S. 164 (1988).

34 Those are her precise words. She seemed to suggest by this that the words were close enough to be constitutional, but her infelicitous choice of language ironically heightened the entire problem with the fast-tracking of this bill, that no one knew what was being said and that to change wording "for the sake of English" might not help at all. It speaks volumes about the pressure the committee chair was under to deliver to the DOJ a bill that they wanted.

35 ORS 163.150(1)(b)(D)(1989).

36 Tape 2, Side B, Conference Committee on HB 2250, 1989 Oregon Legislative Assembly, Oregon State Archives.

37 Letter from James Mountain, Deputy Attorney General, to the Honorable Tom Mason and the Honorable Joyce Cohen, July 1, 1989. Exhibit B, Conference Committee on HB 2250, Oregon State Archives.

38 *Ibid.,* 2.

39 This underscores the suggestion above that the DOJ was seeking a kind of "floating" constitutionality for the capital punishment statute that would impose the possibility of the death penalty on those convicted before 1989 though the statute had to be changed by the legislature in 1989.

CHAPTER 10

The Wagnerian Saga Continues

On Monday, July 3, 1989, the United States Supreme Court granted certiorari in the *Wagner* case on direct appellate review.[1] The U.S. Supreme Court only grants "cert" in about one percent of the cases submitted to it.[2] It almost never grants "cert" to death penalty cases on direct appeal. Because the prisoner has the opportunity to return later to the Court for habeas corpus relief, and because petitions for habeas corpus relief are the vehicles through which one can bring federal constitutional claims, the few death penalty cases the Supreme Court actually reviews are normally the result of a habeas corpus petition.

Usually a direct appeal of a death penalty case to the Supreme Court will be made within three months after an appellate judgment is entered in the state supreme court. The Supreme Court then rejects the appeal within six to nine months after that. In the *Wagner* case, the appeal was duly made in the required time after February 1988 but then was held by the Supreme Court because *Penry*, which implicated the identical Texas statute, had been submitted. Thus, when the Supreme Court handed down its decision in *Penry*, its decision in *Wagner I* would not be far behind. Instead of denying certiorari, the effect of which would be to let the decision of the Oregon Supreme Court stand as good law, the U.S. Supreme Court granted certiorari, as mentioned, but then immediately vacated the decision of the Oregon Supreme Court and remanded the case to Oregon for reconsideration in the light of *Penry*.[3]

By vacating *Wagner I*, the U.S. Supreme Court was saying that Oregon had erred in its decision. Like a good teacher who wants the student to discover the source of her mistake, however, the United States Supreme Court usually does not tell the state court why or how it erred. It just tells the court that it erred and lets it discover for itself how that is the case. In Oregon's case it could have been because the reasoning of the court in *Wagner I* was wrong, the statute on which the reasoning was based was defective, or both. When one considers: 1) that *Penry* held that the three special issues in Texas' capital sentencing statute were constitutionally insufficient to permit full jury consideration of mitigating circumstances in his case, and 2) that certiorari in *Wagner I* was seemingly granted in response to Justice Gillette's plea regarding mitigating circumstances, a logical inference could be drawn that both the reasoning of the Oregon Supreme Court *and* the Oregon statute were defective.[4] What we will see in *Wagner II*, surprisingly, is that the Oregon Supreme Court seemed to affirm *both* the constitutionality of the Oregon statute *and* the reasoning of the court in *Wagner I*.[5]

Wagner II

The Oregon Supreme Court heard oral arguments in *State v. Wagner* (*Wagner II*) on August 14, 1989, and handed down its decision on January 11, 1990.[6] If *Wagner I* was a model of discursiveness and comprehensiveness even though it was incorrectly decided, *Wagner II* was a model of brevity. The majority opinion only took 15 pages, and the dissent by Justice Linde, joined by Justice Fadeley, took another 15 pages. The court majority characterized the case as one of statutory interpretation, and so it spent about two-thirds of its time trying to interpret the statute in place at the time of Wagner's crime ORS 163.150(1985).[7] The opinion concludes with remarks about statutory changes made by legislative introduction of a fourth question in June/July 1989.[8]

The structure of the majority opinion is easy to follow. It states at the outset what the justices thought was the significant question presented by the U.S. Supreme Court's action:

> The first question before us is whether 163.150 (1987 Replacement Part) (in effect for defendant's trial and later amended as of July 24, 1989) permits the trial judge to submit to the sentencing jury a so-called "fourth question," i.e., a query whether the death penalty is appropriate for this defendant, considering all aspects of his life and crime.[9]

After a cursory examination of the text of ORS 163.150(1)(a)–(e), the court held that "on its face, the statute neither precludes nor permits a general mitigation question. Either rendering, then, of the statute can find support." Because of this, the justices figuratively rolled up their sleeves and decided they had to examine the text of the statute more closely.

A Fourth Question Not Precluded

When they did they discovered, first of all, that the statute did not preclude a fourth question. Even though the statute provided for the submission of three issues to the jury, which the court characterized as "two issues and one contingent issue," it nowhere stated that these three are the *only* issues that may be submitted to the jury. Indeed, the text of the statute before 1989 only provided for submission of mitigating circumstances in relation to future dangerousness (special issue 2), but the court had construed the statute in *Wagner I* to include submission of mitigating circumstances in relation to all three special issues.[10]

Emboldened by this expansive move in its statutory construction in *Wagner I*, the court then examined ORS 163.150(1)(e):

> If the jury returns an affirmative finding on each issue considered under this section, the trial judge shall sentence the defendant to death. If the jury returns a negative finding on any issue submitted under this section, the trial judge shall sentence the defendant to imprisonment for life.[11]

Although conceding that this provision is the closest the statute comes to precluding a fourth question, the court pressed on. The words "this section" do not refer solely to (1)(e) nor simply to (1)(b), which is referred to as a "subsection."[12] Therefore the word "section" has an expansive meaning and can relate to any subsection of the statute. Indeed, *Wagner I* recognized that ORS 163.150(1) must permit jury consideration of "any aspect of the defendant's character and record or any circumstances of his offense as an independently mitigating factor."[13] So, to discover if a full instruction on mitigating evidence is not precluded by the statute, one must look at the entire statute.

Reading the Entire Statute

The court then turned to its reading of the entire statute, ORS 163.150(1)(a)–(e)(1987), and concluded that as it stood before 1989 the statute permitted introduction of all constitutionally relevant mitigating evidence.[14] Key to its determination is the presence in ORS 163.150(1)(a) of words allowing presentation at the sentencing proceeding of any matter "that the court deems relevant to sentence."

> Thus far, the terms of the statute support a contention that the trial court has the authority to admit the broadest range

of mitigating evidence and that a defendant may argue to
the jury, based on that evidence, for a life sentence.[15]

Ignoring the fact that the U.S. Supreme Court had vacated the holding in
Wagner I, the court opined that its textual interpretation of ORS 163.150(1)(a)
was fully supported by the holding of *Wagner I*. So it appears that ORS
163.150(1)(a) was sufficient to include all evidence of mitigation that could
be brought up in defense of a capital punishment defendant.

Then the court changed gears a bit. It recognized that *Wagner I* was only
dealing with the constitutionality of the three statutory questions. However,
the U.S. Supreme Court was possibly talking about a fourth question or special issue as a result of *Penry*. The court then tipped its hat to the dissenters in
Wagner I, especially Justice Gillette, who had "read the federal precedents more
insightfully than did the court." Justice Gillette had realized that the federal
precedents could require something more. The Supreme Court in *Penry* "appears to have put its imprimatur on a fourth question," as one mechanism for
the sentencing jury to give consideration to the entire range of possible mitigating evidence.

After a long quotation from Justice Gillette's dissenting opinion in *Wagner
I*, the court held, in a sentence that does not resonate with clarity:

> [I]n view of what we have learned from *Penry*, it is now clear
> that mitigating evidence beyond the scope of the statutory
> issues is indeed constitutionally "relevant to sentence" and,
> accordingly statutorily admissible.[16]

Does that mean that the general jury instruction in ORS 163.150(1)(a),
to consider all relevant evidence in sentencing, means that those words alone
are enough to permit any question in mitigation? Or does it mean that the
current three questions are not sufficient but that a fourth is required? The
court's lack of clarity seems to be related, as will be argued below, to the same
contradiction which enmeshed the DOJ.

A Fourth Question Permitted

After concluding that mitigating evidence beyond the scope of the statutory issues was statutorily admissible, the court went on to conclude that ORS
163.150(1987) permits a general mitigation question. It has been a rule of
hoary age that a jury is charged with the responsibility of considering all relevant evidence, therefore juries in capital punishment cases must also consider
all relevant evidence. Evidence in mitigation is one form of relevant evidence.

The federal constitution requires admission of all mitigating evidence and the Oregon statute permits it. The holding follows:

> We hold that, in such circumstances, the trial court has the statutory authority under ORS 163.150(1), (and the constitutional responsibility if the facts require it[17]), to submit to the sentencing jury a fourth question, in response to which the sentencing jury may spare a defendant from the death penalty, notwithstanding an affirmative finding on the issues listed in subsection (1)(b) of the statute.[18]

So is the Oregon statute, ORS 163.150 (1987), constitutional? In the court's view, yes. If the U.S. Supreme Court wants to overrule *Jurek*, it is welcome to do so. It has not done so. Therefore, *Jurek* is still good law. Since *Wagner I* was based on *Jurek*, and *Wagner I* held ORS 163.150 (1987) to be facially constitutional, the statute is still constitutional today.[19] This was the same argument that the Oregon Supreme Court made in *Wagner I*, which most people would have naturally thought was overruled when the U.S. Supreme Court vacated the judgment on July 3, 1989.

Rewriting the Statute

The Oregon Supreme Court was not yet finished. How should one consider the legislative changes in the 1989 Legislative Assembly? Now, according to ORS 163.150 (1989) the jury must answer four questions and not the three of the 1987 statute. The court had problems with the legislative language passed a few months previously. The statutory language for the fourth question now provided:

> If constitutionally required, considering the extent to which the defendant's character and background, and the circumstances of the offense may reduce the defendant's moral culpability or blameworthiness for the crime, whether a sentence of death be imposed.[20]

The court majority expressed its befuddlement at the words. The sentence, it opined, lacked grammatical clarity. Because of the importance of making sure that juries receive clear guidance in the sentencing process, however, the court would alter the wording of the statute.[21] But it gave the impression that it was not altering the statute. It said it was only giving a suggested jury instruction that may be given but need not be. The sentence wasn't clear, but it was clear enough, apparently, for the supreme court to say that its suggested jury instruction would be "consistent" with the statutory language. The new "suggested" language in place of the statutory fourth question was:

> Should defendant receive a death sentence? You should an-
> swer this question "no" if you find that there is any aspect of
> defendant's character or background, or any circumstances
> of the offense, that you believe would justify a sentence less
> than death.[22]

The statutory words were ungrammatical and unclear, and so the court decided it would lend its hand to the process of shaping the fourth question. What was not particularly clear, however, was whether the Oregon Supreme Court was striking down the fourth question, passed by the legislature in 1989, or only giving interpretive guidance on how that question should be presented, rewriting the statute, or doing all or none of these things. In any case, the final word of the majority of the Oregon Supreme Court in *Wagner II* was that the old statute, ORS 163.150(1987), was facially constitutional and that the new 1989 statute had some problems.[23]

Criticisms of *Wagner II*

Justice Hans Linde, in his last month on the Oregon Supreme Court, issued a stinging dissent, calling the majority opinion "unworthy of this court and of this state."[24] He excoriated the majority for taking extraordinary measures to resuscitate an unconstitutional statute and for failing in its duty not to extend the death penalty law beyond its exact terms. Though several of his criticisms are consistent with those offered here, I prefer to present five easily identifiable major shortcomings of the decision which, in my judgment, should lead the Oregon Supreme Court to revisit whether it still thinks that *Wagner II* was correctly decided.

Ignoring United States Supreme Court Precedents

First, the Oregon Supreme Court's style of analysis is not one that the United States Supreme Court would have recognized. Ever since *Lockett* in 1978, the Supreme Court had been moving toward full consideration of mitigating circumstances, both in explicit statutory provision and in jury instructions. The U.S. Constitution required this kind of explicitness in 1989. This was a significant development from *Jurek* in 1976 and was a development of constitutional proportions.

Instead of using the language of constitutional requirements and explicit statutory provision, however, the Oregon Supreme Court in 1990 used the threefold framework of "not precluding," "general permission," and then "specific permission." It looked at the 1987 statute as if it were some kind of balloon that could be blown up to become much larger than it was. Because the law did not preclude all mitigating measures, and because it permitted them, it must contain them. The small acorn may grow into the towering oak, and the Oregon Supreme Court's jurisprudential theory was that the acorn already was the oak. The Oregon law was a statutory Zelig,[25] infinitely expandable to meet the need of the moment. It was not important that only three issues were provided for in the earlier statute. The statute could expand to contain four.

In order to get to this point the court had to read the general language of ORS 163.150(1)(a) to allow all evidence of mitigation of whatever proportions in considering the special issues. To see the nature of their statutory method, it is necessary to quote the relevant portions of the first section of the statute in place before the legislative changes of 1989.

> (1)(a) Upon a finding that the defendant is guilty of aggravated murder, the court shall conduct a separate sentencing proceeding to determine whether the defendant shall be sentenced to life imprisonment or death. The proceeding shall be conducted before the trial jury as soon as practicable.... *In the proceeding, evidence may be presented as to any matter that the court deems relevant to sentence;...*
> (b) Upon the conclusion of the presentation of the evidence, the court shall submit the following issues to the jury:
> (A) Whether the conduct of the defendant that caused the death of the deceased was committed deliberately and with the reasonable expectation that death of the deceased or another would result;
> (B) Whether there is a probability that the defendant would commit criminal acts of violence that would constitute a continuing threat to society. In determining this issue, the court shall instruct the jury to consider any mitigating circumstances offered in evidence, including, but not limited to, the defendant's age, the extent and severity of the defendant's prior criminal conduct and the extent of the mental and emotional pressure under which the defendant was acting at the time the offense was committed; and
> (C) If raised by the evidence, whether the conduct of the defendant in killing the deceased was unreasonable in response to the provocation, if any, of the deceased.

(c) The state must prove each issue submitted beyond a reasonable doubt, and the jury shall return a special verdict of 'yes' or 'no' on each issue considered.

(d) The court shall charge the jury that it may not answer any issue 'yes' unless it agrees unanimously.

(e) If the jury returns an affirmative finding on each issue considered under this section, the trial judge shall sentence the defendant to imprisonment for life in the custody of the Department of Corrections as provided in ORS 163.105.

In fact, it is the italicized words in subsection (a) that seem to be the catalyst to enable the court to get around the point that only three issues are to be submitted to the jury in subsection (b). An expansive reading of (a) permits anything in mitigation to be presented. This is the holding of the Oregon Supreme Court despite the contrary holding of the U.S. Supreme Court, that a general relevancy instruction in the first part of the statute cannot make up for deficiency in the second part, and the point in *Penry* that it was the explicit words of the three special issues that drove the U.S. Supreme Court's consideration of whether they were broad enough to accommodate the facts of Penry's situation.[26] The Oregon Supreme Court has improperly leveraged subsection (a) to permit more than subsection (b) on its face permits.

Improper Construction of the Statute

Second, the specific statutory construction of the Oregon Supreme Court isn't constitutional. To be more specific, the court is correct for the wrong reason on one issue and wrong on another issue. The court used a very technical textual argument to get to the point that Oregon's capital punishment statute permitted consideration of all mitigating circumstances. It argued that the word "section" in (1)(e) ("each issue considered under this section") meant the entire ORS 163.150(1) and not simply (1)(e).[27] It noted that the word "section" in (1)(e) does not by its terms refer only to (1)(e), but also seems to include (1)(b) and (1)(a). (1)(a) and (1)(b) are referred to as "subsections," and so the word "section" in (1)(e) must refer to a larger portion of text than the word "subsection." Hence, it *does not preclude* a reference to all of ORS 163.150(1). If one brings all of ORS 163.150(1) under the word "section," one also has to see that (1)(a) talks about admission of all evidence "relevant to sentence." Therefore, the "each issue considered under this section" of (1)(e) *does not preclude* its relation to all evidence "relevant to sentence" in (1)(a). Since all evidence "relevant to sentence" *permits* all evidence in mitigation, one seems to have a strong textual chain supporting the expansive argument of the court.

This argument, however, is chimerical. The court is correct that the word "section" in (1)(e) refers to all of ORS 163.150(1) but its reason for it is wrong. The word "section" in (1)(e) refers to the placement of this portion of the statute in the initiative petition submitted to the voters in 1984. The language of the initiative petition approved by the voters in 1984 was published in the 1985 *Oregon Session Laws*.[28] The law as originally passed by the voters in 1984 contained eight sections. The section that eventually was codified at ORS 163.150 was section 3 of the 1984 initiative petition and is section 3 of the 1985 *Oregon Session Laws*. Therefore, when any reference was made in section 3 of the 1984 initiative petition to this "section" it was referring to section 3 of the initiative petition. Section 3 of the petition contained the entire law later codified at ORS 163.150. The reference to "section" in (1)(e) therefore refers to the entire statute.

But on the important issue, the court is incorrect. It argued that "each issue under this section" in (1)(e) by its terms related back to (1)(a) to include all evidence "relevant to sentence," which includes all evidence of mitigation. One needs to become as technical as the court to see that this is not so. Sub-section (1)(e) allows consideration of each *issue* under this section (all of ORS 163.150(1)). The language of (1)(a) speaks of relevant evidence that could be presented under each *matter*. It is only in (1)(b) that the statute speaks of *issues*. When the statute speaks of *issues*, it speaks of three issues and three issues alone—deliberateness, future dangerousness and provocation. As a matter of fact, the text of the statute argues precisely against what the Oregon Supreme Court maintained. The *only* place that issues are considered is in (1)(b). The only way that mitigation evidence can be taken into consideration, then, is in respect to an *issue*. By its terms, then, the statute does not permit mitigation evidence on the basis of (1)(a).

Illogical Results of the Statutory Construction

Third, the use of the phrase "does not preclude" as the first step in its argument that ORS 163.150(1) *permits* and thus *contains* a fourth question is fraught with further difficulties. It strains one's credulity and it proves rather too much. One may use an example from education to illustrate the straining of credulity. Suppose for a moment that one had a professor in college who gave a syllabus to the class at the beginning of the semester and on the syllabus was the statement: "Class Meetings: M-W-F at 2: 00." After handing out the syllabus, the professor then said, "I want you students to know that just because I listed the class as a M-W-F class, I am not precluded by those words from holding the class Tuesday or Thursday on a regular basis. Indeed, since Monday and Friday are the first and last days of the week, the very reference to

M-W-F permits this practice. As a matter of fact, the designation M-W-F actually contains Tuesday and Thursday and so you can expect to meet any day of the week I want." The students would look at each other in bemusement and know that it is the professor who was not clear on what he was trying to say. Their reaction would have been, "You are the professor and you can hold class when you want, but this argument about precluding and permitting when you could just have said what was required is laughable. It just does not make sense. Are you trying to use last year's syllabus for this year's purpose?"

But the worse problem for the Oregon Supreme Court's argument is that it proves too much. If ORS 163.150(1) does not on its face preclude a fourth question, it also does not preclude a fifth question and a sixth question and a 48th question. If it does not preclude but actually permits a fourth question to consider other aspects of mitigation, why not include a fifth question that would negate the first question in some way? And a sixth question to negate the second question? One could imagine six impossible thoughts before breakfast and include them all as questions that were not precluded by the silence of the statute. Once a court begins to argue that a statute may include what the text gives no warrant for including, it has no logical principal to disallow its inclusion of other things. The supreme court's argument on "does not preclude," "permits" and "contains" has no logical stopping place.

Laboring with a Contradiction

Fourth, the court experienced the same problem that dogged the DOJ in its presentation to the Oregon Legislature on June 29, 1989. That is, it had to argue both for the constitutionality of the old statute and the constitutional necessity of changing the statute. Both ends of this contradiction are apparent in the decision. On the one hand, using its "does not preclude," "permits" and "contains" argument, the court held that the old statute remained constitutional. This should have been difficult enough to say persuasively on June 29, 1989, but almost impossible to do convincingly on January 11, 1990. By holding the old (pre-1989) statute constitutional, the Oregon Supreme Court gave no indication that it had responded in any real way to the *Penry* decision of June 26, 1989, or the vacating of its *Wagner I* opinion on July 3, 1989. What did the court think that the vacating of its *Wagner I* opinion meant if not that the reasoning was faulty, the statute defective, or both? So it doggedly held to the constitutionality of a probably discredited statute.

But it did so inconsistently. It said that Justice Michael Gillette had more insightfully read the federal precedents (from 1978 to 1987) and that the federal constitution "could require more" than the old statute permitted.[29] The mere fact that the justices engaged in rewriting the statute passed by the

1989 legislature suggested that the Oregon Supreme Court felt that it was very important for future cases to have clear jury instructions that passed constitutional muster in capital sentencing cases. Indeed, if the old statute was all that was needed, why even turn to consider the work of the 1989 legislature? Since the linchpin of the constitutionality of the statute was the jury's ability to consider all evidence relevant to sentence (ORS 163.150(1)(a)), why even care what the rest of the statute said?

Improper Rewriting of the Statute

Fifth, when one turns to the supreme court's analysis of the 1989 legislative changes, one is left with the eerie sense that the court isn't sure if it is passing judgment on the constitutionality of a new statute, striking it down, upholding it but simply "construing" it in a more grammatically acceptable fashion, or only giving generic advice to lower courts which they were free to accept or reject regarding sentencing in capital sentencing cases.

The 1989 legislature provided for a fourth question, in some cases, in the following words that we have already seen a few times:

> If constitutionally required, considering the extent to which the defendant's character and background, and the circumstances of the offense may reduce the defendant's moral culpability or blameworthiness for the crime, whether a sentence of death be imposed.[30]

The justices said that they were frankly unable to understand the provision grammatically. Since they were conscious of the need for clear direction from the legislature and the courts on the statutory and constitutional mandates in a death penalty case, they would change the wording.[31] But, what did they think they were doing when they changed the wording? It appears that this newly passed statute only functioned for the supreme court as a suggested jury instruction that could be molded by them in accordance with their desires.

But then another contradiction emerges. The court said that the lack of grammatical clarity made the fourth question unintelligible to them, but that they would rewrite it consistently with its meaning. But, if the meaning of the original words is unintelligible, how can you rewrite it consistently without falling prey to that same unintelligibility? Does that mean that they thought they would likewise give an unintelligible product? Presumably not, but if the fourth question was unintelligible to them, how could they understand it well enough to suggest an alternative wording both clear and consistent with the unintelligible statute?

In any case, the court decided it had to rewrite the words of ORS 163.150(1)(b)(D). It never mentioned what authority it had to rewrite the words.[32] The justices appeared to think that they were merely construing the words, or interpreting them consistently with the legislative intent. But if that is what they thought they were doing, why did they give alternative wording that is in quotation marks and is clearly meant to *substitute* for the statute and not *construe* the statute? And, where does their authority come from to change the text of the statute? Isn't that a legislative prerogative? Nevertheless, the Oregon Supreme Court rewrote the statute to replace this fourth question with the following:

> Should defendant receive a death sentence? You should an-
> swer this question 'no' if you find that there is any aspect of
> defendant's character or background, or any circumstances
> of the offense, that you believe would justify a sentence less
> than death.[33]

Yet in rewriting the statute, the court said that this instruction may (but need not) be given to the jury. So, it appears that their rewriting of the statute has authority if the lower courts want it to have authority. Now the supreme court seems to be in the business of rewriting statutes and making them optional. Once one starts down the slippery slope of broad construal, where one can find mitigating circumstances where none are mentioned, perhaps it is not too much of a leap to start writing statutes that are optional.

A plausible explanation for the court's confusion regarding what they were doing with this section of the statute, ORS 163.150(1)(b)(D)(1989), is that they had entitled this subsection (or is it a section?) of their opinion, "Procedural Applications." In legal jargon, "procedural" is often contrasted with "substantive." A procedural rule is sometimes characterized as "merely" procedural whereas a substantive rule gets to the heart of what the statute means. Perhaps the court called this section "procedural applications" because they wanted to give the impression that procedural issues were less important than substantive ones. They had just done the "heavy lifting" in the earlier sections of the opinion; now they could dispense more quickly with the "lighter" issues.

Yet even if this is a correct explanation for their almost incomprehensible treatment of ORS 163.150(1)(b)(D)(1989), it would not excuse it. What never seemed to dawn on the court in the "procedural applications" section of the opinion is that they were dealing with a statute. Courts can find statutes unconstitutional or constitutional, they can construe them narrowly or broadly, they can limit their application in a number of ways but they cannot substantially rewrite statutes because of grammatical unclarity. Justice Hans Linde said it best,

> Here we deal not with evidence, procedure, or even instructions, but with the substance of the statutory test for life or death.[34]

What the Oregon Supreme Court failed to realize in *Wagner II* is that they usurped the legislative function by rewriting the statute in a substantive way.

CODA

The clearest and most honest response to all of this would be for the Oregon Supreme Court to revisit *Wagner II*. Justice Robert Durham has urged his colleagues unsuccessfully, thus far, to do so.[35] If the court chooses to do so, it could make a number of observations which it did not make in 1988–1990 that would help it base its death penalty jurisprudence on a credible decision. In accordance with the argument developed in this book, the Oregon Supreme Court should take cognizance of how the U.S. Supreme Court's jurisprudence of mitigating measures expanded from 1978 to 1987. The court should not focus so exclusively and obsessively, as it did in *Wagner I* and *Wagner II*, on whether the U.S. Supreme Court had explicitly overruled *Jurek*. Like the Oregon Supreme Court, the U.S. Supreme Court is reluctant to overrule its precedents if it does not have to do so. Because of the large number of cases expanding the notion of mitigating circumstances, the U.S. Supreme Court need not rely on *Jurek* when it considers mitigating measures. It has other arrows in its quiver.

The Oregon Supreme Court should revisit the question of what the *Penry* decision required of the court in 1989. The *Penry* decision was too fresh for the 1989 legislature to have been able to do anything constructive about it. Their hastily passed fourth question was an attempt to respond to the turmoil that *Penry* caused, but it really was nothing more than a crude attempt, given extreme pressure, to fashion an appropriate response to an influential case. They should not be faulted for that attempt.

When the Oregon Supreme Court revisits the question of what the *Penry* decision required, it should do so by asking the question of what it meant that the U.S. Supreme Court vacated *Wagner I* on July 3, 1989. I argued above that vacating a decision means that either the reasoning or the statute or both were inadequate. Because *Penry* had to do with the constitutionality of full consideration of mitigating circumstances, Oregon's reexamination of its statute and its reasoning in *Wagner I* should focus on those points. It would probably be to Oregon's benefit to conclude that both the reasoning of *Wagner I* and the statute itself were faulty.

This kind of conclusion may not have been possible for the Oregon Supreme Court to reach in 1988 and 1990. The pace of the court, understood by only a few, the change in court personnel, the relative freshness of the *Penry* decision, may not have permitted the kind of thoughtful reflection that should have gone into *Wagner II*. Now with the perspective of time, the court might well conclude that it was hasty and misguided in its 1990 decision.

The result of this reconsideration of *Wagner II* may, as suggested here, lead to the conclusion that Oregon in fact did not have a constitutional death penalty statute after the *Penry* decision and the vacating of *Wagner I*. The issues which a jury could consider were the same issues as a Texas jury could consider. These three issues were held constitutionally deficient. A fourth issue was one way to solve the constitutional dilemma. Yet to claim that the fourth issue was required but that the old statute was perfectly fine is an exercise of intellectual duplicity that simply will not stand. The old statute was constitutionally infirm in 1989 and, as will be shown in the next chapter, this infirmity was not corrected until the legislature revised ORS 163.150 again in the 1991 Legislative Assesmbly.

The bottom line with this kind of analysis is that the men convicted of aggravated murder and sentenced to death before the passage of a constitutional death penalty statute in 1991 may very well have been improperly sentenced to death. This includes a list of about ten men.[36] Therefore, the reconsideration of *Wagner II* is not simply for the sake of trying to make sure that significant areas of Oregon law are supported by cases with convincing rationales, but is for the sake of the lives of almost a dozen men. The argument of this chapter is that if these men were put to death on the basis of the statute in place in 1989, buttressed by the reasoning of *Wagner II*, a miscarriage of justice would have occurred. *Wagner II*, in the words of Justice Linde, is not worthy of the Oregon Supreme Court or of the citizens of Oregon.[37]

Endnotes

1   492 U.S. 914 (1989). Since the U.S. Supreme Court would immediately vacate the decision of the Oregon Supreme Court, it did not need to hear oral arguments to reach its decision. A grant of certiorari essentially means that the U.S. Supreme Court accepts jurisdiction in the case, a prerequisite to judging the merits of a case.

2   The number of cases granted certiorari is slightly larger than the number heard at oral argument. The Supreme Court can issue a per curiam decision without oral argument, or may summarily affirm or overturn a lower court decision in the light of another case. This latter course was the one followed by the Supreme Court on July 3, 1989. The Supreme Court's docket usually includes about 7,000 cases per year, with a majority of those on its "in forma pauperis" docket. That means that the majority of people who appeal to the Supreme Court are impoverished or in prison. It has been a rare year under the leadership of Chief Justice William Rehnquist when the Supreme Court has heard more than 100 oral arguments in a term.

3   *Wagner v. Oregon* 492 U.S. 914 (1989).

4   "Constitutionally insufficient" means that the then-current sentencing scheme in Texas, where three special issues were submitted, was a violation of the "cruel and unusual punishment" clause of the Eighth Amendment to the United States Constitution.

5   Former Chief Justice Edwin Peterson, the author of *Wagner II*, stresses that the reason the Oregon Supreme Court felt it erred in *Wagner I* was that they had, in that case, erroneously limited the reach of the Oregon statute with respect to mitigating measures. That is, in *Wagner I* the court had construed the statute to include three mitigating measures and three alone. The *Penry* decision required the application of mitigating circumstances to four issues. Hence, the issue the Oregon Supreme Court had to deal with in *Wagner II* was whether the statute as construed in *Wagner I* was also broad enough to include a fourth special issue. Under this reading of the U.S. Supreme Court's decision to vacate *Wagner I*, the Oregon Supreme Court would see their *Wagner I* decision as characterized by *too narrow* a construal of the statute. My presentation in Chapter Eight argues that *Wagner I* already took too many interpretive liberties with the statute by construing mitigating circumstances, which the statute tied to the second question, to all three questions. Interview with Justice Peterson, 24 November 1999.

6   *State v. Wagner,* 309 Or 5, 786 P2d 93 (1990) (Linde, J. dissenting).

7   *Ibid.,* 5–16.

8   *Ibid.,* 17–20.

9   *Ibid.,* 7.

10   The majority of the court never seemed to consider that the United States Supreme Court may have objected to this kind of statutory interpretation. It is fairly radical to hold that a particular feature (mitigation) which is tied to one part of a process (determination of future dangerousness) can be applied to every aspect of the process simply because the court so construes it. This kind of statutory analysis would not be permissible before the court in 2001, because the rule of *PGE v. BOLI,* 317 Or 606, 859 P2d 1143 (1993), is in place. In *PGE* the emphasis is on method of statutory interpretation and most attention is devoted to ascertaining the meaning of the words in their particular statutory context. The contemporary Oregon Supreme Court would be skeptical of taking a word that is embedded in one context, to refer to one thing and removing it to another context without clear legislative signals in the text of the statute that this is what the legislature intended. For a searching criticism of the *PGE* framework, see Jack L. Landau, "Some Observations about Statutory Construction in Oregon," 32 *Willamette Law Review* 1 (1996).

11   ORS 163.150(1)(e)(1987) quoted in *State v. Wagner,* 309 Or 10, 786 P2d 93.

12   *Ibid.* The full text of the ORS 163.150(1)(a)–(e) is provided below in my critique of the court's reasoning and decision.

13   *State v. Wagner*, 305 Or. 160, 752 P2d 1136 (1988).
14   *State v. Wagner*, 309 Or. 11, 786 P2d 93.
15   *Ibid.*, 12.
16   *Ibid.*, 14.
17   The Oregon Supreme Court seems to be making the distinction that the DOJ made before the Oregon Legislature in 1989, which no one explained and no one questioned, that some cases would only require three special issues to be considered (like that of Franklin, in Texas) but in some cases (like that of Penry) four special issues were constitutionally required. By putting this nebulous qualification in parentheses, the supreme court was adding to the air of unreality surrounding the three words, "if constitutionally required." Who makes that determination? Is it the judge or the jury? Because it relates to the "facts" of the case, and since the jury is the ultimate judge of the facts, it would seem that the jury would make this determination. But where are the standards? Because the court seems to want to be solicitous of juries, why doesn't it give juries some advice of which cases require four issues to be considered and which cases require only three? It may not be clear to the court what it means by its statement in parentheses.
18   *Sta\te v. Wagner*, 309 Or 16, 786 P2d 93 (1990).
19   Chief Justice Peterson emphasized that in upholding the "old" ORS 163.150 in *Wagner II*, the Oregon Supreme Court was motivated by the classic principle of statutory construction—that a court ought to construe a statute as constitutional, insofar as it is possible. When in doubt, conclude that a statute is constitutional. While this generally may be good judicial practice, it seems that in the area of death penalty jurisprudence it is not a particularly helpful method because it allows for so much slippage in the interpretation of the statute that the potential for real injustice can result. Because of the uniqueness of the penalty of death, the legislature and the courts owe it to those defendants and their attorneys to flesh out the statutory language as much as possible so that one won't be left with an endless chain of construals that can, as happened in Oregon, construe mitigation in only the second question to refer to all three questions, and then, by further construal, have it refer to a possible fourth question which the statute itself did not provide. The quest to preserve the statute at all costs, which this method encourages, gives the subtle (or not so subtle) message to the legislature that it does not have to take much care in crafting statutes. The courts will "take care" of their shortcomings. Therefore, while the principle has power in the abstract, its applicability to death penalty statutes ought to be very limited. Interview, 24 November 1999.
20   ORS 163.150.(1)(b)(D)(1989).
21   *State v. Wagner*, 109 Or 18–19, 786 P2d 93.
22   *Ibid.*, 19.
23   It is interesting that the court never came out and said the words in 1990 (*Wagner II*) that ORS 163.150 (1987) was facially constitutional. It said that it had determined that the statute was facially unconstitutional in 1988 (*Wagner I*) and decided in 1990 to "adhere" to that decision. It is less than a ringing endorsement of the statute.
24   *State v. Wagner*, 309 Or 21, 786 P2d 93 (Linde, J., dissenting).
25   Zelig refers to the title character in Woody Allen's movie who, because of his personal feelings of inadequacy and eagerness to be accepted by all people he met, could infinitely grow or shrink to approximate the size of the person with whom he was speaking.
26   *Penry v. Lynaugh*, 492 U.S. 322–28.
27   *State v. Wagner*, 309 Or 10, 786 P2d 93.
28   Or Laws 1985, ch. 3, 21–23.
29   *State v. Wagner*, 309 Or 13, 786 P2d 93.
30   ORS 163.150(1)(b)(D)(1989).
31   *State v. Wagner*, 309 Or 18, 786 P2d 93.

32   Indeed, it may not have had authority. "In the construction of a statute, the office of the judge is simply to ascertain and declare what is, in terms or in substance, contained therein, not to insert what has been omitted, or to omit what has been inserted; and where there are several provisions or particulars such construction is, if possible, to be adopted as will give effect to all." ORS 174.010.

33   *Ibid.*, 19.

34   *Ibid.*, 28 (Linde, J., dissenting).

35   In *State v. Montez*, 324 Or 343, 927 P2d 64 (1996), Justice Durham argued in a lengthy footnote some of the points urged above. He said, "*Penry* dictates the conclusion that ORS 163.150(1)(b)(1985) likewise is unconstitutional and that, in 1987, Oregon had enacted no valid statute authorizing a death sentence. In *Wagner II,* a majority of this court evaded that conclusion by purporting to construe ORS 163.150(1)(b)(1985) to require the court to impose a death sentence despite the statute's constitutional defect…. In the author's view, the court should reconsider *Wagner II.*" 342 Or 346, n. 5.

36   I say "about" because some men such as Dallas Ray Stevens, Michael McDonnell, Dayton Leroy Rogers and Robert Langley, who have been on death row and may yet return there, are currently either in general population at the Oregon State Penitentiary or in their local county jails awaiting a new sentencing trial. Apart from these four men, this argument would affect Jesse Pratt, Marco Montez, Mark Pinnell, Jeffrey Williams, David Simonsen and Randy Guzek. All of these men committed their crimes leading to the death penalty before July 1991, when the revised version of ORS 163.150 went into effect.

37   *State v. Wagner,* 309 Or 20.

CHAPTER 11

Developments from 1991 to 2001

Oregon's odyssey with its capital punishment sentencing statute was destined not to end in 1989. The legislature returned to it in 1991 and wrote three more changes into ORS 163.150.[1] The remainder of this chapter will assume that after the 1991 changes Oregon's death penalty law was constitutional. It may well not be, but that is a topic beyond the scope of this book.[2]

In 1993 the statute went unchanged. But then, like an antique car aficionado who simply cannot keep his hands off his 1928 Bentley, the legislature introduced more changes into the law in the 1995, 1997 and 1999 legislative sessions.[3] The 1995 and 1997 changes were largely driven by the triumph in Oregon of the victims' rights movement and its effort to make sure that victim impact evidence was admissible and considered by the jury in deciding whether to put a person to death.[4] A recent decision by the Oregon Court of Appeals, written by Paul DeMuniz who has recently been elected to the Oregon Supreme Court, brings into question whether the victim impact evidence in the penalty phase of a capital sentencing trial is constitutional.[5]

This final chapter on law will discuss briefly the significant changes to Oregon's capital sentencing statute since the 1989 Legislative Assembly. It will then introduce the remainder of the men on death row in Oregon so that the reader can understand who is on death row today and where they are in the ten-step process described in Chapters Four and Five. Finally, this chapter will conclude with a presentation of some of the tragedy, confusion and even wonder that some of the current cases have presented. Though each case has its own special character, the cases of Conan Wayne Hale, Cesar Barone, Alberto Reyes-Camarena, Dallas Ray Stevens and Scott Harberts bring unique dimensions.[6]

Legislative Changes to ORS 163.150

When the legislature convened in 1991 it was asked to make several changes in Oregon's death penalty law. All the changes were presented in House bill 2393, which was referred to the House Judiciary Committee by the Speaker on January 17.[7] Interestingly enough, HB 2393 as originally drafted did not contain any changes to the "fourth question" of ORS 163.150(1)(b) that had been passed with so much haste at the end of the 1989 session and then changed, apparently, by the Oregon Supreme Court in *Wagner II*.[8] The bill as originally presented had to do both with the post-conviction and capital sentencing processes.

The bill proposed a change in ORS 138.580 that would require post-conviction petitioners to raise all issues on which they had claimed relief in their first petitions, thereby waiving any other issues that might arise later.[9] It proposed a change in ORS 138.650, which was resurrected also in 1999, that would skip Step 4 of the process described above by eliminating any court of appeals role in the post-conviction consideration of death penalty cases. It also proposed additions to ORS 163.150 relating to the details of the sentencing process after a remand from the Oregon Supreme Court and the problem of a juror who sat on the panel in the guilt phase of a capital trial but needed to be excused from penalty phase considerations.

All of these changes made it successfully out of the House and were referred to the Senate Judiciary Committee in March 1991. The first two changes were quickly quashed, the first on constitutional grounds and the second after an appearance and testimony by Supreme Court Chief Justice Wallace Carson stating that the court was unanimously opposed to the idea. It was not until June 1991 that the committee began to tinker with the fourth question. This was done at the prodding of Senator Bob Shoemaker who, the reader will recall, was interrupted by the chair in the 1989 session and chided for wanting to change the fourth question "just for the sake of English."

The Senate Judiciary Committee changed the fourth question in a way that conformed largely to the wording of the *Wagner II*. Instead of making a long fourth question, however, the fourth question approved by the committee and ultimately codified into law simply stated: "whether the defendant should receive a sentence of death."[10] Then the legislature added many of the remaining words of Justice Gillette's original fourth question to a separate subsection in ORS 163.150(1)(c). That new provision read:

> In determining the issue in subparagraph (D) of paragraph (b) of this subsection, the court shall instruct the jury to answer the question "no" if one or more of the jurors find there is any aspect of the defendant's character or background, or any circumstances of the offense, that one or more of the jurors believe would justify a sentence less than death.[11]

At the end of the 1991 Legislative Assembly, Oregonians had a capital sentencing statute that looked as follows, in relevant part: In ORS 163.150(1)(a) one had the general instructions to the court on how to proceed in the sentencing phase portion of a capital punishment trial. This section was originally (in 1984) 22 lines in length but had grown to 40 lines by 1991.[12] It was the phrase "relevant to sentence" in this subsection that the Oregon Supreme Court fixed upon in *Wagner II* in holding that the statute permits consideration of all mitigating evidence in a sentencing phase of a capital punishment trial.

The Oregon Revised Statute 163.150(1)(b) provided for the four special issues or statutory questions that a jury was to answer before sentencing a person to death. Originally (in 1984) this subsection only had three questions or issues to present to the jury, but the *Penry* decision as interpreted in Oregon led to the creation of a fourth constitutionally required issue. The fourth issue was added because the *Penry* court held that the three issues in the Texas statute, which Oregon copied, were not sufficient to permit consideration of all mitigating evidence in Penry's case. Therefore, when the Oregon Legislature added the fourth issue or question in 1989 and revised it in 1991, the fourth issue was a "mitigation" issue. It was added to allow consideration of all evidence that might mitigate a sentence of death.

The Oregon Revised Statute 163.150(1)(c)(1989) became a new section in 1989 as a result of the Oregon Supreme Court's decision in *Wagner I*.[13] In that case, the court "construed" the mitigation language that had originally appeared only in the question or special issue relating to future dangerousness, ORS 163.150(1)(b)(B)(1987), to apply to all three issues in ORS 163.150(1)(b). Therefore, as a "housekeeping" move in 1989, the legislature moved the language from the second special issue in ORS 163.150(1)(b)(B)(1987) to a separate section (c) in ORS 163.150 (1989).

In 1991, the legislature kept ORS 163.150(c)(1989) and added the wording quoted above to ORS 163.150(c) to make two subparagraphs to ORS 163.150(c). The 1989 legislative changes, therefore, would make ORS 163.150(1)(c)(A) applicable to all questions or special issues and the 1991 change would make ORS 163.150(1)(c)(B) applicable to the fourth issue only. One therefore will have some overlap in the two subsections of ORS 163.150(c)(1999), which actually can add to the confusion on how to understand the statute. Nevertheless, by the close of the 1991 Legislative Assembly one had a clearer fourth issue and specific instructions to the jury to consider any mitigating evidence with respect to that factor. The requirements of *Penry* had finally been addressed as the Legislative Assembly understood them.

Two changes to the statute in 1995 and 1997 have provoked considerable discussion. One cannot understand these statutory changes without brief reference to the increased role that victims' advocacy groups played in the criminal justice system in the late 1980s and the 1990s. The victims' rights movement arose in the 1980s in response to the assumptions and practices of the criminal justice reform movements in the 1950s and 1960s that were described in Chapter Three. Their major belief, codified in several Oregon statutes and the Oregon Constitution, is that the victim of the crime and his or her loved ones have a significant role to play in the sentencing of convicted criminals. Victim impact statements are the primary vehicle through which this commitment is to be channeled in the sentencing context. This "statement" may include testimony from affected relatives, pictures of the deceased, and testimony from all who knew the victim about the pain that the defendant has caused through his crime.

In the mid-1980s, victim impact evidence was greeted with skepticism by the courts. The United States Supreme Court held in 1987 that victim impact evidence in death penalty cases was irrelevant testimony because it tended to inject a constitutionally unacceptable risk that the jury might impose the death penalty in an arbitrary and capricious manner.[14] In a dramatic change of direction, however, the U.S. Supreme Court reversed itself four years later and held that the Eighth Amendment to the United States Constitution did not erect a per se bar prohibiting a capital sentencing jury from considering victim impact evidence.[15] With the Supreme Court now having reversed itself, the states were free to include victim impact evidence as a part of sentencing procedures.

Oregon did so, with regard to its death penalty statute, both in 1995 and 1997. The 1995 legislature amended ORS 163.150(1)(a) regarding the admissibility of victim impact evidence. It turned to the sentence of the statute upon which the Oregon Supreme Court had put so much weight in *Wagner II* and amended it. The pre-1995 sentence simply read:

> In the [sentencing] proceeding, evidence may be presented as to any matter that the court deems relevant to sentence.[16]

The 1995 change made the statute read:

> In the [sentencing] proceeding, evidence may be presented
> as to any matter that the court deems relevant to sentence
> including, but not limited to, victim impact evidence relat-
> ing to the personal characteristics of the victim or the impact
> of the crime on the victim's family and any aggravating or
> mitigating evidence relevant to the issue in paragraph (b)(D)
> of this subsection.[17]

No change was made to any other part of the statute relating to this issue and
no legal challenge to the wording was forthcoming between 1995 and 1997.
All that this change provided, by its terms, was that aggravating, mitigating
and victim impact evidence could be presented to the sentencing jury. It did
not specifically say that the jury had to take the information into consideration in answering the special issues of ORS 163.150(1)(b).

The positions were drawn more sharply, however, when the legislature
sought to change the law again in 1997. This time the change would be to
ORS 163.150(1)(c)(B), relating specifically to the fourth question: whether
the defendant should receive a death sentence. The pre-session draft of the bill
by the Legislative Counsel indicated the direction that the legislature, prod-
ded by the Department of Justice, would go.[18] ORS 163.150(1)(c)(B)(1995)
had provided:

> In determining the issue in paragraph (b)(D) of this subsec-
> tion [whether the defendant should receive a death sentence],
> the court shall instruct the jury to answer the question "no"
> if one or more of the jurors find there is any aspect of the
> defendant's character or background, or any circumstances
> of the offense, that one or more of the jurors believe would
> justify a sentence less than death.

The "first draft" of the new law would provide:

> The court shall instruct the jury that, in determining the
> issue in paragraph (b)(D) of this subsection, the jury may
> consider any aggravating evidence and any mitigating evi-
> dence concerning any aspect of the defendant's character or
> background, or any circumstances of the offense and any vic-
> tim impact evidence as described in subsection (1)(a) of this
> section.[19]

Though Assistant Attorney General Robert Rocklin characterized the change between 1995 and 1997 as merely a "conforming" amendment fulfilling the intent of the 1995 amendment in an explicit way, opponents of the wording thought that the introduction of these words was a constitutional violation.[20] Opponents of the new law suggested that the 1995 amendment might not have been unconstitutional because it only provided that this kind of evidence could be presented to the jury. But, they claimed, the 1997 changes were clearly unconstitutional because they provided for actual consideration of these types of evidence in jury determination of the fourth issue.

The argument went as follows: The *Penry* decision held that the three statutory special issues in Texas, and thus in Oregon, did not provide a vehicle to consider mitigating circumstances fully in all death penalty cases. When Oregon added a fourth question to its statute in 1989, it was codifying that holding of *Penry*. Oregon's fourth question, therefore, was a "pure mitigation" question. Such a "pure mitigation" question was Oregon's response to a constitutional requirement. It allowed a jury to consider any mitigation evidence that could not be considered in the first three questions. Thus, when the Oregon Legislature in 1997 introduced aggravating and victim impact evidence into jury determination of the answer to the fourth question, it added this kind of evidence to a question that was intended to be a "pure mitigation" question. It injected a balancing test into a statute that was not a balancing statute and gave no guidance to the jury on how to weigh the various aggravating, mitigating and victim impact evidence. In so doing, it vitiated the constitutional holding of *Penry*.[21]

The Oregon Department of Justice and the Oregon Legislature did not read the *Penry* decision in this way. As Robert Rocklin explained in a lengthy memorandum prepared originally for the House Judiciary Committee and later for the Senate Committee on Rules and Elections, the *Penry* decision only required the statute to allow for full consideration of mitigating circumstances. Since the Oregon statute allows that full consideration in ORS 163.150(1)(c)(A)–(B), the additional consideration of aggravating and victim impact evidence does not preclude full consideration of mitigating circumstances.[22] The consideration of aggravating and victim impact evidence is a supplement to the mitigating evidence considered under ORS 163.150(1)(c)(B).

Though one can easily see the intramural character of the disagreement between the DOJ and the State Public Defender's Office on this issue before the committee, the issue finally spilled over to the courts in September 1999.[23] In *State v. Metz*, the Oregon Court of Appeals subjected the *ex post facto* clause of the Oregon Constitution to searching scrutiny and held that victim impact statements violated that clause when the person sentenced for aggravated murder before the effective date of the law was resentenced after the effective date of the law using the new law.[24] The *ex post facto* clause forbids the legislature from passing any law:

> after a fact done by any citizen, which shall have relation to that fact, so as to punish that which was innocent when done; or add to the punishment of that which was criminal; or to increase the malignity of a crime; or to retrench the rules of evidence, so as to make conviction more easy.[25]

In the case at hand, the Oregon Court of Appeals held that to consider victim impact evidence in a post-1995 remand for a crime committed before 1995, when a person was sentenced under the pre-1995 statute, violated the *ex post facto* provision because it affected the nature of what was proved. The 1995 and 1997 changes to the law, although ostensibly a mere change in a rule of evidence, actually changed the fundamental nature of the question the jury was to answer.[26] This case was appealed to the Oregon Supreme Court, but the court declined to review the case in May 2000. The holding of the court of appeals, therefore, may bring even further prospects for longer death penalty appeals.[27]

Death Row—July 2001

In Chapter One we saw that by June 1989 there were 22 men and 0 women on death row. After the *Penry* decision, all of those men either received a new sentencing-phase trial or a completely new trial. Eleven of them came back to death row (Isom, Pratt, Guzek, McDonnell, Montez, Pinnell, Stevens, Simonsen, Williams, Rogers and Langley) during 1990–1994. Six of these men are still on death row (Pratt, Guzek, Montez, Pinnell, Simonsen and Williams). James Isom died in 1997. Dallas Ray Stevens' case has still not been resubmitted to a Linn County jury. Three cases have recently been remanded and may yet appear before the court, if the county courts resentence the men to death (McDonnell, Langley, Rogers). Of the six pre-*Penry* defendants still on death row, one has not yet had his conviction affirmed by the Oregon Supreme Court (Guzek) and five have (Pratt, Pinnell, Montez, Williams and Simonsen). At least five cases, if Stevens' is included, have not advanced appreciably in ten years. Since the *Penry* decision, 25 others have been sentenced to death in Oregon, 19 of whom are still on death row. If Randall Smith is included, this brings to 25 the number of men on death row in Oregon as of July 1, 2001.

The 19 men who were sentenced to death row since 1989 and are still on death row are displayed in the table on page 193. PC stands for "post-conviction relief."

In addition to these 19 men, five others have been added to death row since 1989. Stressla Johnson was removed from death row in 1992 after a Multnomah County jury did not resentence him to death, and Douglas Wright and Harry Moore, who committed their crimes in 1991 and 1992, were executed in 1996 and 1997, respectively. Grant Charboneau and Gregory Wilson of Multnomah County were previously on death row but have now pled to lesser sentences on remand.

In summary then, of the 25 men currently on death row in Oregon, 6 are pre-*Penry* defendants and 19 are post-*Penry* defendants. Three pre-*Penry* defendants recently had their cases remanded and may yet return to death row. As I argued in Chapter Ten, Oregon's death penalty before 1991 was probably not constitutional. Therefore, the death sentences of six of the men on death row should be vacated and resentenced either to life imprisonment or life imprisonment without the possibility of parole. Of the other 19 men, 11 of them have not yet had their cases even argued before the Oregon Supreme Court. The other 8, whose cases have been heard and affirmed by the Oregon Supreme Court (Smith, Cunningham, Barone, Lotches, McNeely, Hayward, Thompson and Reyes-Camarena), committed their crimes between 1990 and 1995 (when other problems began to creep in to the Oregon death penalty statute).

Five Interesting Cases

Many of the cases of men on death row in Oregon today, as I have shown in Chapter Five, have presented interesting issues of substantive law for the Oregon Supreme Court. In this section, I will describe one case that has received national and international attention, one that presents an enormously sad chain of horrors, one that has comic dimensions to it, and two that have presented complex procedural issues for Oregon courts.

The case of Conan Wayne Hale started out as a garden-variety aggravated murder case, if such a case can ever be garden variety. Hale—19 at the time—and companion Jonathan Susbauer killed three young people, Kristal Rene Bendele (15), Brandon Williams (15) and Patrick Finley (13) in Springfield on December 21, 1995. The reason for the murders was that Bendele, Hale's former girlfriend, had taken up with Williams, and Hale and Susbauer wanted to put an end to that. They did so, and Hale ended up getting sentenced to death by a Lane County jury in May 1998.

Table 11–1. People sentenced to death row since 1989 who were still there on April 1, 2001.

Name	Date of Crime	Date of Sentence	Oregon Supreme Court
R. Smith	September 1990	March 1992	affirmed 1994 PC hearing March 2001 sentence vacated, will be removed from death row
C. Barone	(1) April 1991 December 1992 January 1993	December 1995	affirmed July 1999
	(2) October 1992	January 1995	affirmed December 1998
C. Cunningham	October 1991	October 1992	affirmed September 1994 PC case dismissed August 1999
E. Lotches	August 1992	June 1993	affirmed December 2000
M. McNeely	March 1993	October 1994	affirmed August 2000
M. Hayward	April 1994	December 1995	affirmed July 1998
K. Terry	August 1994	November 1995	not yet argued
M. Thompson	November 1994	February 1996	affirmed April 1999
A. Reyes-Camarena	September 1995	January 1997	affirmed July 2000
R. Acremant	December 1995	October 1996	not yet argued
C. Hale	December 1995	May 1998	not yet argued
J. Tiner	1995	May 2000	not yet argued
B. Oatney	August 1996	March 1998	not yet argued
J. Compton	June 1997	November 1998	not yet argued
J. Sparks	April 1998	May 1999	not yet argued
J. Fanus	June 1998	April 1999	not yet argued
E. Running	February 1998	August 2000	not yet argued
D. Cox	September 1998	December 2000	not yet argued
T. Gibson	March 2000	March 2001	not yet argued

The reason it took so long from the commission of the crime to Hale's conviction and sentence was that the Lane County Sheriff's office taped a conversation Hale had with a Catholic priest while the priest was on a sacramental visit to Hale, and the Lane County District Attorney wanted to preserve the tape for Hale's trial.[28] The ensuing storm of controversy evoked national and international attack on the Lane County District Attorney's office.[29] Not well known, however, are some of the facts of the case and the unsettling results for both law and religion. Believers and unbelievers in any religion at all should take pause and wonder if the result in the case was a victory for law or religion or a loss for both.

After Hale was imprisoned in Lane County Jail for unrelated burglary charges but before he had been formally charged with the three murders, he asked for the services of a priest, to whom he wanted to make a confession. On April 22, 1996, the Reverend Timothy Mockaitis, pastor of St. Paul Catholic Church in Eugene, arrived to administer the sacrament of reconciliation to Hale. Part of that sacrament is the hearing of a confession that a penitent gives the priest. The confession/conversation took place in the regular meeting facility between guests and inmates; another room, designated for completely confidential conversations between lawyers and their clients, was not used.[30] The conversation was conducted via phone between the two men, who were separated by a glass partition. Hale was aware that the confession was probably being taped, since the Lane County Sheriff's office had a policy of taping conversations that were made between inmates and guests. Mockaitis was unaware that the confession might have been taped. Before the taping of the confession actually took place, the Sheriff's Department had asked the Lane County District Attorney's office for legal advice on the propriety of the taping. Two deputy district attorneys in that office briefly consulted with Lane County District Attorney Douglas Harcleroad, who told them to make sure, whatever they did, that they were on firm legal ground.

The conversation was taped. On the next day the Lane County District Attorney's office applied for a search warrant to gain access to the tape and its content. The warrant was granted. Subsequently the tape was transcribed. The Catholic Church became aware of the existence of the tape and transcription and moved to intervene in the case that the district attorney was developing against Hale for the three murders. It wanted the tape and the transcription suppressed and destroyed. Lane County Circuit Court Judge Jack Billings returned the papers submitted by the Church telling them that they had no standing to intervene in a criminal case to which they were not a party.

As the case developed, *both* Hale and District Attorney Harcleroad wanted to preserve the tape. Hale wanted to use it because, as he was probably calculating all along, he did not reveal anything incriminating on the tape, and the district attorney wanted to make sure Hale could not argue that he was denied access to evidence. This left the Catholic Church in the unenviable position of being a legal outsider to a case in which both the plaintiff and defendant wanted evidence admitted and it, the Catholic Church, wanted evidence suppressed and destroyed.

At stake for the Catholic Church was a central theological tenet and practice. That tenet was the sacredness of the confession and the sacrament of reconciliation. Confession is one of the seven sacraments of the Catholic Church, and is the means by which Catholics believe that a person's continuing sins are acknowledged, confessed and forgiven. In order for the sacrament to function effectively, in Catholic belief, there has to be full honesty in confession. After the confession, the priest prescribes a penance which, upon being performed by the penitent, leads to full absolution for one's sins.[31]

Of absolute importance for the sacredness of the ritual is the confidentiality of what is said. The priest is normally in a separate compartment from the penitent during confession so that the anonymity of the confession is assured. Anonymity stresses the fact that the priest is simply a channel of God's grace, not dispensing the forgiving favor of God on a penitent because of his own capability but only as a vessel or minister of Jesus Christ. By pronouncing absolution the priest is, as it were, speaking the very words of God to the penitent. You are forgiven. Thanks be to God.

Any interference by the state or another private party to this ritual, either by taping it or otherwise monitoring the confession would, in the view of the Catholic Church, be akin to a sexual violation of a person. So offensive is the taping or divulging of the contents of the confession to the Catholic Church that the Congregation for the Doctrine of the Faith, the body that declares official Church doctrine, has decreed that a person who either tapes or divulges the contents of a confession shall be excommunicated from the church.[32] Such a person has committed a mortal sin. The text of the decree does not state explicitly that someone who "hears" the confession is likewise subject to excommunication, but one could say that taping or divulging also includes hearing. It is a most sober penalty. It is, for a good Catholic, the equivalent to a sentence of death.

Thus, when the Catholic Church was forbidden from intervening in the Lane County case against Hale, it had to act. Had Judge Billings decided to hear the Catholic Church's complaint and then dismissed it, the proper legal channel for the church to pursue would have been an appeal to the Oregon Court of Appeals. Because Judge Billings threw out the Church's complaint without so much as dignifying it with a hearing or reply (he merely had the papers returned to the Church), the Church sought relief in federal court. They filed a complaint in the Federal District Court of Oregon, alleging violations of the Religious Freedom Restoration Act, the Fourth Amendment protection against illegal search and seizure and Federal Wiretap Act.[33] In addition, they claimed that since Judge Billings had summarily decided not even to hear their plea, that it was impossible for them to get a state forum to hear their complaint.

The last point is significant. Federal courts are loath to intervene in state criminal court proceedings unless the person can show that his or her rights would be irremediably damaged by the action or inaction of the state court. This was what the Catholic Church needed to argue before U.S. District Court Judge Owen Panner.

The case was given expedited briefing, hearing and decision. By August 15, 1996, fewer than three months after the taping had taken place, Judge Panner issued his decision and dismissed the Catholic Church's claim. He held that even though the taping of the confession was improper, the priest and archbishop had had an opportunity to raise their issue in state court. Since federal courts are reluctant to intervene in state criminal cases, he would not do so in this case. Rather, the Church could make its point in a pretrial motion to suppress the tape as the product of an illegal search. There was really no need for federal court intervention in the matter. The judge did not explain how the Church would be able to bring such a motion since Judge Billings had not permitted them to intervene in the case at all.

Observers recognized that the situation was getting rather desperate for the Catholic Church. A most sacred ritual had already been severely compromised. The reduction of a sacred confession to a mere "piece of evidence" was a serious affront to the Church's dignity. One might argue that whatever happened next could not really eliminate the damage that had already been done to the Church. In a word, its most sacred ritual had been reduced to an exhibit on the growing list of exhibits being prepared by the Lane County District Attorney's office. It had been stripped of all value, shorn of all dignity, irreparably violated.

In such a case, the Church decided to throw up a "Hail Mary" pass. It appealed to the Ninth Circuit Court of Appeals. Perhaps it might find someone a bit more sympathetic to its claim in the three-judge panel that would be randomly selected to hear the case.[34]

When the dust settled and the three-judge panel had been selected, a prescient observer might begin to wonder if there were forces beyond those of mere chance in the lottery selection of the senior judge in the case. The senior judge and eventual writer of the unanimous decision reversing the federal district court was John T. Noonan, Jr. A brief review of some of Judge Noonan's credentials and past experience might give the reader an impression of the type of judge that would be hearing the appeal. Noonan was born in Boston in October 1926 and holds both a B.A. and LL.B from Harvard. It is not, however, his Harvard credentials that are most impressive in this context.

After graduating from Harvard, he completed an M.A. and Ph.D. at the Catholic University of America. From 1975 to 1990 he received honorary doctorates from the following universities: Catholic University of America, University of Santa Clara, University of Notre Dame, Loyola University South, Holy Cross College, St. Louis University, University of San Francisco, and Gonzaga University. He was a law professor at Notre Dame, and has been the Pope John XXIII lecturer at Catholic University in 1973 and the Cardinal Bellarmine lecturer at St. Louis University Divinity School. Among his many publications were works on the treatment of usury in scholastic theology, the history of contraception in the Catholic Church and a host of other topics on medieval canon law. He has been a consultant to the United States Catholic Conference and secretary treasurer of the Institute for Research in Medieval Canon Law. In 1985 he ascended the federal bench and served a distinguished tenure on the Ninth Circuit Court of Appeals.[35]

It really is not necessary to go through the opinion of the court at length. Noonan showed an impressive display of legal and historical learning. Not surprisingly, the court concluded that the seizure of the tape violated both the Religious Freedom Restoration Act (RFRA) and the Fourth Amendment to the United States Constitution.[36] The preservation of the tape substantially burdened the free exercise of religion. Under the RFRA, if an act by a governmental entity burdened religious expression in this way, it had to show a compelling need in order for the burden to have survived constitutional scrutiny. The state did not make this showing. In addition, the court disagreed with the district court and held that abstaining from this case would inflict an irreparable injury on the Catholic Church.[37] The Ninth Circuit Court of Appeals therefore issued an injunction forbidding the tape from being used as a piece of evidence in Hale's upcoming trial.[38]

One final somber note serves to emphasize the religious as well as the legal dimensions of this case. Recall that in Catholic theology the recording and divulging of the contents of the tape is an offense meriting excommunication. It is, in fact, the Church's death penalty. Shortly after the Ninth Circuit handed down its decision, and shortly before the case against Hale was to be heard by a Lane County jury, the chief prosecutor in the case, one of the two attorneys who had listened to the tape, who was himself a Catholic, and was in good health in the strength of middle age (50), suddenly died.

The Case of Cesar F. Barone

Though the case of Conan Wayne Hale makes one wonder about imponderable things in the connection between religion and law, and of the existence of another dimension to reality superintending or intervening in this dimension of life, the case of Cesar Barone locks us into a hopeless chain of horror on this earth.[39] Barone is a native of Fort Lauderdale, Florida, and grew up under the name of Adolph James Rode. He was expelled from kindergarten and constantly fought with other children, threatening them with knives and poking lighted cigarettes in their eyes.[40] At age 16 he robbed and sexually threatened a retired school teacher who lived across the street from him, and served three years in a correctional facility for the offense. Two weeks after he was released, the same neighbor was brutally raped and murdered. It was not until the mid-1990s, with the advent of DNA testing, when Oregon had already convicted Barone on four murders, that Florida authorities wanted to extradite Barone to Florida to stand trial for the 1979 murder of retired teacher Alice Stock.[41]

While imprisoned in Florida in the early 1980s, he was housed with the infamous Ted Bundy. Barone may have met his future wife by answering a personal ad she placed in a Seattle newspaper that Bundy had passed on to him in the prison. Barone and the woman corresponded, and after his release from prison in Florida he went to Seattle and began dating her. They soon married and moved to Portland.

Changing his name to Cesar Barone and his address to Oregon in the late 1980s could not change the man. As the ancient Stoic philosopher Seneca said, "One needs to change the soul, not the sky." This, obviously, Barone was unable or unwilling to do. From 1991 to 1993 he committed four murders in Oregon before Oregon authorities were able to stop and confine him. Three of the murders, those of Margaret Schmidt in 1991, Chantee Woodman in 1992 and Betty Lee Williams in 1993, were consolidated in one trial. Barone was found guilty of aggravated murder in each of these cases and sentenced to death by a Washington County jury in December 1995. These convictions were affirmed by the Oregon Supreme Court in July 1999.

In order to understand the full chain of horrors leading to the fourth case, in which Barone was also convicted of aggravated murder and sentenced to death, one must go back to 1981 in Oregon. In May 1981 a deranged Lawrence William Moore walked into the Salem Museum Tavern on NE Pine Street in Salem on a crowded Thursday evening and opened fire on the more than two hundred patrons of the popular night-spot. When the shots had stopped and he was apprehended, four people lay dead and twenty were seriously injured. Salemites who look back on that day say it marked a change in Salem life, a realization that Salem was no longer a pleasant small town where people were polite to each other and respected each other's person and privacy. The "big city" had come in an awful way to the state's capital.

Moore committed his crime only four months after the Oregon Supreme Court invalidated Oregon's death penalty.[42] Because of Oregon law in effect at the time, Moore received four consecutive life sentences, each of which required 20 years before the possibility of parole. The judge ordered the sentences to run consecutively. Thus, in fact, Moore received an 80-year sentence.

The mental debility that stalked Moore also bedeviled his sister, Vickie Cutsforth. She lived in Portland and for years had been a nurse at Oregon Health Sciences University. Though she lived in the affluent and comfortable Eastmoreland neighborhood at 7734 SE 36th Avenue, she was also suffering from severe mental disorders. Early in September 1989 she shot and killed her two daughters in the house and then turned the gun on herself. The three slayings added to the tragedy not simply of the Moore/Cutsforth family but to the cup of sorrow of Portland and Salem.

Shortly after the Cutsforth murder-suicide, another nurse moved into the house on 7734 SE 36th Avenue. She, Martha Bryant, was a native of Chicago and, like hundreds of thousands of young people in the 1980s, came to Portland to explore the beauty and experience the lifestyle of the Northwest. She married Rob Crouch and they moved into the house on 36th Avenue. It turned out that Martha Bryant had known Vickie Cutsforth briefly when she worked at OHSU but had changed her job to work as a midwife at Tuality Community Hospital in Hillsboro. Only after Bryant and Crouch lived in the house for a while did they learn of its gruesome history.

On the early morning of October 9, 1992, Bryant left the hospital and drove home. Her car was intercepted not far from the hospital. She was forced from the road, shot and left to die by a man who authorities later identified as Cesar Barone. Shortly after the shooting the police were notified, and an ambulance rushed to the scene on NW 231st Avenue near Cornell Road. Bryant was alive when she was found at 3:25 a.m. but died in intensive care at OHSU three hours later. To further compound the irony and pain, the last person whose baby she had delivered the night she was murdered had vaguely known and disliked Barone when they worked briefly at a Forest Grove care center. The car Barone was driving when he killed Bryant, wierdly enough, had been owned previously by another person whose baby Bryant had delivered. A more oppressive and hopeless chain of events can scarcely be imagined.[43]

Dallas Ray Stevens

The one case of a death row inmate that may be even more complicated and may eventually occasion more delay than that of Michael McDonnell is that of Dallas Ray Stevens. On February 26, 1988, he arrived at a woman friend's home near his house in Oakville. Stevens was married to his friend's estranged husband's sister. His friend had four daughters of her own, and unbeknownst to his friend, Stevens took three of her daughters to his Oakville farmhouse. High on methamphetamine, Stevens killed one of the girls and sexually abused the others. A Linn County jury convicted him of three charges of aggravated murder, four counts of first degree kidnapping, two counts of first degree sexual abuse, one count of first degree rape and two counts of second degree assault. The jury sentenced him to death. He also received lesser prison terms.[44]

In 1991 the Oregon Supreme Court vacated his sentence because of the *Penry* problem. A second Linn County jury resentenced him to death and his case returned to the Oregon Supreme Court in 1994. The court remanded his case again because the jury in the second penalty phase trial did not consider the possible mitigating testimony of Stevens' wife as to the potential effect of Steven's execution on his daughter.[45] In other words, by 1994 the Oregon Supreme Court was reading the *Penry* decision very broadly to include mitigating evidence of how even a person's execution might affect his remaining family members. The circuit court had considered this evidence and rejected it, saying only, "I don't find that the mother's belief about what's in the best interest of the child would relate in any way to the defendant's background or character."[46]

Linn County therefore was required to conduct a third penalty phase trial. But the case ran into severe procedural problems on remand. Before the start of the third penalty phase trial, the defendant filed a motion in limine seeking to suppress 53 items of evidence that the court had admitted in earlier guilt and penalty phases proceedings.[47] The trial court granted the motion in part. In response the state filed two motions: an appeal of the order to the Oregon Court of Appeals, and a motion for summary determination of appealability. The former was an appeal on the merits of the lower court's decision, while the latter was a motion to have it considered expeditiously.

The court of appeals granted the state's motion for summary determination of appealability but dismissed the state's appeal because the state had not, in accordance with the statute, appealed the suppression order "prior to trial." Therefore the state was left with no victory at all. They were in essence told that they could seek a quick or summary judgment by the appeals court about their issue, but they were turned aside with respect to the substance of their appeal.

So, they turned to two more remedies. The state appealed the court of appeals' dismissal to the Oregon Supreme Court and filed a petition for a writ of mandamus. The writ of mandamus is an extraordinary remedy sought by a petitioner when no speedy, plain or adequate remedy exists in the ordinary course of law.

In March 1998 the Oregon Supreme Court refused to grant a writ of mandamus but did reverse the appeals court on the suppression order. The court held that appeal rather than mandamus was the correct route for the state to pursue. More important, however, were two other holdings of the court. First, it held that all evidence properly admitted in earlier guilt and penalty phase proceedings was also admissible in a new penalty phase proceeding.[48] This holding resolved a previously unresolved legal issue, and remains important because many of the death penalty cases have been or may be remanded for a new penalty phase trial.

Second, the court held that Stevens' waiver of any *ex post facto* objection he might have to jury consideration of three sentencing options (life imprisonment, life imprisonment without the possibility of parole, death) did not violate the Oregon or federal constitutions. Therefore, in Stevens' third penalty phase trial, the jury would be instructed that it could consider each of the three sentencing options.

After the Oregon Supreme Court handed down its decision in March 1998, newspaper stories hinted that it might be a few months before the sentencing jury would deliberate in his third penalty phase trial. By late fall 1998, however, the penalty phase had not been held. A new date in July 1999 for the beginning of the penalty phase was set. But the trial still has not begun as of July 2001. The reason for this is that Stevens' attorney has now decided to file his own writ of mandamus with the Oregon Supreme Court. The writ of mandamus claims that Linn County's manner of constituting the jury pool violates the Oregon and United States Constitutions.[49] A similar claim from Clatsop County was filed, as were a number of cases from other Oregon counties. The Oregon Supreme Court agreed to hear the case in 2000.

Oral arguments were scheduled in 2000 on the Clatsop County case. The heart of the case, as argued by Portland attorney Kathleen Correll, was that the U.S. Constitution requires, and Oregon law does not forbid, access to master jury lists and other jury summoning materials generated by each county. On January 3, 2001, the court decided that Oregon law does not prohibit a defendant from acquiring relevant jury selection information in order to determine if, in fact, a representative jury has been selected in his case. Unclear in the decision, however, was whether circuit court judges had discretion to disclose or withhold this information. Most neutral readers of the opinion, however, would say that it requires disclosure.

Over the next month, several circuit court judges decided that the language of the court's opinion allowed them discretion over release of this information. In a rare fit of pique the supreme court, through its own lawyer Keith Garza, ordered Portland attorney Laura Graser on February 8 to write a brief within twelve days that would answer the question of whether disclosure of this jury selection material was constitutionally and statutorily mandated. The Department of Justice was given twelve days to respond, no reply briefs were allowed and oral argument followed on March 2, the earliest possible date. It appeared that the court was going to resolve this issue very quickly. Oral arguments came. Then, nothing happened. As of this writing, the supreme court has still not handed down its decision on the issue.

If the court acts consistently with its January 2001 opinion it will probably decide that defense counsel does have access to jury selection records in their cases. The implications then are unclear. Certainly they will seek to stay any proceedings in order to study whether in fact juries were selected in a constitutional manner. The upshot for the Stevens case is that, after various jury challenges are heard and dealt with, probably not until late 2002 or 2003 will his remanded sentencing-phase trial be held. Then, if a death sentence is reimposed, his case may not return to the Oregon Supreme Court until 2005 or 2006 at the earliest.

Alberto Reyes-Camarena

Though it would be wrong to characterize any of these cases as a comedy, the case of Alberto Reyes-Camarena has had its comic dimensions to it. There was, however, nothing amusing about his crime. While working on a farm in Woodburn as a translator/supervisor of some other Mexican workers, he offered to drive two sisters to Washington where they could find other farm labor. Reyes-Camarena and the son of his girlfriend (Castanas-Bailey) drove the sisters, Maria and Angelica Zetina, to the Oregon Coast and then proceeded south with them. They stabbed and abandoned one of the sisters, Angelica, and stabbed the other to death and dumped her body alongside U.S. 101 near Reedsport. Angelica survived and was instrumental in helping authorities track down Reyes-Camarena and Castanas-Bailey.

Reyes-Camarena was tried in Douglas County Circuit Court in October 1996 and convicted of aggravated murder on Friday, October 25, 1996. The sentencing phase of the trial was scheduled to begin during the next week. On Sunday evening, October 27, Reyes-Camarena and another man, Carlos Gomez Alonso, escaped from the Douglas County Jail. They did so by smuggling in a large wrench, knocking out a security screen over a window, repeatedly smashing the one-inch thick laminated plate glass window until it broke, making a makeshift rope of a bundle of clothes and bedding and lowering themselves out of the third floor window of the jail to freedom. When asked how they could have escaped, the spokesman for the Sheriff's Department said that the jail was understaffed that evening, and that the control room of the jail was located on a different floor from the recreation area, where the break-out occurred. The fact that there had been seven escapes in the previous eighteen years from the Douglas County Jail might have also suggested that the facility was not very secure, the staff not too diligent or both. Nevertheless, Deputy Stratton of the Douglas County Sheriff's Department doggedly insisted that "our jail is just about as secure a facility as you can get."[50]

A manhunt for Reyes-Camarena and Alonso began immediately but by Monday, October 28, the trail seemed cold. Alleged sightings of the pair led to nothing, and a local detective probably exacerbated fears when he described the escapees as "extremely dangerous."[51] After authorities had all but given up hope of finding the fugitives, they ran across Alonso calmly walking down Main Street in Roseburg on November 15. He led them to Reyes-Camarena and both were recaptured. As it turned out, neither man had left town during their 19 days of freedom.

The reason that Alonso and Reyes-Camarena never left Roseburg is that as Reyes-Camarena was lowering himself down the makeshift rope from the third floor window, his hands slipped and he fell at least 20 feet, landing on his back. He was severely injured, unable to walk and in great pain. Alonso, after successfully negotiating his own escape, had to carry Reyes-Camarena away from the jail. Not knowing what to do with him, Alonso finally decided to drag him to the nearby First Christian Church. He forced open a basement window, helped Reyes-Camarena into the church and lay him on his back behind some Christmas ornaments in a basement room of the church.

Thus began an excruciating 19-day ordeal for both Reyes-Camarena and Alonso. Reyes-Camarena went untreated for what would eventually become permanent disabilities and Alonso played the unexpected role of nurse, food-runner and general encourager. Reyes-Camarena was getting no better as the days went on, and it was only a matter of days before they would have been discovered. When asked about it later, the pastor of the church mentioned that the ladies guild of the church would soon have gone into the closet to bring out the ornaments for another Christmas season. One can imagine the surprise on the faces of the good women of First Christian Church when instead of simply finding Mary, Joseph and the angels in the basement they also run across the notorious and extremely dangerous Alberto Reyes-Camarena. The two escapees had been "quiet as a church mouse," according to the pastor.

Reyes-Camarena then underwent costly back surgery and hospitalization. Because Douglas County was responsible for his security and medical care while under its control, the county was eventually socked with a medical bill in excess of $41,000.[52] Before the sentencing phase of the trial began, Douglas County Sheriff John Pardon released the results of a study conducted by a four-officer review board examining jail procedures in the county jail. To no one's surprise, the report indicated that there had been security lapses at the jail. Deputies consistently did not follow procedures, doors were left unlocked, windows had loose bolts, tools could easily be acquired by inmates and even the main control center was vulnerable.[53] Not exactly Alcatraz.

Reyes-Camarena's penalty phase trial was held in early January 1997, and he was sentenced by a jury to death. Despite the fact that he was in a wheelchair during the penalty phase, prosecutor Pat Champion urged the jury: "Do not be misled. This man is so dangerous that there is only one sentence that will ensure there will not be another tragedy as befell…" and then she listed eleven victims of his past violent acts.[54]

The jury might easily have been "misled." It had to find affirmatively that Reyes-Camarena would pose a threat of future dangerousness, and one or more jurors might have concluded that his new physical condition could hinder him from committing violent crimes in the future. Immediately after surgery, the prognosis for Reyes-Camarena's recovery was positive. Figures of between three and five weeks for recovery were mentioned. Yet he was still confined to a wheelchair during the penalty phase of the trial. The jury sentenced him to death, however. Five years later, on death row in the Oregon State Penitentiary, he still uses either a wheelchair or crutches to make his way.

Scott Harberts

One of the most dramatic events of 2000 in the Oregon death penalty arena was the September 14 decision of the Oregon Supreme Court not simply to vacate Harberts' sentence of death but to reverse his conviction, dismiss his indictment and order his release from prison.[55] Though the opinion never said that the court entertained doubts as to Harberts' guilt, those who followed the case closely now believe that there is significant evidence to question the jury verdict in his case.

The court chose the lofty vehicle of the Oregon Constitution, however, to vacate his sentence and overturn his conviction. The court concluded that a delay of five years, from 1989 to 1994, in holding Harberts in jail before bringing him to trial constituted a violation of Article I, section 10, of the Oregon Constitution, which promises an accused will be brought to trial "without delay."

A 2-year-old child was murdered in the early morning hours of July 14, 1989, in the house where Harberts had been living with the child's father and stepmother and three small children of the stepmother. Immediately after the murder, Harberts was taken in for questioning, and a lengthy polygraph examination was administered. He made statements in connection with the examination that some would take as incriminating. As a result of the examination, he was indicted for the murder on July 20, 1989. Trial was set for January 3, 1990.

In a November 1989 pretrial motion, his attorney moved to suppress all statements made by Harberts in connection with the polygraph examination. On March 3, 1990, the trial court granted his motion. The state immediately appealed this decision. It was not until November 1991 that the court of appeals decided that the trial court had erred, and the evidence should be admissible. Harberts' counsel then immediately appealed this decision to the Oregon Supreme Court. The supreme court affirmed the appeals court but remanded the case to the trial court to determine if the incriminating statements made by Harberts could be edited so that all connection with a polygraph examination would be removed.

On remand the trial court decided that it could not edit Harberts' statement without changing its meaning. Therefore, on May 24, 1993, the trial court again suppressed Harberts' statements. The state again immediately appealed this decision. It asked for three extensions to file its briefs but then, late in January 1994, moved to dismiss its appeal. It would be willing to proceed to trial without the possibly incriminating statements. The court granted the state's motion to dismiss the appeal.

When nothing occurred for a few more months, Harberts' attorney wrote to the state court administrator asking where the case was and what was occurring. This got the ball rolling again, and a trial was finally scheduled for July 1994. Harberts was found guilty of aggravated murder and on October 27, 1994, sentenced to death.

In reversing his conviction and ordering his ultimate release, the court was particularly critical of the Department of Justice for its delay in bringing the second challenge to the trial court's motion to suppress Harberts' statement. In the meantime, while the department was dallying one of the significant investigators in the case died. Harberts' ability to get a fair trial was significantly impaired. An interesting attempt to try to repair this problem was House bill 2918, passed by the 2001 legislature in its waning days and sent to the governor for signature, which would require that an appeal of a trial court's decision on suppression of evidence would go dirccetly to the supreme court and must be decided within a year of oral argument.

Harberts therefore was released from prison. New accusations of various acts of sexual abuse arose and in March 2001 he was convicted of one count of sexual abuse of a minor and sentenced to a year in jail with five years probation. He will soon be out on work release and living and working in Clackamas County.

Endnotes

1   These changes had to do with the problem of what to do if a juror in the guilt phase of the trial was unable to serve during the penalty phase, with another rewriting of the "fourth question" in ORS 163.150(1)(b) and with a lengthy rewrite of the 1989 portion of the law dealing with the sentencing-phase process after a decision had been remanded from the Oregon Supreme Court to a county circuit court. Discussion of the "fourth question" change appears below in the text.

2   See, Graser, Laura, "The Worst of All Worlds: The Post 1995 Oregon Death Penalty Statutes," *Defending the Death Penalty Case: Tips, Tactics and Practical Advice* (Eugene, OR: OCDLA, 1998), chapter 8. This discusses a summary of the constitutional difficulties with the 1991 statute, especially after the legislature modified the statute in 1995 and 1997.

3   The 1999 changes had more to do with the process of drawing a death warrant and therefore were changes to ORS 137 and not ORS 163.150. Nevertheless, it shows that the legislature is still interested in doing more than just "tinkering" with the process of putting a person to death in Oregon. Several bills concerning the death penalty were introduced in the 2001 legislative session, only one of which passed. This bill, HB 2092, expands the types of proceedings in which the murder of a juror or witness becomes aggravated murder. It passed both houses and is currently on the Governor's desk. Governor Kitzhaber, however, has vowed to veto it because he opposes the expansion of the death penalty.

4   Indeed, the 1995 change to ORS 163.150(1)(a) and the 1997 change to ORS 163.150(1)(c)(B) have been subject to increasing opposition among those who are closest to the issue and may soon cause ripple effects beyond the rather narrow circle of death penalty attorneys. In brief the issue has to do with the propriety of a jury's consideration of aggravating and victim impact evidence when it answers the fourth question or special issue in its capital punishment deliberations. The 1995 and 1997 changes will be discussed below.

5   In *State v. Metz*, 162 Or App 448, 986 P2d 714 (1999), Judge Paul DeMuniz, writing for a unanimous three-judge panel of the Oregon Court of Appeals, held that presentation of victim impact evidence in resentencing under ORS 163.150 violates the *ex post facto* provision of the Oregon Constitution, when the resentencing is for a crime committed prior to 1995. Oregon Constitution Article 1, section 21.

6   The interesting issue in Conan Wayne Hale's case is that members of the Lane County Sheriff's Department illegally taped his confession to a Catholic priest in May 1996. The string of tragedies connected with Cesar Barone's October 1992 killing of Martha Bryant is shocking. Procedural snafus in the Stevens and Charboneau/Wilson cases add to the cost of the process. Finally, Alberto Reyes-Camarena's escape from the Douglas County Jail the weekend after he was convicted of aggravated murder set the stage for a series of almost comic human errors until he was recaptured a few weeks later fewer than 100 yards from the county jail.

7   House Journal, 1991 Legislative Assembly (Salem: Legislative Counsel Committee, 1991), H-77.

8   See the discussion in Chapter Ten.

9   HB 2393, Original Bill. Original bill file, 1991 Legislative Assembly, Oregon State Archives.

10   ORS 163.150(1)(b)(D)(1991).

11   ORS 163.150(1)(c)(B)(1991).

12   It is 44 lines in the session laws for the 1997 Legislative Assembly. This will mean, of course, that the subsection will soon be divided into (1)(a)(1) and so forth so that the specific instructions to the court may be enumerated more precisely. As each session of the legislature seems intent on expanding the law to meet exigencies unforeseen in the previous session, the issue of statutory expansion is a serious one. Currently the laws of Oregon expand about 5% (500–600 pages) each session. What was four volumes of laws in 1953, the last statutory codification of the laws, has become 18 volumes in 1999. I have likened the expansion of statutes in Oregon to the filling of a Victorian mansion one has purchased and which one fills over the years simply because there is space in which to put all one's "junk." Very little effort has been

spent on cleaning up the Oregon statutes. See my article, "Cleaning Up the Oregon Revised Statutes: A Modest Proposal on Public Bodies," 36 *Willamette Law Review*, 83 (2000).

[13]   There was a ORS 163.150(1)(c) before 1989, but the 1989 legislature or, more accurately, the Office of Legislative Counsel, moved the former ORS 163.150(c) to ORS 163.150(d) to accommodate the new ORS 163.150(c). The Office of Legislative Counsel codifies and publishes the Oregon Revised Statutes in November or December after the Legislative Assembly has adjourned.

[14]   *Booth v. Maryland*, 482 U.S. 496 (1987); affirmed by *South Carolina v. Gathers*, 490 U.S. 805 (1989).

[15]   *Payne v. Tennessee*, 501 U.S. 808 (1991). The *Booth* margin of victory was 5–4; the *Payne* decision by a 6–3 majority. Three of the four dissenters in *Payne* (Marshall, Blackmun and Stevens) were in the majority in *Booth*. That majority also consisted of Brennan, who retired in 1990, and Powell, who retired in 1987. The six Justices who became the majority in *Payne* consisted of the four dissenters in 1987 (White, Rehnquist, O'Connor and Scalia) and the two Justices who had replaced Powell and Brennan: Kennedy and Souter, respectively. Kennedy had been appointed by President Ronald Reagan and Souter by President George Bush.

[16]   ORS 163.150(1)(a)(1993).

[17]   ORS 163.150(1)(a)(1995).

[18]   Pre-session drafts of bills are known not by their bill number, since they have not yet been given a number, but only by the Legislative Counsel, or "LC" number. This one, LC 1635, dated 12/19/96 is in the original bill file for HB 2393, 1997 Legislative Assembly, Oregon State Archives.

[19]   LC 1635, 12/19/96, 3.

[20]   Testimony of Robert Rocklin, Assistant Attorney General, to the Senate Committee on Rules and Elections, July 1, 1997. Tape 130, Side A, Senate Committee on Rules and Elections, July 1, 1997, 1997 Legislative Assembly, Oregon State Archives. Major opponents of the wording, in addition to the two committee senators who dissented (Trow and Leonard) were David Groom of the State Public Defender's Office and David Fidanque of the Oregon chapter of the American Civil Liberties Union. The final changes to the bill, agreed to on July 4, 1997, differed slightly from the first draft but these changes do not materially affect the debate as it took place in 1997 or today. The final wording provided: "The court shall instruct the jury to answer the question in paragraph (b)(D) of this subsection 'no' if, after considering any aggravating evidence and any mitigating evidence concerning any aspect of the defendant's character or background, or any circumstances of the offense and any victim impact evidence as described in subsection (1)(a) of this section, one or more of the jurors believe that the defendant should not receive a death sentence." ORS 163.150(1)(c)(B)(1997). A helpful overview of these legislative changes is in Laura Graser's memorandum, "The Worst of All Worlds: The Post 1995 Oregon Death Penalty Statutes," *Defending the Death Penalty Case: Tips, Tactics and Practical Advice* (Eugene, OR: OCDLA, 1998), chapter 8. She also launched a well argued attack on the constitutionality of these changes, based primarily on the point that the fourth issue or question was supposed to be a "mitigation only" question and that the Oregon Legislature has made it a "balancing" question. This, she claims, contradicts the specific constitutional holding of *Penry*. This argument is evaluated immediately below.

[21]   Texas has avoided this constitutional problem. When they modified their capital sentencing statute in 1991 as a result of the *Penry* decision, their alterations in the first part of the statute (corresponding to ORS 163.150(1)(a)) only provided: "In the [sentencing] proceeding, evidence may be presented by the state and the defendant or the defendant's counsel as to any matter that the court deems relevant to sentence, including evidence of the defendant's background or character or the circumstances of the offense that mitigates against the imposition of the death penalty." *Vernon's Texas Statutes Annotated*, Code of Criminal Procedure, Art. 30.071, Sec. 2(a) (West 1981 and Supp. 1998). Later sections of the statute, revised in 1991, give copious mention to jury consideration of mitigating circumstances but no mention is made

about victim impact evidence or the weighing of aggravating evidence. Curiously then, Oregon's capital sentencing statute, which is the only one in the nation that used the Texas statute as its model, is more severe than even the Texas statute. It is a rather strange position for Oregon to occupy.

22   Memorandum of Mr. Robert Rocklin, Assistant Attorney General, January 30, 1997, in HB 2317 Exhibit I, pp. 2–3, House Judiciary Committee, 1997 Legislative Assembly, Oregon State Archives.

23   The Oregon Supreme Court briefly considered a challenge to the constitutionality of victim impact evidence in the sentencing phase of a capital punishment trial in *State v. Hayward*, 327 Or 397, 963 P2d 667 (1998), but concluded in that case that the defendant's attorney had not properly preserved his constitutional objections at trial. The constitutional objections that the attorney made in vain at trial were that the 1995 and 1997 laws were *ex post facto* laws, in violation of both the Oregon and United States Constitutions.

24   162 Or App 448 986 P2d 714 (1999).

25   *Ibid., 456,* Quoting *Strong v. The State*, 1 Blackf 193 (1822).

26   *Ibid.,* 460.

27   The court of appeals decision did not reach a host of interesting questions. Is it the 1995 or 1997 statutory change, or both, that is problematic? To which cases does the law apply? The court held that the law violated the *ex post facto* clause of the constitution when applied to a remand situation for a person originally sentenced under a previous version of the law, but it did not reach the question of whether the law is per se unconstitutional. Those who argue that question four is a pure mitigation question have constitutional difficulties, of the Eighth Amendment variety, with the statute irrespective of its application to a remand situation like that in *Metz*. If the law is only unconstitutional when it is applied to a remand situation, what about a remand that was reconsidered by the trial court between 1995 and 1997? Was it the 1995 law that triggered the *ex post facto* violation or only the 1997 law?

28   A technical question on which the case did not ultimately turn but still had legal implications is whether the words that Hale uttered were actually a confession and the act that was performed on Hale's behalf that day was the Catholic sacrament of reconciliation. The Lane County Court found that the Reverend Mockaitis often came to the Lane County Jail to administer this sacrament and he intended to do it for Hale on April 22. On the other hand, Hale is not a baptized Catholic and his participation in the ritual would have been performed in a way reflecting no knowledge of the proper response of a Catholic penitent in this situation. The federal judge declined to listen to the tape and make a determination for himself, calling it only an "intended confession." I will remain agnostic on the issue, referring to the act alternatively as a conversation or a confession. Certainly Judge Noonan of the Ninth Circuit Court of Appeals considered the act a confession in the Catholic sense.

29   A searching analysis of the religious and legal implications of the taped confession appears in an article by Tom Bates, Mark O'Keefe and David Hogan, "Lane Taping of Confession Sets Church Against State," *Oregonian*, 19 May 1996, A1.

30   Interview with Gregory Chaimov, now Legislative Counsel of the State of Oregon, and then the attorney with the Oregon Department of Justice who handled the case for the DOJ. 5 October 1999 and 17 November 1999.

31   This brief summary of the essence of the sacrament of reconciliation or confession is derived from the *Oregonian* article mentioned above and the summary in the federal court of appeals opinion on the case, *Mockaitis v. Harcleroad,* 104 F3d 1522 (1997).

32   The heavy words of Ecclesiastical Latin are appended to the federal district court's case in this matter. *Mockaitis v. Harcleroad,* 938 F Supp 1516 (1996). The specific words are that anyone ("quicumque") who either tapes a confession ("per instrumenta technica") or divulges the content of it through any means ("per communicationis socialis instrumenta evulgat") will be excommunicated ("excommunicatio latae sententiae").

33   *Mockaitis v. Harcleroad,* 938 F Supp 1516 (1996).

34   The case is *Mockaitis v. Harcleroad,*, 104 F3d 1522 (1997).
35   His brief biographical sketch, about two to three times as long as the average lawyer, appears in *Who's Who in American Law 1998–99*, 10th Ed. (Reed Elsevier: New Providence, NJ 1998), 570.
36   Within six months of the Ninth Circuit's decision, the United States Supreme Court held that the RFRA was unconstitutional. *City of Boerne v. Flores*, 521 U.S. 507 (1997). Nevertheless, since the Ninth Circuit's decision was made before the law was declared unconstitutional, the decision remains. One has the slightest suspicion, however, that even without the RFRA the Ninth Circuit would have found a constitutional violation.
37   104 F3d 1528–30.
38   *Mockaitis v. Harcleroad*, 104 F. 3d 1522 (9th Cir 1997).
39   As with Hale's case, general information on Barone may be found by consulting an *Oregonian* index under his name and reading the articles listed there. In addition, the Oregon Supreme Court has handed down two decisions affirming his convictions and sentences of death. *State v. Barone*, 328 Or 68, 969 P2d 1013 (1998) and *State v. Barone*, 329 Or 210, 986 P2d 5 (1999).
40   Holly Danks, "Four-time Oregon Murderer Tries to Hasten Florida Trial," *Oregonian*, 9 April 1996, B1.
41   A letter to the editor of the Fort Lauderdale *Sun-Sentinel* early in 1997, when Barone's extradition to Florida was planned, complained about Florida residents having to pay the costs of extraditing and trying Barone for the 1979 crime. He still has not been extradited to stand trial. It may never take place.
42   The death penalty was passed by citizen vote in November 1978 but was declared unconstitutional, on state constitutional grounds, in January 1981.
43   A reflective piece on the life and work of Martha Bryant, written by Nena Baker, appeared as "Murder of a Midwife," *Oregonian*, 20 December 1992, NW Living, 1. Barone is a very intelligent man who married a legal assistant from a prominent Portland law firm and had a child with her before the Oregon murders occurred. They separated late in 1991 and their divorce became final in May 1992. Holly Danks, "Barone Father-Son Ploy for Sympathy Misfires," *Oregonian*, 25 January 1995, B2.
44   *State v. Stevens*, 311 Or 119, 806 P2d 92 (1991).
45   *State v. Stevens*, 319 Or 573, 879 P2d 162 (1994).
46   *Ibid.*, 579.
47   *State ex rel. Carlile v. Frost*, 326 Or 607, 956 P2d 202 (1998).
48   *Ibid.*, 617–18.
49   Phone interview with Jason Carlile, Linn County District Attorney, 16 November 1999.
50   Dana Tims of the *Oregonian* followed the story closely and reported on the escape in "Murderer Escapes from Jail in Roseburg," 29 October 1996, B2.
51   *Ibid.*
52   Janet Filips, "Jury Issues Death Penalty for Woman's Killer," *Oregonian*, 16 January 1997, E6.
53   "Douglas County Sheriff Lauds Report on Lax Jail Security," *Oregonian*, 8 January 1997, B7.
54   Janet Filips, "Jury Issues Death Penalty for Woman's Killer," *Oregonian* 16 January 1997, E6.
55   *State v. Harberts*, 331 Or 72, 11 P3d 641 (2000).

Part IV
Conclusion

CHAPTER 12

Conclusions and Future Possibilities

The purpose of this chapter is to weave together some results of this study on the Oregon death penalty. Though several of the following observations are scattered throughout the book, it might be helpful to bring them together so that the cumulative effect may be evident.

First, the most overwhelming reality confronting the student of Oregon's modern death penalty is the cost that it exacts to implement it. I have stressed the enormous monetary costs in Chapter One, but a few other costs should be listed. Difficulty of precise calibration of these costs should not be confused with their existence and their reality.

There is the cost to the victim's family, especially if the cases are remanded from the Oregon Supreme Court for resentencing. It is wrenching enough for the family to testify at the original trial and sentencing. The wound is so fresh, the violation so extreme, the anguish so overwhelming. But, as more than one family can affirm, the reality of testifying at subsequent resentencing hearings is even worse than at the original trial. Take the family of Anne Gray, who was brutally murdered in Salem by Robert Langley late in 1987 and buried in a shallow grave behind the house of Langley's aunt on NE Broadway. Langley was convicted of the crime in 1989 and sentenced to death. The case had a *Penry* problem and so resentencing had to occur. That resentencing finally happened late in 1994.

The reaction of the family to the resentencing hearing is stunning. They thought that they would be able to get some closure after Anne's death when they testified at the first trial. Although they never were able to forget "Annie," they felt that they were able to start moving forward with their lives. Then came the resentencing and they were called upon to testify again. One of her sisters said,

> You try so hard to put it in a place that makes it OK to go on with your life. To have to remember it again is horrible. I've suffered more anxiety this time than the first time.[1]

In the same article, the district attorney predicted that it could take up to seven years after the 1994 sentencing for Langley to be put to death. It has now been seven years since that resentencing, and Langley's case has been remanded once again to the Marion County Circuit Court. One wonders if this time the family and the state will push for another sentence of death or will seek a plea for a lesser sentence, such as life without the possibility of parole. If they do the former, it will be yet another three or four years before the supreme court will be called upon to reconsider the sentencing decision.

Then there are the hidden costs to the system of justice itself. Attorneys on both sides of the issue burn out with regularity because of the intensity of death penalty issues and the stakes involved. Perhaps the public finds it difficult to conjure up much support for lawyer burnout, but one must consider that this includes prosecuting and defense attorneys as well as judges who hear these cases along the way. It is not difficult to find a defense attorney who will say that the costs on lawyers are too great, but it would take a courageous district attorney to say the same. The Oregon Supreme Court, already burdened with cases galore to which priority has to be accorded,[2] is one of the bodies which disproportionately bears the costs of Oregon's death penalty. Though many of the justices have their own personal reservations about the death penalty, their conscientious effort to apply and interpret the death penalty law is increasingly demanding a larger and larger amount of their time and effort. With up to 15 cases not yet affirmed and with the possibility of all 25 cases returning to the court at the post-conviction stage, one has all the makings for major gridlock at the top of Oregon's judicial system.

Finally, there are the hidden costs on the people of the state of Oregon. Of course these costs are not borne by many and may be very small, but they are especially borne in the preparation for and aftermath of executions. Over one hundred extra staff are required to facilitate all aspects of an execution. Many of the people involved in executions have had to seek professional counseling as a result of it dawning on them that they were actually participating, in an intimate and irreversible way, in putting a person to death. Those affected are not simply Corrections Department people. They are lawyers from the Justice

Department, newscasters, journalists, clergy and counselors themselves. The alluringly sweet song of simply doing one's duty as a loyal public servant plays off-key when an execution is imminent.

Unintended Consequences

Perhaps the most unexpected result of this study, an unintended consequence if you will, is the sheer number, magnitude and irony of the unexpected consequences of implementing the 1984 death penalty statute in Oregon. The first major unexpected consequence was the 1989 *Penry* decision of the U.S. Supreme Court. This added at least five years and up to a decade or more to the process for all those sentenced to death upon their resentencing after *Penry*. A second unintended consequence was the results of poor drafting of Ballot Measure 40 by supporters of victims' rights. A third consequence is that the inordinate delays may lead to executions of people who themselves would die within a short time if the state does not choose to execute them. A fourth consequence is only beginning to unfold now and may relate to the efforts of victims' rights supporters to change the death penalty statute in 1995 and 1997 so that aggravation evidence and victims' impact evidence may be considered under the fourth question in Oregon's death penalty statute. As the process becomes longer and longer for more and more death row inmates, one can only imagine what other hurdles to delay the process will arise. It is simply naïve to believe, on the basis of past history, that "all the problems" with the statute are now solved.

The Effect of Post-Conviction

Although it is not an unexpected consequence of the death penalty statute, the existence of post-conviction relief was a hidden cost in 1984 that has finally come to the surface. Post-conviction was only a small cloud on the horizon, no larger than a man's hand, when Oregon's death penalty was abolished in 1964. Supporters of restoration of the penalty in the 1983 legislature were aware that post-conviction relief was available to those sentenced to death, but they imagined that the process would be dispatched rather summarily. The average length of the first of four steps in post-conviction relief for those sentenced to death since 1984, however, has been 4.5 years. The entire state post-conviction process may add eight to ten years to the death penalty process.

One might respond to the reality of delays and costs and unintended consequences in three ways. One approach might be to conclude that this enormous expenditure of economic and social capital on a few men is an expense well worth it. If society holds certain values very dear, it is willing to expend a lot of resources, economic and otherwise, to see that its values are implemented. Justice is costly in America. Due process requires that extreme vigilance be practiced, especially in death penalty cases where the risk of mistake is a cost almost too unbearable to endure. Therefore, the system is basically even though it requires considerable time and expense to implement it.

Asecond approach might be to try to hasten the process. This approach would recognize that the people of Oregon have unequivocally chosen to have a death penalty and that the citizens of Oregon, therefore, deserve to have a penalty that is implemented, if the crime fits the legal criteria, in a just *and* expeditious manner. Delay in rendering justice is not necessarily an indication of judicial care. It may be a reflection of judicial interest in undermining the statute, in opposing the clear directive of the people of Oregon. Justice delayed may be justice denied. Therefore, keep the death penalty but speed up the process in a major way.

If one approaches the issue in this way, one would have to seek major statutory changes to make the system hum more smoothly. Fiscally conservative people who support the death penalty are certainly not getting the bang for their buck under the current system. Therefore, according to this approach, the system needs to change in a dramatic way. One could require the Oregon Supreme Court, as did the original version of the statute passed by the voters in 1978, to handle direct and automatic review within a specified time after sentence of death is imposed. One could require them to make a decision within a short time after that. One could try to eliminate one or more steps from the post-conviction process, though with our current understanding of the right to appeal circuit court judgments, only one step could plausibly be eliminated. One could try to cut the budget of the indigent defense services division, so as to encourage lawyers and the system to realize that fewer resources are available.

Some of these efforts are fraught with difficulty. Indeed, opponents of the current system are caught in somewhat of a Catch-22 situation. If they want to cut the budgets of various people along the way that would lead to lesser remuneration for attorneys arguing death penalty cases, it could also lead to more plausible cases of ineffective assistance of counsel later in the process. More delays. If one tries to eliminate Step 4 of the process, appeal to the Oregon Court of Appeals, one may have to do so in the face of a unanimous Oregon Supreme Court opposing one in the legislature. The only place in the system at this point where significant savings of time can probably be brought into the system without huge difficulty is in Step 3 of the process, post-conviction relief in the Marion County Circuit Court. The quick dismissal of Jeffrey Williams' claim, fewer than three years after he sought post-conviction relief, may be an indication that Marion County will be doing just this.

The third response considers that the excessive costs and delays in implementing Oregon's 1984 statute are really an indication of the significant ambivalence the judiciary and the people of Oregon have toward the death penalty. Proponents of this approach would maintain that the 1984 vote, overwhelming as it was, was simply a clear and powerful expression of popular dissatisfaction with a criminal justice system that seemed unable, for whatever reason, to keep its most dangerous people locked up and secure. Proponents would stress that the passage of the 1989 law permitting life imprisonment without the possibility of parole has solved the problem that Oregonians in 1984 were clamoring to have solved. About 70–80 people in Oregon are now serving life sentences without the possibility of parole. This penalty, proponents argue, deals with the issues of justice and safety all at once. In addition, it saves an immense amount of money.[3]

Future Issues

In June 2001 the Oregon Supreme Court certified the ballot title for a constitutional amendment, to be submitted to the voters in November 2002, which would eliminate the death penalty in Oregon. This amendment would have the effect of repealing Article I, section 40, of the Oregon Constitution, the section that exempted the death penalty from an attack based on Article 1, sections 15 and 16, of the Oregon Constitution in effect in 1984.[4] Proponents of the ballot measure are now free to collect signatures and must collect around 90,000 valid signatures by July 2002 in order to qualify for the November ballot. If the proponents surmount this hurdle, the people of Oregon will vote on the issue for the first time since 1984.

Interesting to note is a major decision that backers of the measure, the Oregon Coalition to Abolish the Death Penalty, had to make in shaping the measure. Their approach would eliminate not only the punishment of death for those convicted of aggravated murder but also the option of life imprisonment with a possibility of parole after 30 years. In essence, then, if a person were convicted of aggravated murder under the provision now being circulated, that person would automatically receive a sentence of life imprisonment without the possibility of parole. In addition, such a person would be required to make restitution to the state of Oregon for their incarceration and to the victim's heirs for their crime. Proponents felt that by tailoring the measure to capture the sentiment of those supportive of restorative justice, as well as those who were still worried that life imprisonment means the person will only serve a few years in jail, they have a chance of success in 2002. In other words, enough "fence-sitters" would be persuaded by this approach to eliminate the death penalty from Oregon.

Though this is not the forum to debate the various options that were open to the committee, their focus on life imprisonment without the possibility of parole shows that we may be mired in a second-generation reaction to the liberal penological theories of the 1960s and 1970s. Those theories, rampant in Oregon at the time of eliminating the death penalty in 1964 (as shown in Chapter Three) were based on a notion of human perfectability and rehabilitation. Uncritical acceptance of these theories led to unwise parole policies and to some of the most memorable and chilling murders in recent Oregon history. As a result Oregonians were hurt so deeply, either because they suffered directly from this policy (and became victims or acquaintances of victims) or indirectly, through fear, that they just were not going to let this happen again. The enormous strength of the victims' rights movement in this state during the late 1980s and 1990s is a testimony to this commitment.

By 2001 that movement may have crested in the public's mind, and "victims" of the victims' rights movement are starting to gain their voices.[5] The fact that the Oregon Coalition to Abolish the Death Penalty feels that it is time to bring the measure to the public again, with the support of former Senator Mark Hatfield and a host of other people, bespeaks a confidence that simply was not there a few years ago. But it is clearly a measure shaped by the history of the past 40 years in Oregon. There are probably very few people on the OCADP who believe that the only punishment for aggravated murder *ought* to be life imprisonment without the possibility of parole. Their measure is therefore a political compromise, a necessary one in their judgment, to eliminate the death penalty.

Finally, it will be interesting to see what kinds of arguments are made by proponents and opponents of the death penalty in the next year as the issue makes its way to the ballot.[6] The traditional arguments that were made in the 1960s—that the death penalty does not deter a person from violent crime, or that the death penalty disproportionately falls upon the poor or racial minorities, or that the death penalty may be executed against an innocent person— may not resonate as well with Oregonians in 2002. Deterrence only works as an argument for either side if there is a significant number of executions so that one can collect statistical samples and measure the effect, or lack thereof, of those executions. There have been only two executions in Oregon in the last 35 years. Deterrence statistics will tell us nothing.

In addition, the argument regarding disproportionate effect of the death penalty on racial or ethnic minorities will have no resonance here as there is only one African-American on death row in Oregon, and the number of Hispanics (2) or Native Americans (1) on death row is not grossly disproportional to their population in the state. Proponents of the ballot measure to abolish the death penalty might try to argue for the possibility of mistake, and the case of Scott Harberts lends some credibility to that possibility, but the diligence of the Oregon Supreme Court over the last decade in death penalty cases leaves that possibility somewhat remote at this point.

These proponents are on firmer ground, I believe, in trying to make the point that Oregon finally has a law assuring life imprisonment without the possibility of parole and that the law is actually working effectively. To that end, a desideratum would be a study in Oregon of the use of this as a sentencing option since its passage by the Oregon Legislature in 1989. Opponents of the death penalty ought not be too elated about the virtue of such a law, however. Some convicted aggravated murderers, if they considered the choice at age 25 between execution and life imprisonment without the possibility of parole, might choose the former.

A contribution of this work, I believe, is that the economic argument should play a role in the debate about the death penalty in 2002. Economic arguments have become central to setting public policy in America in the 1990s. Schools must be efficient, businesses must be efficient, systems of all kinds must run economically. That is the way arguments are made in the 1990s. Why shouldn't the criminal justice system also be efficient, especially in death penalty cases? Whatever the arguments advanced, the issue of whether Oregonians want capital punishment to continue is with us again—for the eighth time.

Endnotes

1   Janet Davies, "Family Waits for Closure After Killing," *Statesman Journal,* 19 November 1994, A1.

2   An example of this are the numerous ballot measure title approvals that take up at least one month of each year of the court's time and must be resolved expeditiously in order for ballot supporters to begin to collect voter signatures for these measures. The Oregon Supreme Court spent a considerable portion of the months of October and November 1999 certifying ballot measure titles.

3   An intermediate legal suggestion that has not been given much attention but deserves consideration would be that if the state (through a circuit court jury) sentences a person to death, the state would only have a certain amount of time, say 15 years, to put the person to death, or else the interminable waiting becomes, as it were, cruel and unusual punishment. If justice delayed is justice denied, and if a death sentence constantly delayed is tantamount to injustice, why shouldn't there be an outer timelimit, except in exceptional cases, within which a sentence of death must be carried out?

4   Chapter Four dealt with the constitutional amendment passed in 1984 which limited the effect of Article 1, sections 15 and 16 in cases of aggravated murder.

5   An indication of this effort was the attempt made in 2000 to repeal Measure 11, the mandatory minimum sentencing law for about 15 very serious felonies which the citizens of Oregon passed by a large margin in 1994. Some of the most vociferous opponents of Ballot Measure 11 are women whose sons (almost exclusively) have been sentenced, they believe unfairly, under this new law. This measure was defeated by a 3–1 margin in November 2000.

6   As with every ballot measure, of course, there is a significant chance that it will not garner a sufficient number of valid signatures to get on the ballot. It is a constitutional amendment, and so will require more valid signatures than a mere statutory change. An issue that will probably cause considerable debate within OCADP will be the propriety of using paid signature-gatherers for their effort. The "old" Oregon way is to do it with volunteers who are committed to the cause. The "new" way is to get it on the ballot in whatever way you can, legally, even if this means that you will pay someone a certain amount for gathering signatures. So, various layers of values are intertwined in this issue.

APPENDIX

The Developments of the Modern Oregon Death Penalty Statute

The 1978 Initiative Petition

Passed handily 573,707 - 318,610

This was Section 3 of a much longer act passed by the people.

SECTION 3. (1) Upon a finding that the defendant is guilty of murder, the court shall conduct a separate sentencing proceeding to determine whether the defendant shall be sentenced to life imprisonment or death. The proceeding shall be conducted in the trial court before the trial judge as soon as practicable. In the proceeding, evidence may be presented as to any matter that the court deems relevant to sentence. This subsection shall not be construed to authorize the introduction of any evidence secured in violation of the Constitution of the United States or of the State of Oregon. The state and the defendant or his counsel shall be permitted to present arguments for or against a sentence of death.

　　　(2) Upon conclusion of the presentation of the evidence, the trial court shall consider:

　　　(a) Whether the conduct of the defendant that caused the death of the deceased was committed deliberately and with the reasonable expectation that death of the deceased or another would result;

(b) Whether there is a probability that the defendant would commit criminal acts of violence that would constitute a continuing threat to society. In determining this issue, the trial judge shall consider any mitigating circumstances offered by the defendant, including, but not limited to, the defendant's age, the extent and severity of his prior criminal conduct and the extent of the mental and emotional pressure under which the defendant was acting at the time the offense was committed; and

(c) If raised by the evidence, whether the conduct of the defendant in killing the deceased was unreasonable in response to the provocation, if any, by the deceased.

(3) The state must prove each issue submitted beyond a reasonable doubt, and the trial judge shall render a judgment of "yes" or "no" on each issue considered.

(4) If the trial judge renders an affirmative finding on each issue considered under this section, the trial judge shall sentence the defendant to death. If the trial judge renders a negative finding on any issue submitted under this section, the trial judge shall sentence the defendant to imprisonment for life in the custody of the Corrections Division.

(5) The judgment of conviction and sentence of death shall be subject to automatic review by the Supreme Court within 60 days after certification of the entire record by the sentencing court, unless an additional period not exceeding 30 days is extended by the Supreme Court for good cause. The review by the Supreme Court shall have priority over all other cases, and shall be heard in accordance with rules promulgated by the Supreme Court.

1984 Initiative Petition

Passed handily: 893,818 - 295,988

Section 3. (1) Upon a finding that the defendant is guilty of aggravated murder, the court shall conduct a separate sentencing proceeding to determine whether the defendant shall be sentenced to life imprisonment or death. The proceeding shall be conducted in the trial court before the trial jury as soon as practicable. If the defendant has pleaded guilty, the sentencing proceeding shall be conducted before a jury impaneled for that purpose. In the proceeding, evidence may be presented as to any matter that the court deems relevant to sentence; however, neither the state nor the defendant shall be allowed to introduce repetitive evidence that has previously been offered and received during the trial on the issue of guilt. The court shall instruct the jury that all evidence previously offered and received may be considered for purposes of the sentencing hearing. This subsection shall not be construed to authorize the introduction of any evidence secured in violation of the Constitution of the United States or of the State of Oregon. The state and the defendant or the counsel of the defendant shall be permitted to present arguments for or against a sentence of death.

(2) Upon the conclusion of the presentation of the evidence, the court shall submit the following issues to the jury:

(a) Whether the conduct of the defendant that caused the death of the deceased was committed deliberately and with the reasonable expectation that death of the deceased or another would result;

(b) Whether there is a probability that the defendant would commit criminal acts of violence that would constitute a continuing threat to society. In determining this issue, the court shall instruct the jury to consider any mitigating circumstances offered in evidence, including, but not limited to, the defendant's age, the extent and severity of the defendant's prior criminal conduct and the extent of the mental and emotional pressure under which the defendant was acting at the time the offense was committed; and

(c) If raised by the evidence, whether the conduct of the defendant in killing the deceased was unreasonable in response to the provocation, if any, by the deceased.

(3) The state must prove each issue submitted beyond a reasonable doubt, and the jury shall return a special verdict of "yes" or "no" on each issue considered.

(4) The court shall charge the jury that it may not answer any issue "yes" unless it agrees unanimously.

(5) If the jury returns an affirmative finding on each issue considered under this section, the trial judge shall sentence the defendant to death. If the jury returns a negative finding on any issue submitted under this section, the trial judge shall sentence the defendant to imprisonment for life in the custody of the Corrections Division as provided in ORS 163.105.

(6) The judgment of conviction and sentence of death shall be subject to automatic and direct review by the Supreme Court. The review by the Supreme Court shall have priority over all other cases, and shall be heard in accordance with rules promulgated by the Supreme Court.

Law after 1987 Legislative Assembly

ORS 163.150(1987) Sentencing for aggravated murder; proceedings; issues for jury; review by Supreme Court: effect of plea of guilty or no contest.

(1)(a) Upon a finding that the defendant is guilty of aggravated murder, the court, except as otherwise provided in subsection (2) of this section, shall conduct a separate sentencing proceeding to determine whether the defendant shall be sentenced to life imprisonment or death. The proceeding shall be conducted in the trial court before the trial jury as soon as practicable. If the defendant has pleaded guilty, the sentencing proceeding shall be conducted before a jury impaneled for that purpose. In the proceeding, evidence may be presented as to any matter that the court deems relevant to sentence; however, neither the state nor the defendant shall be allowed to introduce repetitive evidence that has previously been offered and received during the trial on the issue of guilt. The court shall instruct the jury that all evidence previously offered and received may be considered for purposes of the sentencing hearing. This subsection shall not be construed to authorize the introduction of any evidence secured in violation of the Constitution of the United States or of the State of Oregon. The state and the defendant or the counsel of the defendant shall be permitted to present arguments for or against a sentence of death.

(b) Upon the conclusion of the presentation of the evidence, the court shall submit the following issues to the jury:

(A) Whether the conduct of the defendant that caused the death of the deceased was committed deliberately and with the reasonable expectation that death of the deceased or another would result;

(B) Whether there is a probability that the defendant would commit criminal acts of violence that would constitute a continuing threat to society. In determining this issue, the court shall instruct the jury to consider any mitigating circumstances offered in evidence, including, but not limited to, the defendant's age, the extent and severity of the defendant's prior criminal conduct and the extent of the mental and emotional pressure under which the defendant was acting at the time the offense was committed; and

(C) If raised by the evidence, whether the conduct of the defendant in killing the deceased was unreasonable in response to the provocation, if any, by the deceased.

(c) The state must prove each issue submitted beyond a reasonable doubt, and the jury shall return a special verdict of "yes" or "no" on each issue considered.

(d) The court shall charge the jury that it may not answer any issue "yes" unless it agrees unanimously.

(e) If the jury returns an affirmative finding on each issue considered under this section, the trial judge shall sentence the defendant to death. If the jury returns a negative finding on any issue submitted under this section, the trial judge shall sentence the defendant to imprisonment for life in the custody of the Department of Corrections as provided in ORS 163.105.

(f) The judgment of conviction and sentence of death shall be subject to automatic and direct review by the Supreme Court. The review by the

Supreme Court shall have priority over all other cases, and shall be heard in accordance with rules promulgated by the Supreme Court.

(2) When the defendant is fuond guilty of aggravated murder upon a plea of guulty or not contest prior to the introduction of evidence before the trier of fact and the state advises the court on the record that the state declines to present evidence for purposes of sentencing, the court shall not conduct a sentencing proceeding as descried in subsection (1) of this section, but the court shall sentence the defendant to life imprisonment as prescribed by ORS 163.105. (1985 c. 3 sec 3; 1987 c. 320 sec 86; 1987 c. 557 sec 1.

The Law after 1989 Legislative Assembly

163.150. Sentencing for aggravated murder; proceedings; issues for jury; review by Supreme Court; effect of plea of guilty or no contest.

(1)(a) Upon a finding that the defendant is guilty of aggravated murder, the court, except as otherwise provided in subsection (3) of this section, shall conduct a separate sentencing proceeding to determine whether the defendant shall be sentenced to life imprisonment, as described in ORS 163.105 (1)(c), life imprisonment without the possibility of release or parole, as described in ORS 163.105 (1)(b), or death. The proceeding shall be conducted in the trial court before the trial jury as soon as practicable. If the defendant has pleaded guilty, the sentencing proceeding shall be conducted before a jury impaneled for that purpose. In the proceeding, evidence may be presented as to any matter that the court deems relevant to sentence; however, neither the state nor the defendant shall be allowed to introduce repetitive evidence that has previously been offered and received during the trial on the issue of guilt. The court shall instruct the jury that all evidence previously offered and received may be considered for purposes of the sentencing hearing. This subsection shall not be construed to authorize the introduction of any evidence secured in violation of the Constitution of the United States or of the State of Oregon. The state and the defendant or the counsel of the defendant shall be permitted to present arguments for or against a sentence of death and for or against a sentence of life imprisonment with or without the possibility of release or parole.

(b) Upon the conclusion of the presentation of the evidence, the court shall submit the following issues to the jury:

(A) Whether the conduct of the defendant that caused the death of the deceased was committed deliberately and with the reasonable expectation that death of the deceased or another would result;

(B) Whether there is a probability that the defendant would commit criminal acts of violence that would constitute a continuing threat to society;

(C) If raised by the evidence, whether the conduct of the defendant in killing the deceased was unreasonable in response to the provocation, if any, by the deceased; and

(D) If constitutionally required, considering the extent to which the defendant's character and background, and the circumstances of the offense may reduce the defendant's moral culpability or blameworthiness for the crime, whether a sentence of death be imposed.

(c) In determining the issues in paragraph (b) of this subsection, the court shall instruct the jury to consider any mitigating circumstances offered in evidence, including but not limited to the defendant's age, the extent and severity of the defendant's prior criminal conduct and the extent of the mental and emotional pressure under which the defendant was acting at the time the offense was committed.

(d) The state must prove each issue submitted under subparagraphs (A) to (C) of paragraph (b) of this subsection beyond a reasonable doubt, and the jury shall return a special verdict of "yes" or "no" on each issue considered.

(e) The court shall charge the jury that it may not answer any issue "yes," under paragraph (b) of this subsection unless it agrees unanimously.

(f) If the jury returns an affirmative finding on each issue considered under paragraph (b) of this subsection, the trial judge shall sentence the defendant to death.

(g) The judgment of conviction and sentence of death shall be subject to automatic and direct review by the Supreme Court. The review by the Supreme Court shall have priority over all other cases, and shall be heard in accordance with rules promulgated by the Supreme Court.

(2)(a) Upon the conclusion of the presentation of the evidence, the court shall also instruct the jury that if it reaches a negative finding on any issue under paragraph (b) of subsection (1) of this section, the trial court shall sentence the defendant to life imprisonment without the possibility of release or parole, as described in ORS 163.105 (1)(b), unless 10 or more members of the jury further find that there are sufficient mitigating circumstances to warrant life imprisonment, in which case the trial court shall sentence the defendant to life imprisonment as described in ORS 163.105 (1)(c).

(b) If the jury returns a negative finding on any issue under paragraph (b) of subsection (1) of this section and further finds that there are sufficient mitigating circumstances to warrant life imprisonment, the trial court shall sentence the defendant to life imprisonment in the custody of the Department of Corrections as provided in ORS 163.105 (1)(c).

(3)(a) When the defendant is found guilty of aggravated murder upon a plea of guilty or no contest prior to the introduction of evidence before the trier of fact, and the state advises the court on the record that the state declines to present evidence for purposes of sentencing the defendant to death, the court:

(A) Shall not conduct a sentencing proceeding as described in subsection (1) of this section, and a sentence of death shall not be ordered.

(B) Shall conduct a sentencing proceeding to determine whether the defendant shall be sentenced to life imprisonment without the possibility of release or parole as described in ORS 163.105 (1)(b) or life imprisonment as described in ORS 163.105 (1)(c). If the defendant waives all rights to a jury sentencing proceeding, the court shall conduct the sentencing proceeding as the trier of fact. The procedure for the sentencing proceeding, whether before a court or a jury, shall follow the procedure of paragraph (a) of subsection (1) and subsection (2) of this section, as modified by this subsection which prohibits a sentence of death when the state declines to present evidence.

(b) Nothing in this subsection shall preclude the court from sentencing the defendant to life imprisonment, as described in ORS 163.105 (1)(c), or life imprisonment without the possibility of release or parole, as described in ORS 163.105 (1)(b), pursuant to a stipulation of sentence or stipulation of sentencing facts agreed to and offered by both parties if the defendant waives all rights to a jury sentencing proceeding.

(4) If any part of subsection (2) of this section is held invalid and as a result thereof a defendant who has been sentenced to life imprisonment without possibility of release or parole will instead be sentenced to life imprisonment in the custody of the Department of Corrections as provided in ORS 163.105 (2), the defendant shall be confined for a minimum of 30 years without possibility of parole, release on work release or any form of temporary leave or employment at a forest or work camp. Subsection (2) of this section shall apply only to trials commencing on or after July 19, 1989.

(5) Notwithstanding paragraph (a) of subsection (1) of this section, the following shall apply:

(a) If a reviewing court finds prejudicial error in the sentencing proceeding only, the court may set aside the sentence of death and remand the case to the trial court. No error in the sentencing proceeding shall result in reversal of the defendant's conviction for aggravated murder. Upon remand and at the election of the state, the trial court shall either:

(A) Sentence the defendant to imprisonment for life in the custody of the Department of Corrections as provided in ORS 163.105 (1)(c); or

(B) Impanel a new sentencing jury for the purpose of conducting a new sentencing proceeding.

(b) The new sentencing proceeding shall be governed by the provisions of subsections (1) and (2) of this section. A transcript of all testimony and all exhibits and other evidence properly admitted in the prior trial and sentencing proceeding shall be admissible in the new sentencing proceeding. Either party may recall any witness who testified at the prior trial or sentencing proceeding and may present additional relevant evidence.

(c) The provisions of this section are procedural and shall apply to any defendant sentenced to death after December 6, 1984. (1985 c.3 sec 3; 1987 c.320 sec 86; 1987 c.557 sec 1; 1989 c.720 sec 2; 1989 c.790 sec 135b.)

The Law after 1991 Legislative Assembly

Note the continual expansion.

ORS 163.150 (1992) Sentencing for aggravated murder; proceedings; issues for jury; review by Supreme Court; effect of plea of guilty or no contest.

(1)(a) Upon a finding that the defendant is guilty of aggravated murder, the court, except as otherwise provided in subsection (3) of this section, shall conduct a separate sentencing proceeding to determine whether the defendant shall be sentenced to life imprisonment, as described in ORS 163.105 (1)(c), life imprisonment without the possibility of release or parole, as described in ORS 163.105 (1)(b), or death. The proceeding shall be conducted in the trial court before the trial jury as soon as practicable. If a juror for any reason is unable to perform the function of a juror, the juror shall be dismissed from the sentencing proceeding. The court shall cause to be drawn the name of one of the alternate jurors, who shall then become a member of the jury for the sentencing proceeding notwithstanding the fact that the alternate juror did not deliberate on the issue of guilt. The substitution of an alternate juror shall be allowed only if the jury has not begun to deliberate on the issue of the sentence. If the defendant has pleaded guilty, the sentencing proceeding shall be conducted before a jury impaneled for that purpose. In the proceeding, evidence may be presented as to any matter that the court deems relevant to sentence; however, neither the state nor the defendant shall be allowed to introduce repetitive evidence that has previously been offered and received during the trial on the issue of guilt. The court shall instruct the jury that all evidence previously offered and received may be considered for purposes of the sentencing hearing. This subsection shall not be construed to authorize the introduction of any evidence secured in violation of the Constitution of the United States or of the State of Oregon. The state and the defendant or the counsel of the defendant shall be permitted to present arguments for or against a sentence of death and for or against a sentence of life imprisonment with or without the possibility of release or parole.

(b) Upon the conclusion of the presentation of the evidence, the court shall submit the following issues to the jury:

(A) Whether the conduct of the defendant that caused the death of the deceased was committed deliberately and with the reasonable expectation that death of the deceased or another would result;

(B) Whether there is a probability that the defendant would commit criminal acts of violence that would constitute a continuing threat to society;

(C) If raised by the evidence, whether the conduct of the defendant in killing the deceased was unreasonable in response to the provocation, if any, by the deceased; and

(D) Whether the defendant should receive a death sentence.

(c)(A) In determining the issues in paragraph (b) of this subsection, the court shall instruct the jury to consider any mitigating circumstances offered in evidence, including but not limited to the defendant's age, the extent and severity of the defendant's prior criminal conduct and the extent of the mental and emotional pressure under which the defendant was acting at the time the offense was committed.

(B) In determining the issue in subparagraph (D) of paragraph (b) of this subsection, the court shall instruct the jury to answer the question "no" if one or more of the jurors find there is any aspect of the defendant's character or background, or any circumstances of the offense, that one or more of the jurors believe would justify a sentence less than death.   (d) The state must prove each issue submitted under subparagraphs (A) to (C) of paragraph (b) of this subsection beyond a reasonable doubt, and the jury shall return a special verdict of "yes" or "no" on each issue considered.

(e) The court shall charge the jury that it may not answer any issue "yes," under paragraph (b) of this subsection unless it agrees unanimously.

(f) If the jury returns an affirmative finding on each issue considered under paragraph (b) of this subsection, the trial judge shall sentence the defendant to death.

(g) The judgment of conviction and sentence of death shall be subject to automatic and direct review by the Supreme Court. The review by the Supreme Court shall have priority over all other cases, and shall be heard in accordance with rules promulgated by the Supreme Court. A sentence of death shall be automatically stayed if the defendant seeks review by the United States Supreme Court on a direct appeal. The stay shall remain in effect until:

(A) The defendant's time for filing a petition for certiorari or an appeal expires;

(B) The United States Supreme Court acts to decline to consider the case further; or

(C) The United States Supreme Court resolves the case on the merits.

(2)(a) Upon the conclusion of the presentation of the evidence, the court shall also instruct the jury that if it reaches a negative finding on any issue under paragraph (b) of subsection (1) of this section, the trial court shall sentence the defendant to life imprisonment without the possibility of release or parole, as described in ORS 163.105 (1)(b), unless 10 or more members of the jury further find that there are sufficient mitigating circumstances to warrant life imprisonment, in which case the trial court shall sentence the defendant to life imprisonment as described in ORS 163.105 (1)(c).

(b) If the jury returns a negative finding on any issue under paragraph (b) of subsection (1) of this section and further finds that there are sufficient mitigating circumstances to warrant life imprisonment, the trial court shall sentence the defendant to life imprisonment in the custody of the Department of Corrections as provided in ORS 163.105 (1)(c).

(3)(a) When the defendant is found guilty of aggravated murder upon a plea of guilty or no contest prior to the introduction of evidence before the trier of fact, and the state advises the court on the record that the state declines to present evidence for purposes of sentencing the defendant to death, the court:

(A) Shall not conduct a sentencing proceeding as described in subsection (1) of this section, and a sentence of death shall not be ordered.

(B) Shall conduct a sentencing proceeding to determine whether the defendant shall be sentenced to life imprisonment without the possibility of release or parole as described in ORS 163.105 (1)(b) or life imprisonment as described in ORS 163.105 (1)(c). If the defendant waives all rights to a jury sentencing proceeding, the court shall conduct the sentencing proceeding as the trier of fact. The procedure for the sentencing proceeding, whether before a court or a jury, shall follow the procedure of paragraph (a) of subsection (1) and subsection (2) of this section, as modified by this subsection which prohibits a sentence of death when the state declines to present evidence.

(b) Nothing in this subsection shall preclude the court from sentencing the defendant to life imprisonment, as described in ORS 163.105 (1)(c), or life imprisonment without the possibility of release or parole, as described in ORS 163.105 (1)(b), pursuant to a stipulation of sentence or stipulation of sentencing facts agreed to and offered by both parties if the defendant waives all rights to a jury sentencing proceeding.

(4) If any part of subsection (2) of this section is held invalid and as a result thereof a defendant who has been sentenced to life imprisonment without possibility of release or parole will instead be sentenced to life imprisonment in the custody of the Department of Corrections as provided in ORS

163.105 (2), the defendant shall be confined for a minimum of 30 years without possibility of parole, release on work release or any form of temporary leave or employment at a forest or work camp. Subsection (2) of this section shall apply only to trials commencing on or after July 19, 1989.

(5) Notwithstanding paragraph (a) of subsection (1) of this section, the following shall apply:

(a) If a reviewing court finds prejudicial error in the sentencing proceeding only, the court may set aside the sentence of death and remand the case to the trial court. No error in the sentencing proceeding shall result in reversal of the defendant's conviction for aggravated murder. Upon remand and at the election of the state, the trial court shall either:

(A) Sentence the defendant to imprisonment for life in the custody of the Department of Corrections as provided in ORS 163.105 (1)(c); or

(B) Impanel a new sentencing jury for the purpose of conducting a new sentencing proceeding to determine if the defendant should be sentenced to:

(i) Death;

(ii) Imprisonment for life without the possibility of release or parole as provided in ORS 163.105 (1)(b); or

(iii) Imprisonment for life in the custody of the Department of Corrections as provided in ORS 163.105 (1)(c).

(b) If the trial court grants a mistrial during the sentencing proceeding, the trial court, at the election of the state, shall either:

(A) Sentence the defendant to imprisonment for life in the custody of the Department of Corrections as provided in ORS 163.105 (1)(c); or

(B) Impanel a new sentencing jury for the purpose of conducting a new sentencing proceeding to determine if the defendant should be sentenced to:

(i) Death;

(ii) Imprisonment for life without the possibility of release or parole as provided in ORS 163.105 (1)(b); or

(iii) Imprisonment for life in the custody of the Department of Corrections as provided in ORS 163.105 (1)(c).

(c) Nothing in this subsection shall preclude the court from sentencing the defendant to life imprisonment without the possibility of release or parole, as described in ORS 163.105 (1)(b), pursuant to a stipulation of sentence if the defendant waives all rights to a jury sentencing proceeding.

(d) The new sentencing proceeding shall be governed by the provisions of subsections (1) and (2) of this section. A transcript of all testimony and all exhibits and other evidence properly admitted in the prior trial and sentencing proceeding shall be admissible in the new sentencing proceeding. Either party may recall any witness who testified at the prior trial or sentencing proceeding and may present additional relevant evidence.

(e) The provisions of this section are procedural and shall apply to any defendant sentenced to death after December 6, 1984. (1985 c.3 sec 3; 1987 c.320 sec 86; 1987 c.557 sec 1; 1989 c.720 sec 2; 1989 c.790 sec 135b; 1991 c.725 sec 2; 1991 c.885 sec 2 .)

Law after 1995 Legislative Assembly

(There were no changes to the law in the 1993 session.)

ORS 163.150 (1996) Sentencing for aggravated murder; proceedings; issues for jury; review by Supreme Court; effect of plea of guilty or no contest.

(1)(a) Upon a finding that the defendant is guilty of aggravated murder, the court, except as otherwise provided in subsection (3) of this section, shall conduct a separate sentencing proceeding to determine whether the defendant shall be sentenced to life imprisonment, as described in ORS 163.105 (1)(c), life imprisonment without the possibility of release or parole, as described in ORS 163.105 (1)(b), or death. The proceeding shall be conducted in the trial court before the trial jury as soon as practicable. If a juror for any reason is unable to perform the function of a juror, the juror shall be dismissed from the sentencing proceeding. The court shall cause to be drawn the name of one of the alternate jurors, who shall then become a member of the jury for the sentencing proceeding notwithstanding the fact that the alternate juror did not deliberate on the issue of guilt. The substitution of an alternate juror shall be allowed only if the jury has not begun to deliberate on the issue of the sentence. If the defendant has pleaded guilty, the sentencing proceeding shall be conducted before a jury impaneled for that purpose. In the proceeding, evidence may be presented as to any matter that the court deems relevant to sentence including, but not limited to, victim impact evidence relating to the personal characteristics of the victim or the impact of the crime on the victim's family and any aggravating or mitigating evidence relevant to the issue in paragraph (b)(D) of this subsection; however, neither the state nor the defendant shall be allowed to introduce repetitive evidence that has previously been offered and received during the trial on the issue of guilt. The court shall instruct the jury that all evidence previously offered and received may be considered for purposes of the sentencing hearing. This subsection shall not be construed to authorize the introduction of any evidence secured in violation of the Constitution of the United States or of the State of Oregon. The state and the defendant or the counsel of the defendant shall be permitted to present arguments for or against a sentence of death and for or against a sentence of life imprisonment with or without the possibility of release or parole.

(b) Upon the conclusion of the presentation of the evidence, the court shall submit the following issues to the jury:

(A) Whether the conduct of the defendant that caused the death of the deceased was committed deliberately and with the reasonable expectation that death of the deceased or another would result;

(B) Whether there is a probability that the defendant would commit criminal acts of violence that would constitute a continuing threat to society;

(C) If raised by the evidence, whether the conduct of the defendant in killing the deceased was unreasonable in response to the provocation, if any, by the deceased; and

(D) Whether the defendant should receive a death sentence.

(c)(A) In determining the issues in paragraph (b) of this subsection, the court shall instruct the jury to consider any mitigating circumstances offered in evidence, including but not limited to the defendant's age, the extent and severity of the defendant's prior criminal conduct and the extent of the mental and emotional pressure under which the defendant was acting at the time the offense was committed.

(B) In determining the issue in paragraph (b)(D) of this subsection, the court shall instruct the jury to answer the question "no" if one or more of the jurors find there is any aspect of the defendant's character or background, or any circumstances of the offense, that one or more of the jurors believe would justify a sentence less than death.

(d) The state must prove each issue submitted under paragraph (b)(A) to (C) of this subsection beyond a reasonable doubt, and the jury shall return a special verdict of "yes" or "no" on each issue considered.

(e) The court shall charge the jury that it may not answer any issue "yes," under paragraph (b) of this subsection unless it agrees unanimously.

(f) If the jury returns an affirmative finding on each issue considered under paragraph (b) of this subsection, the trial judge shall sentence the defendant to death.

(g) The judgment of conviction and sentence of death shall be subject to automatic and direct review by the Supreme Court. The review by the Supreme Court shall have priority over all other cases, and shall be heard in accordance with rules promulgated by the Supreme Court. A sentence of death shall be automatically stayed if the defendant seeks review by the United States Supreme Court on a direct appeal. The stay shall remain in effect until:

(A) The defendant's time for filing a petition for certiorari or an appeal expires;

(B) The United States Supreme Court acts to decline to consider the case further; or

(C) The United States Supreme Court resolves the case on the merits.

(2)(a) Upon the conclusion of the presentation of the evidence, the court shall also instruct the jury that if it reaches a negative finding on any issue under subsection (1)(b) of this section, the trial court shall sentence the defendant to life imprisonment without the possibility of release or parole, as described in ORS 163.105 (1)(b), unless 10 or more members of the jury further find that there are sufficient mitigating circumstances to warrant life imprisonment, in which case the trial court shall sentence the defendant to life imprisonment as described in ORS 163.105 (1)(c).

(b) If the jury returns a negative finding on any issue under subsection (1)(b) of this section and further finds that there are sufficient mitigating circumstances to warrant life imprisonment, the trial court shall sentence the defendant to life imprisonment in the custody of the Department of Corrections as provided in ORS 163.105 (1)(c).

(3)(a) When the defendant is found guilty of aggravated murder upon a plea of guilty or no contest prior to the introduction of evidence before the trier of fact, and the state advises the court on the record that the state declines to present evidence for purposes of sentencing the defendant to death, the court:

(A) Shall not conduct a sentencing proceeding as described in subsection (1) of this section, and a sentence of death shall not be ordered.

(B) Shall conduct a sentencing proceeding to determine whether the defendant shall be sentenced to life imprisonment without the possibility of release or parole as described in ORS 163.105 (1)(b) or life imprisonment as described in ORS 163.105 (1)(c). If the defendant waives all rights to a jury sentencing proceeding, the court shall conduct the sentencing proceeding as the trier of fact. The procedure for the sentencing proceeding, whether before a court or a jury, shall follow the procedure of subsection (1)(a) and subsection (2) of this section, as modified by this subsection which prohibits a sentence of death when the state declines to present evidence.

(b) Nothing in this subsection shall preclude the court from sentencing the defendant to life imprisonment, as described in ORS 163.105 (1)(c), or life imprisonment without the possibility of release or parole, as described in ORS 163.105 (1)(b), pursuant to a stipulation of sentence or stipulation of sentencing facts agreed to and offered by both parties if the defendant waives all rights to a jury sentencing proceeding.

(4) If any part of subsection (2) of this section is held invalid and as a result thereof a defendant who has been sentenced to life imprisonment without possibility of release or parole will instead be sentenced to life imprisonment in the custody of the Department of Corrections as provided in ORS 163.105 (2), the defendant shall be confined for a minimum of 30 years without possibility of parole, release on work release or any form of temporary leave or employment at a forest or work camp. Subsection (2) of this section shall apply only to trials commencing on or after July 19, 1989.

(5) Notwithstanding subsection (1)(a) of this section, the following shall apply:

(a) If a reviewing court finds prejudicial error in the sentencing proceeding only, the court may set aside the sentence of death and remand the case to the trial court. No error in the sentencing proceeding shall result in reversal of the defendant's conviction for aggravated murder. Upon remand and at the election of the state, the trial court shall either:

(A) Sentence the defendant to imprisonment for life in the custody of the Department of Corrections as provided in ORS 163.105 (1)(c); or

(B) Impanel a new sentencing jury for the purpose of conducting a new sentencing proceeding to determine if the defendant should be sentenced to:

(i) Death;

(ii) Imprisonment for life without the possibility of release or parole as provided in ORS 163.105 (1)(b); or

(iii) Imprisonment for life in the custody of the Department of Corrections as provided in ORS 163.105 (1)(c).

(b) If the trial court grants a mistrial during the sentencing proceeding, the trial court, at the election of the state, shall either:

(A) Sentence the defendant to imprisonment for life in the custody of the Department of Corrections as provided in ORS 163.105 (1)(c); or

(B) Impanel a new sentencing jury for the purpose of conducting a new sentencing proceeding to determine if the defendant should be sentenced to:

(i) Death;

(ii) Imprisonment for life without the possibility of release or parole as provided in ORS 163.105 (1)(b); or

(iii) Imprisonment for life in the custody of the Department of Corrections as provided in ORS 163.105 (1)(c).

(c) Nothing in this subsection shall preclude the court from sentencing the defendant to life imprisonment without the possibility of release or parole, as described in ORS 163.105 (1)(b), pursuant to a stipulation of sentence if the defendant waives all rights to a jury sentencing proceeding.

(d) The new sentencing proceeding shall be governed by the provisions of subsections (1) and (2) of this section. A transcript of all testimony and all exhibits and other evidence properly admitted in the prior trial and sentencing proceeding shall be admissible in the new sentencing proceeding. Either party may recall any witness who testified at the prior trial or sentencing proceeding and may present additional relevant evidence.

(e) The provisions of this section are procedural and shall apply to any defendant sentenced to death after December 6, 1984. (1985 c.3 sec 3; 1987 c.320 sec 86; 1987 c.557 sec 1; 1989 c.720 sec 2; 1989 c.790 sec 135b; 1991 c.725 sec 2; 1991 c.885 sec 2; 1995 c.531 sec 2; 1995 c.657 sec 23)

Law after 1997 Legislative Assembly

ORS 163.150 (1997) Sentencing for aggravated murder; proceedings; issues for jury; review by Supreme Court; effect of plea of guilty or no contest.

(1)(a) Upon a finding that the defendant is guilty of aggravated murder, the court, except as otherwise provided in subsection (3) of this section, shall conduct a separate sentencing proceeding to determine whether the defendant shall be sentenced to life imprisonment, as described in ORS 163.105 (1)(c), life imprisonment without the possibility of release or parole, as described in ORS 163.105 (1)(b), or death. The proceeding shall be conducted in the trial court before the trial jury as soon as practicable. If a juror for any reason is unable to perform the function of a juror, the juror shall be dismissed from the sentencing proceeding. The court shall cause to be drawn the name of one of the alternate jurors, who shall then become a member of the jury for the sentencing proceeding notwithstanding the fact that the alternate juror did not deliberate on the issue of guilt. The substitution of an alternate juror shall be allowed only if the jury has not begun to deliberate on the issue of the sentence. If the defendant has pleaded guilty, the sentencing proceeding shall be conducted before a jury impaneled for that purpose. In the proceeding, evidence may be presented as to any matter that the court deems relevant to sentence including, but not limited to, victim impact evidence relating to the personal characteristics of the victim or the impact of the crime on the victim's family and any aggravating or mitigating evidence relevant to the issue in paragraph (b)(D) of this subsection; however, neither the state nor the defendant shall be allowed to introduce repetitive evidence that has previously been offered and received during the trial on the issue of guilt. The court shall instruct the jury that all evidence previously offered and received may be considered for purposes of the sentencing hearing. This subsection shall not be construed to authorize the introduction of any evidence secured in violation of the Constitution of the United States or of the State of Oregon. The state and the defendant or the counsel of the defendant shall be permitted to present arguments for or against a sentence of death and for or against a sentence of life imprisonment with or without the possibility of release or parole.

(b) Upon the conclusion of the presentation of the evidence, the court shall submit the following issues to the jury:

(A) Whether the conduct of the defendant that caused the death of the deceased was committed deliberately and with the reasonable expectation that death of the deceased or another would result;

(B) Whether there is a probability that the defendant would commit criminal acts of violence that would constitute a continuing threat to society;

(C) If raised by the evidence, whether the conduct of the defendant in killing the deceased was unreasonable in response to the provocation, if any, by the deceased; and

(D) Whether the defendant should receive a death sentence.

(c)(A) The court shall instruct the jury to consider, in determining the issues in paragraph (b) of this subsection, any mitigating circumstances offered in evidence, including but not limited to the defendant's age, the extent and severity of the defendant's prior criminal conduct and the extent of the mental and emotional pressure under which the defendant was acting at the time the offense was committed.

(B) The court shall instruct the jury to answer the question in paragraph (b)(D) of this subsection "no" if, after considering any aggravating evidence and any mitigating evidence concerning any aspect of the defendant's character or background, or any circumstances of the offense and any victim impact evidence as described in subsection (1)(a) of this section, one or more of the jurors believe that the defendant should not receive a death sentence.

(d) The state must prove each issue submitted under paragraph (b)(A) to (C) of this subsection beyond a reasonable doubt, and the jury shall return a special verdict of "yes" or "no" on each issue considered.

(e) The court shall charge the jury that it may not answer any issue "yes," under paragraph (b) of this subsection unless it agrees unanimously.

(f) If the jury returns an affirmative finding on each issue considered under paragraph (b) of this subsection, the trial judge shall sentence the defendant to death.

(g) The judgment of conviction and sentence of death shall be subject to automatic and direct review by the Supreme Court. The review by the Supreme Court shall have priority over all other cases, and shall be heard in accordance with rules promulgated by the Supreme Court. A sentence of death shall be automatically stayed if the defendant seeks review by the United States Supreme Court on a direct appeal. The stay shall remain in effect until:

(A) The defendant's time for filing a petition for certiorari or an appeal expires;

(B) The United States Supreme Court acts to decline to consider the case further; or

(C) The United States Supreme Court resolves the case on the merits.

(2)(a) Upon the conclusion of the presentation of the evidence, the court shall also instruct the jury that if it reaches a negative finding on any issue under subsection (1)(b) of this section, the trial court shall sentence the defendant to life imprisonment without the possibility of release or parole, as described in ORS 163.105 (1)(b), unless 10 or more members of the jury further find that there are sufficient mitigating circumstances to warrant life imprisonment, in which case the trial court shall sentence the defendant to life imprisonment as described in ORS 163.105 (1)(c).

(b) If the jury returns a negative finding on any issue under subsection (1)(b) of this section and further finds that there are sufficient mitigating circumstances to warrant life imprisonment, the trial court shall sentence the defendant to life imprisonment in the custody of the Department of Corrections as provided in ORS 163.105 (1)(c).

(3)(a) When the defendant is found guilty of aggravated murder upon a plea of guilty or no contest prior to the introduction of evidence before the trier of fact, and the state advises the court on the record that the state declines to present evidence for purposes of sentencing the defendant to death, the court:

(A) Shall not conduct a sentencing proceeding as described in subsection (1) of this section, and a sentence of death shall not be ordered.

(B) Shall conduct a sentencing proceeding to determine whether the defendant shall be sentenced to life imprisonment without the possibility of release or parole as described in ORS 163.105 (1)(b) or life imprisonment as described in ORS 163.105 (1)(c). If the defendant waives all rights to a jury sentencing proceeding, the court shall conduct the sentencing proceeding as the trier of fact. The procedure for the sentencing proceeding, whether before a court or a jury, shall follow the procedure of subsection (1)(a) and subsection (2) of this section, as modified by this subsection which prohibits a sentence of death when the state declines to present evidence.

(b) Nothing in this subsection shall preclude the court from sentencing the defendant to life imprisonment, as described in ORS 163.105 (1)(c), or life imprisonment without the possibility of release or parole, as described in ORS 163.105 (1)(b), pursuant to a stipulation of sentence or stipulation of sentencing facts agreed to and offered by both parties if the defendant waives all rights to a jury sentencing proceeding.

(4) If any part of subsection (2) of this section is held invalid and as a result thereof a defendant who has been sentenced to life imprisonment without possibility of release or parole will instead be sentenced to life imprisonment in the custody of the Department of Corrections as provided in ORS 163.105 (2), the defendant shall be confined for a minimum of 30 years without possibility of parole, release on work release or any form of temporary leave or employment at a forest or work camp. Subsection (2) of this section shall apply only to trials commencing on or after July 19, 1989.

(5) Notwithstanding subsection (1)(a) of this section, the following shall apply:

(a) If a reviewing court finds prejudicial error in the sentencing proceeding only, the court may set aside the sentence of death and remand the case to the trial court. No error in the sentencing proceeding shall result in reversal of the defendant's conviction for aggravated murder. Upon remand and at the election of the state, the trial court shall either:

(A) Sentence the defendant to imprisonment for life in the custody of the Department of Corrections as provided in ORS 163.105 (1)(c); or

(B) Impanel a new sentencing jury for the purpose of conducting a new sentencing proceeding to determine if the defendant should be sentenced to:

(i) Death;

(ii) Imprisonment for life without the possibility of release or parole as provided in ORS 163.105 (1)(b); or

(iii) Imprisonment for life in the custody of the Department of Corrections as provided in ORS 163.105 (1)(c).

(b) If the trial court grants a mistrial during the sentencing proceeding, the trial court, at the election of the state, shall either:

(A) Sentence the defendant to imprisonment for life in the custody of the Department of Corrections as provided in ORS 163.105 (1)(c); or

(B) Impanel a new sentencing jury for the purpose of conducting a new sentencing proceeding to determine if the defendant should be sentenced to:

(i) Death;

(ii) Imprisonment for life without the possibility of release or parole as provided in ORS 163.105 (1)(b); or

(iii) Imprisonment for life in the custody of the Department of Corrections as provided in ORS 163.105 (1)(c).

(c) Nothing in this subsection shall preclude the court from sentencing the defendant to life imprisonment without the possibility of release or parole, as described in ORS 163.105 (1)(b), pursuant to a stipulation of sentence if the defendant waives all rights to a jury sentencing proceeding.

(d) The new sentencing proceeding shall be governed by the provisions of subsections (1) and (2) of this section. A transcript of all testimony and all exhibits and other evidence properly admitted in the prior trial and sentencing proceeding shall be admissible in the new sentencing proceeding. Either party may recall any witness who testified at the prior trial or sentencing proceeding and may present additional relevant evidence.

(e) The provisions of this section are procedural and shall apply to any defendant sentenced to death after December 6, 1984. (1985 c.3 :sec.3; 1987 c.320 :sec.86; 1987 c.557 :sec.1; 1989 c.720 :sec.2; 1989 c.790 :sec.135b; 1991 c.725 :sec.2; 1991 c.885 :sec.2; 1995 c.531 :sec.2; 1995 c.657 :sec 23; 1997 c.784 :sec 1)

After 1999 Legislative Session

ORS 163.150 (1999)

Sentencing for aggravated murder; proceedings; issues for jury.

(1)(a) Upon a finding that the defendant is guilty of aggravated murder, the court, except as otherwise provided in subsection (3) of this section, shall conduct a separate sentencing proceeding to determine whether the defendant shall be sentenced to life imprisonment, as described in ORS 163.105 (1)(c), life imprisonment without the possibility of release or parole, as described in ORS 163.105 (1)(b), or death. The proceeding shall be conducted in the trial court before the trial jury as soon as practicable. If a juror for any reason is unable to perform the function of a juror, the juror shall be dismissed from the sentencing proceeding. The court shall cause to be drawn the name of one of the alternate jurors, who shall then become a member of the jury for the sentencing proceeding notwithstanding the fact that the alternate juror did not deliberate on the issue of guilt. The substitution of an alternate juror shall be allowed only if the jury has not begun to deliberate on the issue of the sentence. If the defendant has pleaded guilty, the sentencing proceeding shall be conducted before a jury impaneled for that purpose. In the proceeding, evidence may be presented as to any matter that the court deems relevant to sentence including, but not limited to, victim impact evidence relating to the personal characteristics of the victim or the impact of the crime on the victim's family and any aggravating or mitigating evidence relevant to the issue in paragraph (b)(D) of this subsection; however, neither the state nor the defendant shall be allowed to introduce repetitive evidence that has previously been offered and received during the trial on the issue of guilt. The court shall instruct the jury that all evidence previously offered and received may be considered for purposes of the sentencing hearing. This subsection shall not be construed to authorize the introduction of any evidence secured in violation of the Constitution of the United States or of the State of Oregon. The state and the defendant or the counsel of the defendant shall be permitted to present arguments for or against a sentence of death and for or against a sentence of life imprisonment with or without the possibility of release or parole.

(b) Upon the conclusion of the presentation of the evidence, the court shall submit the following issues to the jury:

(A) Whether the conduct of the defendant that caused the death of the deceased was committed deliberately and with the reasonable expectation that death of the deceased or another would result;

(B) Whether there is a probability that the defendant would commit criminal acts of violence that would constitute a continuing threat to society;

(C) If raised by the evidence, whether the conduct of the defendant in killing the deceased was unreasonable in response to the provocation, if any, by the deceased; and

(D) Whether the defendant should receive a death sentence.

(c)(A) The court shall instruct the jury to consider, in determining the issues in paragraph (b) of this subsection, any mitigating circumstances offered in evidence, including but not limited to the defendant's age, the extent and severity of the defendant's prior criminal conduct and the extent of the mental and emotional pressure under which the defendant was acting at the time the offense was committed.

(B) The court shall instruct the jury to answer the question in paragraph (b)(D) of this subsection "no" if, after considering any aggravating evidence and any mitigating evidence concerning any aspect of the defendant's character or background, or any circumstances of the offense and any victim impact evidence as described in subsection (1)(a) of this section, one or more of the jurors believe that the defendant should not receive a death sentence.

(d) The state must prove each issue submitted under paragraph (b)(A) to (C) of this subsection beyond a reasonable doubt, and the jury shall return a special verdict of "yes" or "no" on each issue considered.

(e) The court shall charge the jury that it may not answer any issue "yes," under paragraph (b) of this subsection unless it agrees unanimously.

(f) If the jury returns an affirmative finding on each issue considered under paragraph (b) of this subsection, the trial judge shall sentence the defendant to death.

(2)(a) Upon the conclusion of the presentation of the evidence, the court shall also instruct the jury that if it reaches a negative finding on any issue under subsection (1)(b) of this section, the trial court shall sentence the defendant to life imprisonment without the possibility of release or parole, as described in ORS 163.105 (1)(b), unless 10 or more members of the jury further find that there are sufficient mitigating circumstances to warrant life imprisonment, in which case the trial court shall sentence the defendant to life imprisonment as described in ORS 163.105 (1)(c).

(b) If the jury returns a negative finding on any issue under subsection (1)(b) of this section and further finds that there are sufficient mitigating circumstances to warrant life imprisonment, the trial court shall sentence the defendant to life imprisonment in the custody of the Department of Corrections as provided in ORS 163.105 (1)(c).

(3)(a) When the defendant is found guilty of aggravated murder, and the state advises the court on the record that the state declines to present evidence for purposes of sentencing the defendant to death, the court:

(A) Shall not conduct a sentencing proceeding as described in subsection (1) of this section, and a sentence of death shall not be ordered.

(B) Shall conduct a sentencing proceeding to determine whether the defendant shall be sentenced to life imprisonment without the possibility of release or parole as described in ORS 163.105 (1)(b) or life imprisonment as described in ORS 163.105 (1)(c). If the defendant waives all rights to a jury sentencing proceeding, the court shall conduct the sentencing proceeding as the trier of fact. The procedure for the sentencing proceeding, whether before a court or a jury, shall follow the procedure of subsection (1)(a) and subsection (2) of this section, as modified by this subsection which prohibits a sentence of death when the state declines to present evidence.

(b) Nothing in this subsection shall preclude the court from sentencing the defendant to life imprisonment, as described in ORS 163.105 (1)(c), or life imprisonment without the possibility of release or parole, as described in ORS 163.105 (1)(b), pursuant to a stipulation of sentence or stipulation of sentencing facts agreed to and offered by both parties if the defendant waives all rights to a jury sentencing proceeding.

(4) If any part of subsection (2) of this section is held invalid and as a result thereof a defendant who has been sentenced to life imprisonment without possibility of release or parole will instead be sentenced to life imprisonment in the custody of the Department of Corrections as provided in ORS 163.105 (2), the defendant shall be confined for a minimum of 30 years without possibility of parole, release on work release or any form of temporary leave or employment at a forest or work camp. Subsection (2) of this section shall apply only to trials commencing on or after July 19, 1989.

(5) Notwithstanding subsection (1)(a) of this section, if the trial court grants a mistrial during the sentencing proceeding, the trial court, at the election of the state, shall either:

(a) Sentence the defendant to imprisonment for life in the custody of the Department of Corrections as provided in ORS 163.105 (1)(c); or

(b) Impanel a new sentencing jury for the purpose of conducting a new sentencing proceeding to determine if the defendant should be sentenced to:

(A) Death;

(B) Imprisonment for life without the possibility of release or parole as provided in ORS 163.105 (1)(b); or

(C) Imprisonment for life in the custody of the Department of Corrections as provided in ORS 163.105 (1)(c). (1985 c.3 sec 3; 1987 c.320 sec 86; 1987 c.557 sec 1; 1989 c.720 sec 2; 1989 c.790 sec 135b; 1991 c.725 sec 2; 1991 c.885 sec 2; 1995 c.531 sec 2; 1995 c.657 sec 23; 1997 c.784 sec 1; 1999 c.1055 sec 1).